EROS, MAGIC,

AND THE

MURDER OF

PROFESSOR

CULIANU

TED ANTON

EROS, MAGIC, & THE
MURDER
OF PROFESSOR
CULIANU

Northwestern University Press *Evanston*

Northwestern University Press
Evanston, Illinois 60208-4210
Copyright © 1996 by Ted Anton
All rights reserved
Printed in the United States of America
ISBN 0-8101-1396-1
Library of Congress Cataloging-in-Publication Data
Anton, Ted.
    Eros, magic, and the murder of Professor Culianu / Ted Anton.
    p. cm.
    ISBN 0-8101-1396-1 (alk. paper)
    1. Culianu, Ioan P. 2. Culianu, Ioan P. — Assassination. 3. Religion
historians — United States — Biography. 4. Religion historians — Romania —
Biography. 5. Murder victims — United States — Biography. 6. Occultism —
Study and teaching — History — 20th century. 7. Magic — Study and
teaching — History — 20th century. 8. Religion — Study and teaching —
History — 20th century. 9. Romania — Politics and government — 20th
century. I. Title.
BL43.C84A3 1996
200'.92 — dc 20   96-9432
                                                           CIP

The paper used in this publication meets the minimum requirements of the
American National Standard for Information Sciences — Permanence of Paper for
Printed Library Materials, ANSI Z39.48-1984.

Imaginary universes
are so much more beautiful
than this stupidly constructed
real one.

— *G. H. Hardy,*
   A Mathematician's Apology

CONTENTS

. . . . . .

ACKNOWLEDGMENTS

During nearly five years of research I incurred debts to countless people. First among them was the family of Ioan Petru Culianu. Thereza Culianu-Petrescu and Hillary Wiesner devoted long, patient hours to this project, offering tremendous assistance. I also thank Elena Bogdan and Dan Petrescu in Romania; Nikki Wiesner and Dorothy and Kurt Hertzfeld in the United States; and Carmen Georgescu and her son, Andrei Westerink, in Holland. In three homes in three countries, I was welcomed not only as a researcher but also as a friend, and for this support I am grateful.

Among the people who helped me were those who read drafts of the manuscript or portions thereof. They include Andrei Codrescu, Mircea Sabau, Norman Manea, Vladimir Tismaneanu, Dumitru Radu Popa, Mircea Raceanu, Sorin Antohi, Carlin Romano, Ilinca Zarifopol-Johnston, Mac Linscott Ricketts, Ken Starck, Jim Fairhall, Anne Calcagno, Ara Sismanian, Andrei Oişteanu, Greg Spinner, Michael Allocca, and Gwendolyn Barnes. They offered criticism, translation skills, and encouragement. Others who gave their time to this book include Umberto Eco and John Crowley.

I offer tremendous thanks to my research assistant Eileen Murphy and to several translators. Mac Linscott Ricketts translated Culianu's political articles. Other translators included Marian Stan, Olga Stefan, Anne François-Nizou, Cristina Bellu, Viurica Seceleanu, Alexander Cepeda, Clement Mirza, my Romanian students while I was on my Fulbright grant, and the late Virgil Stefanescu. I offer a very special thanks to Jacqueline Renowden.

For financial support, I want to thank the United States Information Service and its Fulbright Program, particularly Raluca Vasiliu, as well as the Fund for Investigative Journalism, and the DePaul University Summer Research Program. I give the deepest thanks to my friends at DePaul who expressed encouragement at every moment it was needed, especially Gerald Mulderig, Richard Jones, Eileen Seifert, and Stan Damberger.

In the distinguished circle of Ioan Culianu's friends, I wish to acknowledge Miron Bogdan, Şerban Anghelescu, Silviu Angelescu, Gustavo Casadio, Elémire Zolla, Grazia Marchiano, Gianpaolo Romanato, David Brent, Jennifer Stevenson, Michel Meslin, and Stelian Plesoiu. I also want to thank David Funderburk, Jonathan Rickert, Matei Calinescu, Cristina Ilioia, Leon Volovici, Victor Ivanovici, Moshe Idel, Horia Patapeivici, Anca Giurescu, Peter Gross, Willem Noomen, Cicerone Poghirc, Nestor Ratesh, Vasilei Boiluanu, Ion Coja, Petre Bacanu, Ion Pacepa, Liviu Cangeopol, Alexander Ronnett, Mircea Marghescu, Jean Ancel, Gabriella Adameşteanu, and Cornel Dumitrescu. Others who assisted me included Petre Roman, Dan Petreanu, Dana Sismanian, Carmen Sabau, Dorothy Margraf, and Sorin Avram.

Among historians of religion, I want to thank Jerry Brauer, Michael Fishbane, John Collins, Lawrence Sullivan, Carol Zaleski, Wendy Doniger, Franklin Gamwell, Clark Gilpin, Alan Segal, Anthony Yu, and David Tracy. And in the very special world of Culianu's University of Chicago students, I owe a huge debt to Nathaniel Deutsch, Joel Sweek, Karen Anderson, Jim Egge, Karen de Leon Jones, Margaret Arndt-Caddigan, Alexander Arguelles, Stephanie Stamm, Liz Wilson, Elise La Rose, and others.

I want especially to thank Cathy O'Leary and Erika Schluntz for telling me of their memories.

In law enforcement, I wish to thank police detective Robert A. McGuire, retired police captain Frederick Miller, the late Robert Stein, and FBI special agents Paul Dimura and especially John L. Bertulis. To all those who shared their time with me, I offer my gratitude. And I remind the reader that any mistakes are purely my own.

For support of this project, I thank the magazines *Chicago* and *Lingua Franca*, including editors Gretchen Reynolds and Margaret Talbot. The biggest note of appreciation goes to my editor Susan Harris, with a very special thanks to Angela Ray. To my publisher, Nicholas Weir-Williams, I offer fondest gratitude. I offer deepest acknowledgment to my agent, Ellen Levine, her associates, and to a longtime mentor, Sam Vaughan.

At home I want to thank my DePaul University graduate students who read parts of the manuscript.

Most of all, I want to thank the people who put up with me during these past five years. My parents, Bertha and Gus Anton, came to my home and helped when I left for Romania. With heartfelt love for her understanding, criticism, and support, I thank my wife, Maja.

NOTE ON METHOD

I began work on the story of Ioan Culianu in July 1991. In four and
half years I tape-recorded more than 150 conversations and interviews in five different countries, and conducted many more. A work
that uses participants' memories and quotes conversations at which
the author was not present naturally evokes questions: How could
you know what a person was thinking, or what someone said in a
conversation more than twenty years before the interview?

Relying in many cases on personal interviews, I checked what
I heard against statements of other participants and published
sources. Though individual recollections can be affected by the va-
garies of perception or the passage of time, my best response was to
try to talk again and again to as many different people as I could—
from government officials to family members—and to address conflicting versions of any single event.

Still, the memories of different people, or accounts of historical
events, conflicted on occasion. In such cases, or of the seeming
random coincidences to which Culianu or others attached significance, I have attempted to present here more than one possible
interpretation of an event's meaning. I have also changed the names
of two minor figures and some details of their lives to protect their
privacy. What follows is my attempt to explain the intersection of
historical, intellectual, and personal forces so intricate they ultimately address the question: What is truth? This book cannot answer that question. It can, however, invite readers to explore a story
of religion, politics, and passion and draw their own conclusions.

There was one notable exception to my goal of speaking to everyone, that of Ioan Culianu himself. While he left a detailed record of
his thoughts and feelings from adolescence until his death, he also
cautioned students to understand that, if language constructs a
world, then any story is in part an artifice and a seduction. To draw
my portrait I relied on his letters, journals, scholarly writings, and
autobiographical stories, as well as on the testimony of people who
knew him. Such material has its strengths and its limits, but it helped
that up to his last days Ioan Culianu was writing notes he did not

expect others to read. He did so playfully, to test his understanding of his and our lives. These writings illuminated his inner journey almost as clearly as I might speak of my own.

I never met Ioan Culianu. I watched him on video, heard him on tape, listened to hundreds of accounts of him, read countless critical analyses of his scholarship and teaching, and read and reread his work. My distance from a man who seemed so different to people at different times meant that I did not view him through one particular lens, but rather through as many different lenses as I found. Compiling a composite portrait filled with ambiguity and contradiction, I turned to a theory of science or history called complexity that Culianu advocated for new scholars. While a traditionalist works backward, knowing the ending and fitting each piece into a puzzle that explains it, a complexity scholar weighs different versions from the viewpoints of many different players, working *forward* to see each action as a product of chance and constantly shifting choices.

This book is about the ways perceptions shape history, time reveals truth, and forgeries can become self-fulfilling. Ioan Culianu spent a lifetime exploring the degree to which truth and fiction can be the opposite of what we think. My goal here is to preserve the questions about him as faithfully as I illuminate my answers.

EROS, MAGIC,

AND THE

MURDER OF

PROFESSOR

CULIANU

October, 1989. Chicago

Prince's "Dirty Mind" played on the stereo, and the smell of cigarettes and wine hung in the air. The apartment's living room featured dark oak paneling in what was once a luxury building in Chicago's Hyde Park, now given over to gloom and shadow. A large
mirror flanked by wooden pillars reflected the partygoers' faces. A
few students stood in a small knot around Professor Culianu. He
specialized in divination practices. Some of them were trying to get
him to tell their futures. He kept shaking his head no. They kept
working on him. No no, he said. You won't like it.

Finally he agreed to demonstrate the ancient Islamic art called
geomancy. A few students followed him into the bedroom, where
they sat on the floor or on a platform bed where people had thrown
their coats. Everyone felt a little giddy. Culianu pulled a deck of
cards from his European-cut sport jacket and sat crosslegged on the
floor. He took off his loafers. At the party he had been so unassum-
ing that many of them had not realized he was a professor.

He had found the cards in a back stall in Paris, he said, explaining
that normally geomancy was practiced by drawing dots and lines
in the sand. Originating in the Middle East, the art had been rediscovered late in the Middle Ages and flourished during the Renaissance in Italy. The cards were four inches high. Stars flickered
against a deep blue background on the back. On the front was either
a single black dot or two black dots. When the thinking behind
geomancy's modernist wisdom — that the cosmos was connected by
invisible patterns and human events could be predicted based on
simple, repeated mathematical steps — was absorbed by philosophers in Renaissance Florence, it sparked a flowering of magic that
paralleled the rise of science.

Culianu was a shy man with a funny accent who was unusually
quiet about his life, although he was one of the only teachers who
was ready to chat with students about their lives. He had a dimpled
smile and dark eyes that seemed to look beyond you when he spoke.
He had pale skin and high cheekbones and a gentle, enthusiastic,

open manner. In his lectures he digressed too much; other faculty members prepared students better for exams. But to many students Culianu, author of thirteen books and translations in five languages, was the only scholar they knew who studied religion as a real entity, a driving force, in people's lives.

Once he had given a talk to the Divinity School's History of Religions Club. "What is religion?" he had asked. "Why do rational people still buy into it? Why do all religions of humankind, at all times, show striking similarities to each other?" Most modern scholars avoided such sweeping questions, seeking instead the cultural differences that influenced specific faiths. Yet he claimed that these broad questions "had practically called the discipline of the history of religions into being." He said the reason for the similarity in many beliefs lay in the "unity of the operations of the human mind." One implication of his theory was that any "change in the system of religion would immediately affect all the other systems that create history." The mind shaped action, and religion programmed the mind.

Flanking him in the apartment bedroom were Greg Spinner, in shoulder-length hair, and Michael Allocca, with his beard and long black curls. They had asked Culianu to teach them a reading course on divination that quarter. To their surprise he had agreed, setting only one condition: he expected them to tell the future in order to finish the course. So they in particular hoped he would say something accurate tonight. It would make the party.

He began with the party host, who was intrigued. He asked her to concentrate on one question that was most on her mind, and to pick out her cards. Slowly he laid out her cards on the floor. He paused, studying them. "You're concerned that someone with some power in your life is going to hurt you," he said. "You don't have to worry about it."

Her heart leaped. She felt she knew exactly which professor he was talking about.

Culianu said.

"I need a cigarette," she said.

He read some other people's cards, some impressively, some not. When he uncovered another student's concealed panic over his graduate studies, for instance, no one was surprised. Anyone could have told you that. When the party was in full swing, a new student who had been hanging back asked him to try for her. Again he told her to concentrate on the question that was most on her mind. Spinner and Allocca sat behind him, each watching over a shoulder as he laid out her cards. He studied them. "You're sure you want others to hear this?" he asked. She shrugged and laughed nervously. "I think we should send the others out," he said.

"No, no, my life's an open book," she said.

"All right, close the door." He turned to them: Greg Spinner, Michael Allocca, a few others. "What is said here does not leave this room." They smiled uncertainly. "You're humiliating yourself," he said. "It's really painful, and it's getting worse."

"Whoa."

"You're involved in a love triangle, and it's coloring your life. You've got to get out of it."

Her face went white. She looked around in panic. His accuracy "knocked the wind out of me," she later said. Greg leaned forward to check the cards. But Ioan cut him off before he could say anything.

At the end of the party, Greg spotted Culianu putting on his shoes to leave. "Ioan!" he called. "Come on, how does it work?"

"It works because it works."

"That's not what I mean. You read those cards exactly as they were laid out."

"It's mind. It's all in the mind."

Greg Spinner could never accept that answer, though he had often heard it. His teacher always said it with a smile of irony. Once, driving with Culianu, Spinner had stumbled onto the bluntest way to ask his question: "Look, Ioan, if I shot you in the head, would that be in the mind too?"

He smiled. "Well, yes and no," he said.

They never knew when he was playing and when he was being what he normally was — a serious scholar at one of the world's leading divinity schools. He began his career as a follower of school legend Mircea Eliade, one of the world's premier historians of religions of the twentieth century. Culianu was bidding to become a seminal if controversial thinker in his own right, proposing in his books a paradigm shift in the study of history and ideas. Some, especially in Europe, thought he offered an important new approach. Others, even on the faculty, criticized his methods and advised students not to take his courses. The tension was so obvious that no one commented on it, observed one student. But if you wanted to position yourself well, students learned, you did not work with Culianu.

To a select group of students and scholars, though, Ioan Culianu was what higher education was all about. To understand a field truly, he said, you had to practice it. He was interested in the occult because to him it worked more often than could be explained rationally. He wanted to understand why, but that was only a small part of what he wanted. He wanted to understand the logic systems *behind* prophecy and religious movements and the reason for their hold on believers and influence over events. He reminded students that science was, in its beginning, considered an occult art. In fact, it was the Renaissance magicians' image of the universe, that events could be manipulated by theorems, that set the stage for Galileo.

"He was on a quest," was how student Karen Anderson put it. "Not an academic quest, but a real quest."

But did he really believe in that stuff? *That* was their question. Or was it all, really, just a game?

THE CRIME, MAY 21, 1991

I expected to wake up and see my good mother

bending protectively over my bed at home. And so it

will be to the end, and I will expect her cool and soft

hand to dispel evil even at the hour of my death.

—*I. P. Culianu and H. S. Wiesner,*

"The Emerald Game"

* * * * * * * *

RELIGION AS A SYSTEM

Every once in a while a Chicago spring offers one perfectly mica-bright, warm gift of a day. The air will be cool and fragrant with smells of cottonwood, prairie wind, and whitefish off the inland sea of Lake Michigan. The sun will glint off the lake with a hint of immortality, casting such sharply geometric shadows on the dramatic skyline that the city will look surreally emerald, as if rousing itself again to reclaim the great romance it once offered—of nature's metropolis, gangsters, and new schools of art, literature, and economics.

If there was a place where one might look for that promise to be reclaimed in 1991, it was the campus of the University of Chicago. Founded one hundred years earlier, the school boasted 64 Nobel laureates, 113 American Academy of Arts and Sciences members, alumni who included Philip Glass and Susan Sontag, and teachers like the late Enrico Fermi and Leon Lederman. Isolated on the city's South Side, the campus neighborhood featured the most seminaries per square mile of any spot in the world.

The reason for the clustering of seminaries around campus was the university's Divinity School, home of scholars like Paul Tillich, who popularized a vision of Christian faith in the atomic era; Paul Ricoeur, the French thinker on theological philosophy; and Mircea Eliade, the Romanian "exile from eternity," as he was dubbed by the *New York Times*. No one thinker had so profoundly studied the lost power of the "sacred" or the deeper level of life in modern times as the author of such widely read books as *The Sacred and the Profane* and *The Myth of the Eternal Return*.

May 21 at the Divinity School was marked by the excitement of the annual book sale and the anticipation of term's end. Outside the gothic Swift Hall, graduate students chatted in groups or lounged on the stone steps. Leafy oak trees shaded a tour guide who discussed campus safety with a group of high school juniors and their parents.

Inside Room 202 of Swift Hall, Ioan Culianu was finishing up his class Fundamentals of Comparative Religion, in which the day's subject was gnosticism. He discussed the Nag Hammadi texts, rediscovered in the modern era in 1945. "As if in a classic detective story, these scrolls had been hidden for centuries because they offered variations of the Bible, challenging the Christian church's idea of truth," he said. The gnostics saw life as sabotage, rebellion, and escape from the ignorant gods who ruled the world. "The point of gnostic knowledge," he concluded, "was to *use* it. It was meant to change the world." He read aloud from the prologue of one text: " 'These are an offering to an ideal order that completely transcends life as we know it. . . . Whoever finds the interpretation of these texts will not experience death.' "

After class Culianu and some of his students headed down to the book sale. It was a Hyde Park event, attracting students, staff members, retired professors, scholars, and others who toiled in or lived near the great university's offices and labs. The crowd filed into the Swift Common room, lined with oppressive oak wainscoting, where castoffs like Kenneth Clark's *The Nude* or Herbert Marcuse's *One-Dimensional Man* lay stacked on tables and chairs, and on the floor. On stereo speakers Ice-T blared, rattling the dust off portraits of past deans.

At the sale graduate student Alexander Arguelles approached Culianu. That afternoon Arguelles was to give his first thesis talk to the faculty, so he sought advice from his closest friend among the professors. "I'm nervous about this," he said.

"It's just a rite of passage." Culianu smiled and patted him on the back. "It's nothing to fear. You'll do fine. See you in a couple hours."

Arguelles watched him walk to the stairs, trying to feel reassured.

Culianu bounded up the main stairwell. For several weeks he had been juggling a dozen different projects. Earlier in the week he had sponsored an international scholarly conference on "after-death journeys," the first religion conference on campus in years. Entitled Other Realms: Death, Ecstasy, and Otherworldly Journeys in Recent Scholarship, it featured speakers from Barnard College, Hebrew University, Princeton, Notre Dame, and other schools. The talks had titles such as "The Ascent of the Visionary" and "Transcendence of Death." His students Greg Spinner and Michael Allocca catered the final dinner. "He demonstrated the worldwide continuities in reports of otherworldly journeys and demanded an explanation," said a reviewer of Culianu's later book on the subject. A university press wanted to publish the conference papers.

He had three books in press at once — the book on otherworldly journeys, another on gnosticism, and a dictionary of religions. He had several more close to contract, including a multivolume encyclopedia of magic for Oxford University Press. He was teaching two courses, Otherworldly Journeys and Out-of-Body Experiences and Fundamentals of Comparative Religions, supervising several doctoral students, and planning his first trip in nineteen years back to his home country of Romania. He was also planning to get married.

His fiancée was Hillary Wiesner, a graduate divinity student at Harvard. Quiet and distant, she had blossomed in their relationship. His coauthor on two of the forthcoming books and numerous pieces of short fiction, she was planning to travel with him to Europe that summer and to meet his family for the first time. "We're going to have such a party!" he would exclaim when he was feeling good about the trip. They would see Transylvania and his hometown of Iași, where his grandfather and great-grandfather had directed the country's oldest university. Ioan and Hillary had discussed such a trip often since the country's 1989 revolution.

Culianu made long telephone calls to his sister late at night. She pressed him to return. He kept changing his mind. Three days before, he told her he was being threatened by a far rightist group with which a former professor of his was closely associated. She downplayed the danger: people were threatened all the time. So he kept his plane tickets. But he was more worried than he let on.

"We cannot say *where* these after-death journeys take place," he had said in his concluding remarks at the conference. "Although we still mistake the space of the mind in these tales for the space outside, we are learning the former is no less powerful than the latter. Identity, power, and historical truth have their roots in these imaginative realms. Every individual thinks part of a tradition and therefore is thought by it, allowing us to perceive the obscure roots of history which go back to the dawn of *Homo sapiens*. And yet, the exploration of our mind space is only at the beginning."

Culianu was also having some fun. Earlier in the month he had been the featured scholar at a national science fiction conference at the Hilton in Schaumburg, Illinois. He lectured on the Renaissance and participated in a panel exploring questions such as "Is all magic bad magic?" He defended magical practice: "Magic is not about disorder," he said. "On the contrary, it reestablishes a peaceful coexistence between the conscious and unconscious when this coexistence is under attack."

The conference's featured author, science fiction writer John Crowley, had asked Culianu to be the Special Scholar Guest. Crowley had read Culianu's *Eros and Magic in the Renaissance* and had been eager to meet its author. The book was dense and difficult, but it captured Crowley's imagination. "He suggested a kind of mass hypnosis was possible, by means the Renaissance called magical but we call psychological, through the use of erotically charged images," Crowley said. The two had met a year earlier, becoming close friends. "I never had such an intense, sudden friendship in my life," Crowley said. For Culianu, who secretly wanted most of all to be a fantasy writer, the conference was a great inspiration. Participants in his conference sessions felt the same way about him. Conference organizer Jennifer Stevenson said that Culianu "hit you with such an impact, he made the world seem somehow much richer and more mysterious than you ever imagined."

On the last night of the conference, Culianu read his fiction for the first time in America to a packed audience in a suite nicknamed the Dharma Buns Café. Cowritten with Hillary, the story was called "The Language of Creation" and was to be published in National Public Radio columnist Andrei Codrescu's magazine, *Exquisite Corpse*. It describes a scholar very much like Culianu, "forty years old, living in a high-rise security building on a Lake," teaching at a "grey and renowned Midwestern University," to whom many strange coincidences occur, almost all of which were based on his real life. The story's main character comes to possess an ancient music box, which he believes contains a key to the language spoken by God: the Language of Creation. Yet the three former owners of the box each met with murder.

Although the narrator tries to break the code, he cannot. Gradually, however, he begins to feel threatened by the strange occurrences or "charismata" he associates with the box, wondering whether they signal some greater meaning than he realizes. The "charisms" included the ability to divine events, but only petty ones like whether his doorman will shave his mustache, and a "misplaced love charism," which caused certain female students to develop unwanted crushes on him. Culianu read: "After a certain moment my conviction of an occult connection between the charismata and the box had become so solid that I was tempted to make a test of its powers against a distasteful political regime. . . . The hypothesis that I might imminently resume the fate of [the former owners] came to haunt me." After much indecision, the narrator leaves the music box at a yard sale and escapes to freedom from what had become an intellectual prison posed by its secret.

At the end of the conference, Hillary Wiesner noticed that her fiancé seemed terribly distracted. He locked the keys in their rented red Toyota while it was still running. He could not remember when they were to see each other next. He kept pressing her to stay, not to return to Cambridge. When he saw her off at O'Hare airport, he looked sadder than she had ever seen him, as though he carried the weight of the world on his shoulders. What he desperately needed, she thought, was a good vacation.

❋ ❋ ❋

At about quarter to one on May 21, Culianu was in the Swift Hall canteen — a small, crowded, stuffy basement coffee shop with plastic-sealed Danish but good Kona coffee, falafel, and a buzz of heated conversation. There he chatted with students, then took the main stairwell up two steps at a time back to the third floor.

He stopped in his secretary's office at the end of the hall. It was quieter up here. Classes were in session, and seminar room doors were closed. He asked if he had any messages, picked up his mail, and walked to his office a few yards away.

Sitting at her desk, secretary Gwen Barnes listened to the droning voice of another faculty member dictating his book chapter on her headphones. She often worked through lunch because it was the only way to stay ahead of her assignments. Of the three faculty members she served, Ioan Culianu was by far her favorite. Raised in black South Side Chicago, she had felt an instinctive empathy with him when they first met. He greeted her in the morning with a bright "Good morning, Gwendolyn!" and treated her as a colleague. He had made her an editorial associate on his scholarly quarterly, *Incognita: International Journal for Cognitive Studies in the Humanities*. He took her to lunch and remembered her birthday. He encouraged her to earn her masters' degree. A university secretary for twelve years, she knew the academic world well enough to recognize that his attitude toward his secretary was not typical.

Across from her another secretary was mouthing something at her. Gwen Barnes looked up and pulled off the headphones.

"What?"

"Did you hear that?"

"Car backfiring," said the third secretary in the room.

"It sounded like a firecracker. Only more high-pitched."

❀   ❀   ❀

Professor Jerry Brauer sat in his corner office, wearing his trademark bow tie as he prepared for his seminar. He had opened his tall, lead glass windows to look out over the sunny quad. A former dean and a specialist in Puritanism, he had his yellowed lecture outline out and was reviewing it, concentrating. He gradually became aware that he was going to have to go to the men's room. He decided to finish what he was working on.

It was a little after one o'clock when he heard the loud pop. He kept working, but a part of his mind went off on its own. He tried to decide what could cause such a sound: Car backfire? No. Can't be, road's too far away. Gunshot? No. Can't be. Swift Hall, one o'clock.

It was not more than five minutes later when he decided he couldn't wait. He had to use the men's room. He headed up through the swinging doors, taking the steep service stairs. The steps echoed. Downstairs an overflowing dumpster stood beside a door that opened into the lobby; up above was another set of swinging doors. The stairs were deserted. He came out on the third floor, directly opposite the men's room. A tall, lanky young man whom Brauer did not recognize stood out in front. Brauer pushed the bathroom door. The student grabbed his arm. "Don't go in, Professor Brauer."

Brauer had already pushed in far enough to see the familiar lavatory with its blue stalls, yellow tile, fluorescent lights. A student peered at the second stall from the window. It was deathly quiet. A hand dangled beneath the stall door, with curled white fingers poking out from a turquoise shirt cuff. Blood made a small pool on the floor.

"Something terrible's happened," said the student.

"I can see that! We gotta help!" Brauer said.

"We already called for help."

The student turned toward Brauer. He was short, blond, and very scared. It was Jim Egge. He looked white as a sheet. "Dr. Brauer!" he said. "He's dead."

"Who? *Who's* dead?

"I'm not sure."

Suddenly a congregation of firemen, campus security officers, and paramedics came running down the hall. At first there were perhaps five people, followed quickly by another group that included a Chicago police sergeant and two beat cops. Everything happened quickly. Within minutes a paramedic wheeled in a stretcher. After a moment two Chicago detectives stepped in. By then there was a melee in the hall. Clark Gilpin, the current dean, had arrived. "Jerry!" he said. "What is it?"

Brauer pushed him toward the detective. "This is our dean," he said. "What's going on? We have to know who it is."

"Sure, but not right now. We're too busy."

Following them out came the paramedics with the stretcher. An oxygen mask covered the victim's face. Clark Gilpin asked to look at the face. The paramedic removed the mask. Gilpin peered down. The victim's face had swollen gray and expressionless. He looked like a fifty- or sixty-year-old man. No blood-soaked cavity or glaring wound revealed the violence of the death. Gilpin turned to Brauer. "I don't know him," he said.

"Well then, who does?" Brauer asked.

Jerry Brauer returned to the seminar room where his students waited, but no one wanted to discuss American revivalism. They kept hearing footsteps moving outside and a low hubbub. The book sale continued. Afterward Brauer would think: Why had no one come running when the shot was fired? Why did it take the police so long to cordon off the building's exits? If only he had not waited to complete his review of his notes, he might have seen the killer. He could not stop thinking about it.

❋　❋　❋

Gwen Barnes never heard the shot. She first learned of it from another secretary. Only two yards from the bathroom, they never thought of it as a gunshot. A young man came running in, telling her to call the university police. It seemed to her that the security officers took forever to come. She called again. After hanging up she hesitated, then went to look. In the men's room sunlight streamed from the courtyard window, bathing the 1950s floor tile. Blood was spreading from the fourth stall, shining in the fluorescent light. For a long moment the scene held her — the yellow and black specked tile, the hand, and an unusual opal watch that looked somehow familiar. Just then a loud rushing sound made her jump out of her skin — the urinals' automatic flush. She left.

Later she too saw the body on the stretcher. Despite the khaki trousers, turquoise striped shirt, yellow tie, maroon-bordered socks, and watch, she did not know who it was. It was almost 2:00 P.M. when a Chicago patrolman asked to use her phone. As she talked with another secretary, she overheard him spelling a name.

"C-u-l-i-a, n-o, a, n-u-u, no, U!"

A wave swept her up and carried her forward. She ran down the main steps, tears streaming down her face, not hearing herself screaming: "Oh God, oh God. It's Mr. Culianu! No, no, not Mr. Culianu! Not Mr. Culianu!" In the hall conversations stopped. Gwen rushed into Dean Gilpin's office, her cries rising in a loud wail. "It's Mr. Culianu!" she said.

"No, no, it's not."

"Yes it is! Yes it is!"

❊   ❊   ❊

At 3:30 when his seminar had a break, Jerry Brauer strode down to the dean's office. By then the rumor was spreading around the building that someone, maybe Ioan Culianu, had committed suicide. Most students could not believe it. Culianu? One of the happiest professors there? Small groups milled in the lobby and on the front steps. The book sale crowd still moved freely in and out; the stereo belted out concert announcements for the month. A few policemen patrolled the building while detectives Ellen Weiss and Al McGuire questioned a student who had made the error of telephoning, hyperventilating in his fear, to find out if the rumor was true.

In his somber office Gilpin sat quietly in a swivel chair. Ashen, he took a minute between telephone calls. He stared at Brauer. "It was Ioan Culianu, Jerry," he said. "And I didn't even recognize him . . ."

. . . . . .

"What happened?"

"Well, the police think it might be suicide."

"Did they find the gun?"

"No, no, there's no gun."

"Where do they think the gun is?"

"They say maybe he had a friend . . . who took it away."

"And implicate oneself in something like this? Suicide? He's just got his green card, he's going back to see his family, he's getting married . . . Wasn't he sitting on the toilet?"

"Yeah."

"Come on, what human being would go in, pull his pants down, take a gun, and stick it in the back of his head? Where are these guys coming from?"

"Well, it might be murder."

"*Might* be?"

The initial suicide report was in the newspapers, and it was on television. After twenty-four hours, though, when the medical examiner's report came in, there was no question. It was murder.

* * *

Greg Spinner and Michael Allocca noticed an ambulance outside Swift Hall when they unpacked groceries for the weekly Wednesday lunch for divinity students and faculty. That week's lunch talk was to cover the theology of the ABC television series *Twin Peaks*. After they finished, Patty Mitchell approached Greg out in front of building.

"Greg? Did you hear?"

"Hear what?"

"Ioan committed suicide."

"Ioan? Don't be ridiculous. I just saw him this morning. He's the last person in the world who would commit suicide."

Mitchell gave him a funny look.

Greg walked across the leafy quad to the Regenstein Library, hardly giving a thought to Patty's rumor. He remembered to note in his calendar a reminder to call Ioan; they had a longstanding date to get together as soon as his teacher's hectic life calmed down. After settling into his study carrel, Greg saw another Divinity School friend, Jason Gerber, approaching him. Jason's eyes were red. "Greg," he burst out. "Ioan's committed suicide!"

"Who's spreading this rumor? I just heard it from Patty Mitchell. It's ridiculous. Ioan did not, would not, could not, ever commit suicide." But slowly Greg rose and headed back to find out exactly what was going on.

Out on the quad the spring air carried something soft, like the breath of memory. His mind started to race. Without knowing it he ran a series of deductions, just as Ioan claimed the history of an idea or religion would follow. Number one: Ioan would not commit suicide. Number two: here were ambulance and, now, squad cars. Number three: two people had repeated a rumor Ioan was dead. If it was true, if Ioan was dead, then it had to be murder. If it was murder . . . Who would murder Ioan? A year earlier he had told Greg he was getting into "dangerous territory" in some writing . . . But what writing? Greg was running over now. One look at Gwen Barnes's stricken face and his neat train of thought abruptly ended.

❊ ❊ ❊

Later that day Culianu's students gathered on the steps of Swift Hall, crying, trying to console each other. "We just sat there, hugging each other. We couldn't speak," said Greg. Other students came up, each pressing the other for news. There was little. No gun, no money stolen, no sign of struggle.

In the evening the group headed over to Jimmy's, a favorite student bar where Ioan had often gone with them after class. Sitting apart from them in the dark, seedy front room, amid the scattered tables and some broken chairs, was Nathaniel Deutsch, assistant editor of *Incognita*. He did not join in their reminiscing and questioning. Nathaniel's mother was East European, and partly for that reason Ioan Culianu had shared a special relationship with him. In the darkness Nathaniel listened to the others and stared blankly at the dusty editions of baseball encyclopedias and almanacs kept on the shelf to settle bar arguments. He rested his head on his arms and began crying for relatives lost in the Holocaust. He did not, exactly, know why.

❊ ❊ ❊

In Cambridge, Massachusetts, Culianu's twenty-seven-year-old fiancée, Hillary Wiesner, was in a deep afternoon sleep. Often Ioan would telephone her after he woke from a nap, describing a dream that would be exactly what she was doing, or explaining something significant about his next publishing move or some obscure cosmology. It was part of the fabric of life with him. Before Ioan, Hillary had hardly held hands with a man. Her friends described her as intense, otherworldly, and one of the smartest women at Radcliffe College. Incredibly funny. But men? No, none, not before Ioan.

The phone rang, and she jumped. Her sleep had been dreamless. She sat bolt upright, frozen. It was Wendy Doniger, Ioan's colleague, holder of the Mircea Eliade chair in the faculty of the Divinity School, a powerful department member. "Hillary? Hillary, you better sit down. Are you sitting down?"

"What?"

There was a silence. "I'm afraid I have to tell you . . . Ioan has been killed."

"What?"

"I . . . I . . . Hillary, the police are asking if you know of anyone who would do such a thing. I'm so terribly sorry . . ."

For about one minute she couldn't breathe. Maybe it was ten minutes. Oh, she finally thought. Tears couldn't come. She looked at her wall, covered with pictures of him — from Milan, Madrid, Cairo, from the Metra train in Chicago, from Rome and Courmayeur and Paris. He was grinning in front of the big American flag she had bought him, "flown over the Capitol!" he liked to tell visitors. He was giving her the V for Victory sign he liked to make. He was probably America's biggest patriot . . . Slowly, methodically, she began taking the pictures down.

She hung up and telephoned her mother at work in the Board of Trustees office at Amherst College. By the time she had hung up again, her mother saying she was on her way, Hillary was already thinking about packing her bags. She pulled out her suitcase, still with the O'Hare destination tag from her last visit. It dawned on her very easily, very clearly, as one might figure out a difficult mathematics problem and know instantly that the solution was right and true and something more, fated. She had thought about it before, tried to prepare herself, even discussed it with her friends. You had to have a myth for your life, he once told her, some story you discover to live by and turn to at your darkest moments. Now, after all this time, just when everything seemed to have become so wonderful for them, she remembered. She had never taken the time to find one.

Mnemosyne, said the Greeks, is the mother of

the Muses; the history of the training of this most

fundamental and elusive of human powers will

plunge us into deep waters.

— *Frances Yates*, The Art of Memory

* * * * * * * *

THE AFTERMATH

Every day students left roses, lilies, fresh bouquets, and scattered petals at Culianu's office door. Chicago detectives Ellen Weiss and Al McGuire stayed past midnight the first few nights, sifting through the evidence and conflicting rumors. The killer had apparently walked past Culianu's stall, entered the next stall, perched on a toilet seat, and pointed the gun down at the professor's head. From the entry and exit wounds, the killer appeared to be left-handed.

The police district known as Area One on Chicago's South Side averaged some two hundred murders a year, mostly drug and gang killings. This one was unlike any other the police had encountered. It yielded virtually no solid evidence. Detectives found a note requesting that no one lock Culianu's office door; his secretary told them that the professor had commissioned a change in door locks. They found in his desk three walnuts from his family yard in Romania — evidence only of a close emotional link with events five thousand miles away. In Culianu's apartment a fax arrived from the office of the exiled king of Romania. Your box arrived, the fax said, but it was opened and empty. What did you send?

The coroner's report offered few clues. The autopsy found no "stippling" or gunpowder burns on the entrance wound, suggesting that the unusually small gun, a .25 caliber Beretta, was shot from a point at least eighteen inches from Culianu's head. "To kill with one shot from a .25 at that distance, that's not easy," said Cook County medical examiner Robert Stein. He called it "an expert shot, like a gangland execution."

On network television and in newspapers from the *Chicago Tribune* to the *New York Times*, Culianu's friends and family maintained the killing was the first political assassination of a professor on American soil. In articles and short stories in Italy and America and on BBC broadcasts, they said, Culianu had called the 1989 revolution in his home country a bitter failure. He attacked the new Romanian government with almost prophetic insight. He received death threats, as did other writers, and he attributed these to a new far right in his country, linked to the old Communist security police, or Securitate.

But investigators found no record of the threats. Culianu never reported them to the FBI or the police. He never showed anyone any letters. Detectives found his airplane and car reservations for a trip home still intact. While the killing stunned the school, terrified students, and stumped police, the FBI flew in a special Romanian-speaking agent named Gabriella Burger. The murder *looked* like an assassination, but not like any the FBI had ever seen. A professional killer would have chosen a higher-caliber gun and a far less conspicuous site. He would have fired more than once. He might not have even been a "he." The .25 was small enough to fit into a woman's purse.

If the killing was a political crime, then the biggest question was Why? Ioan Culianu was becoming well known in a special international circle of scholars, but he was not a major player in politics. The crime seemed to pose what Culianu would have called a ludibrium, a high Renaissance riddle that reveals a mystery of the universe in its unraveling. Why would a historian of religions and a would-be fantasy writer who had arrived in the United States with a dream of making the best-seller list have seemed so dangerous to someone?

* * *

While the FBI focused on the idea of a political murder, Chicago detectives McGuire and Weiss worked on theories of a disgruntled student or colleague, an occult fanatic, a homosexual lover, an interrupted mugging, or a drug deal gone sour. Right before Ioan Culianu was killed, they discovered, he placed a call from his Swift Hall office to someone in Medellín, Colombia. The call lasted one minute.

Culianu was an enthusiastic and sympathetic friend, detectives learned, and a groundbreaking thinker who specialized in dualism, astral religion, and the Renaissance magic arts of memory or "mnemonics" refined by a sixteenth-century philosopher named Giordano Bruno. Scholars praised his creativity, boldness, and linguistic command. "He had a rare ability," recalled Dean Gilpin, "to show how his and his students' work could be connected to larger events in the outside world." His courses on such subjects were extremely popular. Students adored him. "He was one of the few faculty members who actually just talked to students," said Karen Anderson. "He met us at the seminar door and greeted us by name," said Michael Allocca. Greg Spinner added, "I'll just never know anyone like him again." Recalling his teacher's willingness to buy him breakfast, Nathaniel Deutsch said, "He was a mensch."

As a teacher he was open, funny, and controversial. As a friend, however, he was secretive and insular. He seemed as if he was hiding something. "He was very complicated really, very difficult to know," said one faculty member, who saw him as a consummate academic hustler. He was suspected of seducing female students, or of trying the drug-induced ecstasies he wrote about. "A couple of faculty really hated him," said a student who did not want to be named. "He had just been tenured. My first thought when he was killed was Well, now they'll be happy."

Criticized as a "yuppie exile" and a self-promoter, he left behind totally conflicting impressions of who, exactly, he *was*. He was a charismatic forty-one-year-old émigré fluent in six languages who had earned three Ph.D.'s, including the *doctorat d'état* from the Sorbonne. His supporters considered his work to be brilliant, original, "a seminal contribution on the history of hermetic (magical) thought," according to his friend Umberto Eco. His life was a spiritual quest, taking him from Romania to Italy, France, the Netherlands, and the United States, as he sought a key to universal patterns in daily life. He claimed to have found that key in the imagination. Divinity School dean Clark Gilpin summed up the crime's themes at the university memorial service on June 3, 1991. As students, friends, and university administrators packed into Rockefeller Chapel, Gilpin spoke not of politics or motives but of the relation of ideas to the world: "The university's reason for being displays helplessness before a violent power that ideas could not foresee, could not deflect, could not comprehend. . . . The relation of human thought to the mysterious power at the heart of creation takes on new urgency. Is there any enduring connection between the human ideas to which universities are accountable and some eternal wisdom present at the primordium, when God 'set a compass upon the face of the deep'?"

* * *

Around the world the crime set off a wave of telephone calls between Culianu's friends and fellow exiles, including Andrei Codrescu and Saul Bellow. Their suspicions rested on the ex-Communist secret police, a force so vicious even their counterparts in other East European countries did not trust them. Others suspected Romania's fascists, who may have once counted Mircea Eliade, Culianu's gentle, renowned mentor, as one of them. Many members of the Iron Guard had settled in North America's Midwest, evading responsibility for one of history's least-known holocausts. Ioan Culianu lectured all over the world about the power of the past, while acting as though someone from the past was always at his heels. Whatever

its motive, his murder sounded most of all like the plot of one of the
fantasy novels he was writing, an enigma eerily foreseen by the
victim himself.

Like his mentor, or the mystics, or the romantic poets, Culianu
felt that the details and coincidences in our lives offer an answer to
the most fundamental questions of who we are. It was the prophetic
quality of his fiction and political statements that added the strang-
est dimension to his story. He wrote of political events that mate-
rialized months or years later, of secret sects, and of murders remarkably like his own. This legacy offered clues to anyone who
cared to look — to the logic of our universe, to our psyches, and,
perhaps, to the identity of his killers.

In the last chapters he wrote before his death, he almost seemed
to explain the proliferation of theories about his murder. In "Games
People Play," from *The Tree of Gnosis*, he began with the story of a
Chicago gangster who decided his next move by flipping a coin.
Culianu compared his idea of historical movements branching into
more permutations to the decisions of the gangster flipping his coin.
He called the process the "multiplication of theories." He claimed
that the twentieth century's fascination with "archetypes, formalism
and structuralism" demonstrated a conviction that in moments of
upheaval, such as a revolution, we can most clearly see deeper processes operating in history. He wrote that such convulsions reveal
systems of thought, each functioning almost as "an object coming
from outside and crossing our space in an apparently disconnected
way, in which there is a hidden logic which we can reveal *only if we
are able to move out of our space.*"

Other scholars found such formulations either exciting and profound or unproved and bizarre. In the space of a few months investigators would have two suspects and, much later, a young man, with
the same birthday as Ioan Culianu, offering evidence from a strange
series of experiences. No one, though, could see the background of a
life that cut across boundaries of time and geography, the experience
from which Culianu's thought sprang.

YOUTH, 1950–1972

The world is a chiaroscuro: *there are enough traces*

and signs of a superior presence to make it bearable.

—*I. P. Culianu,* Eros and Magic in the Renaissance

* * * * * * * * *

THE ART OF MEMORY

Culianu was born in a once-beautiful home on a hill in eastern Moldavia. He came from the most intellectual branch of a *boyar*, or noble, family in Iaşi, or Jassy, a cultural and scientific center near the Soviet border. If the most striking thing about his life was its extraordinary unity, then its themes were set in a region "where streams sprang up and swift rivers poured down, whispering secrets," as the Moldavian author Ion Creangă wrote.

Spanning part of Europe's eastern frontier, Romania is a fertile land long pressed by empires, from the Roman to the Soviet. "The history of Romania," reads an official guide brochure, "is undoubtedly one of the most tormented parts of European history." Enclosed by Bulgaria, Serbia, Hungary, Ukraine, and Moldovia, the country is an outpost — a Latin people set the farthest north of any Latin, a European land set the farthest east of any European. With a culture poised between the Orient and the West, Romanians "can be counted among the great practitioners of the . . . art of survival," observed historian Istvan Deak.

Dominated by foreign power and subjected to corrupt leadership, first foreign and then native, Romanians survived as a people primarily through the shared experience of telling stories. "Our weapons of sabotage were ambiguity, humor, mystery, poetry, song, and magic," wrote Andrei Codrescu. The most famous Romanian in the West, Dracula, is a fictional character based on the aptly named fifteenth-century prince Vlad Ţepeş, or Vlad the Impaler. The most emblematic national symbol to many Romanians is an enchanted sheep, Miorița, who foresees the murder of her beloved shepherd at the hands of his brothers. Instead of resisting his fate, the shepherd instructs Miorița to transform his tragedy into triumph through myth. "Tell my mother the murder was really a wedding presided over by the sun and the moon." The Romanian poet Lucian Blaga adopted the shepherd for a national "mioritic space," a world of the imagination no conqueror can violate. Mircea Eliade saw in him a national escape from history. A Westerner would see him as mad.

Culianu's home town of Iaşi was a provincial capital and center of "the holy land of nationalism," with cobblestone boulevards and trolley cars, a domed synagogue, and statues of heroes like Ştefan the Great (1457–1504). Dominated by the stately white Metropolitan cathedral, the intricately carved Trei Ierarhi, or Three Hierarchs church, and the fantastic, enormous Palace of Culture, Iaşi featured some of the country's great institutions of literature and its oldest university, presided over by Culianu's grandfather and great-grandfather.

The Culianu family had escaped to Romania from Greece in 1721, fleeing Ottoman persecution. In Iaşi they entered a world of *boyars* and peasants, of church privilege and deep class divisions, of narrow rutted roads, shrouded valleys, steep mountains, and broad melancholy plains. Nearly four-fifths of the population were peasants, and most of them were uneducated. Out of the mountains their carts puttered along as they had for centuries, driven by men wearing fur hats and layers of wool coats, their women seated beside them in bundles of wool. The surrounding plains in winter smelled of wind, snow, and charcoal fires.

In the nineteenth century Culianu's great-grandfather Neculai Culianu helped found the Junimea Society, or Young Conservatives. These privileged young men joined the pressing debate about whether their country should follow the East or West as a cultural model. The Junimeists voted for the West, donning tight-collared Parisian shirts while many of their fathers still wore Turkish pashas' robes. They proposed a democratic program promoting the nation's arts while preserving their privileges. As the University of Iaşi's president from 1880 to 1898, Neculai ("Papa") Culianu ceremoniously rode his horsedrawn carriage the five blocks from his home to the university, wearing a black greatcoat and top hat, demonstrating to a primitive region the perquisites and power of higher learning.

It was a good time to be a *boyar*. At Christmas the streets filled with gypsy or Roma men playing drums, accordions, and saxophones, pushing real dancing bears. A pretty six-year-old Roma girl might come into the inn, plant her feet firmly, and play a haunting melody on an exquisite miniature violin. Carolers came frequently to the door, singing songs like "Moş Crăciun" (Old Man Christmas) that sounded otherworldly. There were big barrels of pickled cabbage, peppers, and cucumbers. On Christmas Eve a beautiful snow might fall as smells of roast lamb and pork, *tsuica* or plum brandy, church incense and hearth fires, rose beneath the stars.

By the early years of the twentieth century the Culianus featured prominently in physics, chemistry, mathematics, and law. They sent their children to the best universities in Bonn and Paris. They ruled comfortable estates, farming, horse trading, and helping to build a modern infrastructure in science and law. They were related to or friendly with prominent people, including the literary critic Paul Zarifopol, King Carol's controversial mistress and first wife, Zizi Lambrino, and the novelist Mihail Sadoveanu. As a boy growing up in the Communist world, Ioan Culianu learned early that he belonged to a high tradition in a country where intellectuals served as political leaders.

* * *

In contrast, his mother's father, the physicist and chemist Petru Bogdan, was a peasant orphan who built his career through talent, risk-taking, and savvy socializing. Bogdan married the daughter of an orthodox priest, a beautiful Paris-trained pianist. They raised seven children, all of whom went on to become medical doctors, scientists, or attorneys. Sporting a busy white mustache and patrician belly, Bogdan rose to the position of university rector in 1927.

His fourth child was a funny, talented girl. Slight, dark, and graceful, Elena Bogdan was fiercely loyal to friends and family. She earned a doctorate and professorship in inorganic chemistry, also developing a keen interest in photography. Her photograph albums captured a world of picnics in the meadows of the Jiu Valley, at the medieval castle at Hunnedoara, or at the beaches of Constanza. Her girlfriends posed with dresses lifted high or arm in arm with handsome young men wearing white flannels. In half-lit prints she explored the family house, with its winding porch balustrade and labyrinthine rooms shaded by oak and walnut trees. It was said to be the former home of the poet Veronica Micle, illicit lover of the national poet Mihai Eminescu. The garden where the literary couple met secretly, immortalized in their love poems, stood a few streets away.

The 1920s offered a period of freedom, unrest, and rising wealth. After the breakup of the Austro-Hungarian Empire, Greater Romania increased in size by almost a third, poised to play the leading role it had long expected. An oligarchy helped subsidize railroads and factories, while newly landed peasants suffered under onerous bank rates. Avant-garde artists like the sculptor Constantin Brâncuşi, the playwright Eugène Ionesco, and the young novelist Mircea Eliade vaulted the culture into the twentieth century while extolling the best of its unique, wild past.

Yet democratic traditions never really took root. Anti-Semitism rose with the millions of ethnic minorities who joined the nation in its new territories. At the University of Iaşi, a charismatic student named Corneliu Codreanu founded a fascist movement called the Legion of the Archangel Michael, later the Iron Guard. One of the oldest of European fascist movements, the Iron Guard called for a new politics and a "new man" of moral, and ethnic, purity. The Iron Guard's mystical nationalism appealed to many of the young intellectuals dissatisfied with social corruption, including young writers E. M. Cioran and Mircea Eliade. Evolving into what political scientist Vladimir Tismaneanu called "the most straightforward expression of national anti-Semitism in Eastern Europe," the Iron Guard drew on a volatile and "temporary alliance between the mob and the elite."

As university rector, Petru Bogdan faced the Iron Guard's influence in his faculty and student body, and he brokered increasingly violent clashes between Codreanu's followers and student socialists and Communists. Twice the university had to be closed. As the country tilted toward alliance with the Axis powers, Bogdan became known for defending some of Iaşi's Jews one day by wielding his marble-handled cane against their tormentors.

Against this backdrop of fear Elena Bogdan began dating the son of Iaşi's leading family. Sergiu Culianu had a fragile physique, a military bearing, and owlish glasses. Because of ill health he had returned from his studies of advanced differential calculus at the Sorbonne in Paris. He suffered from asthma and later, under Communist rule, tuberculosis. In Iaşi he drove an old Citroën that made him a character in the neighborhood. When it stopped its engine loudly sputtered and died unless his brother Henri jumped out to crank it. Arriving home, Henri or Sergiu leaped out while the car still moved, rousing chickens as they flung open their driveway gate.

During the summer of 1938 Sergiu and Elena took to swimming together in a nearby stream. One day they stayed late with her sister and had to take a small horsedrawn cab home in the dark. The cab was built for two, and after much shifting, Elena ended up on Sergiu's lap. "I'm not hurting you?" she asked, laughing.

"Not yet!" he called.

Two years later they were married.

* * *

In 1938 King Carol had the handsome young Corneliu Codreanu assassinated. In the public backlash Romania's Iron Guard found its moment. It allied with the military dictator Ion Antonescu, who took over from Carol in 1940. Within a few months, though, Antonescu and his new ally Adolf Hitler decided the Guardists were too unstable a force to harness. Mired in blood-and-soil mythology, the Iron Guard "brought a death cult to Romanian politics," wrote the historian Vlad Georgescu. When the Guardists failed to overthrow Antonescu, they took out their anger in vicious pogroms. What had begun as an idealistic movement of nationalist pride veered into something shrouded in history's silence. One American journalist reported that Jews in Bucharest were killed in a beef slaughtering plant, their bodies hung from meathooks. In June 1941 the Iron Guard followed with a pogrom in its home base of Iaşi.* As a government prosecutor, Henri Culianu received death threats from the Guardist killers he pursued.

In the turbulence of Europe the story of this holocaust remained lost to the larger world. After 1942, official government policy under Ion Antonescu resulted in an even greater loss of life, accounting for the deaths of 250,000–300,000 Jews and tens of thousands of Romas. The Iron Guard continued on its own, assassinating the historian Nicolae Iorga, who had once been a sympathizer.

Shortly thereafter the fortunes of war turned against Germany, and King Carol's son Michael removed Antonescu. Michael switched sides in August 1944, declaring war on the Axis. Already, the Soviets were advancing on Iaşi from the east. Petru Bogdan, seventy-two years old and director of Iaşi's Royal Cultural Foundation and university library, had to save his family and the university's rare manuscripts.

At home his daughters followed radio reports of the Soviet army's advance, while Bogdan boarded up the university library. Each train leaving Iaşi was jammed with fleeing women and children. When Bogdan pounded the last nail home, the family raced to the train station. In the chaos, dust rose with the smells of bodies, death, and fear. Thieves stole family heirlooms as people climbed on top of each other, squeezing into the last train cars, hanging from the luggage racks. Over the shouts and curses, Soviet warplanes thundered. Bogdan shoved his wife and three daughters onto the very last train and jumped in beside them.

* Aron Hirt-Manheimer, introduction to *Jagendorf's Foundry*, by Siegfried Jagendorf (New York: HarperCollins, 1991), xxii–xxiii.

Their second night in a small hotel in Transylvania, Petru Bogdan died in his sleep. He may have felt he had saved his family from the final scourge of a troubled century. Within twenty months, though, the Soviet-backed Communist Party seized Romania's parliament. Antonescu was interrogated and tortured in Russia, and eventually shot by a military tribunal. The country's best hope, King Michael, was twenty-five years old, and with no support from the Allies, he abdicated. The Soviets imposed a Communist government, seizing from families like the Bogdans and the Culianus most everything they owned. The day the law "nationalizing" their home went into effect in Iaşi, January 5, 1950, Elena gave birth to her second and last child: Alexandru Ioan Petru Culianu.

❀　❀　❀

Born late in his parents' lives, Ioan Culianu was the product of a conscious effort to continue the family line. His mother was forty-two, and his sister was four years older than he was. His family baptized him Alexandru for a famous relative, Alexandru Ioan Cuza, hero of the nationalist movement of the nineteenth century. From the moment he opened his eyes, the child was imbued with a grandiose destiny to fulfill.

The home at 13 Strada Sfîntul Athanasie (Saint Athanasius Street, named for the family church) was a much poorer place than it once had been, but it still was impressive. Its most arresting feature was a long, winding porch with an intricately carved rail, overlooking a towering walnut tree planted by Culianu's great-grandfather. Behind this house stood another, larger brick home that had also belonged to the family, where his great-grandfather had helped found the Freemasons, an institution useful in the drive for nationhood in the nineteenth century. Iaşi featured several other family homes, peopled by elderly relatives who, in their quirks and pretensions of aristocracy, provided a fertile ground for a young child's imaginative world. "That house was a paradise," said his cousin Miron Bogdan, a Paris-trained pulmonary specialist. "There, on holidays, we managed to stop history."

History to the family was what in *Ulysses* Stephen Dedalus called a "nightmare from which I'm trying to awake." The government confined them to "four rooms suffused with the smell of decomposing upholstery," Culianu wrote. They lived in poverty and in fear of Securitate, the secret police trained by the Soviets. It was a time of banging on the door at night, disappearances, mock trials, imprisonment, forced labor, and death. Prevented from finding a job, Sergiu Culianu withdrew into a separate home, where he pursued his mathematics problems. The burden of carrying on the family name fell to his young son.

The boy was raised by three women: his mother, her sister Ana Bogdan — a medical professor, fired in 1950 by the Communists — and his nanny, who had been with the family thirty years. The children called their nanny Manea. Instilled with a burning drive to succeed, Ioan was a bright, funny child. Forbidden to play with other children, he amused himself with solitary games in the walled garden. Life was difficult without a father. Once when he was three years old, the boy hoisted himself by a coffee table. He sidled to one end, pointing to a picture of his father. "Nene!" he said, calling his invented word for his father. "Nene!" It became Ioan's nickname.

He looked up to his older sister, Tess, picking up on her resentment of their mother's aristocratic pretensions, and moving with her from the family's passion for the sciences to art and literature. They played in the few rooms to which the family was relegated — the kitchen, the drawing room, a hallway with a huge potbellied stove, and a spare bedroom with its high arched white ceiling. Even though the family shared the house with worker-tenants, it was still a place of mystery, of windows swinging open suddenly in an evening breeze.

Even with the scant heat, their mother made sure to invoke the family's heyday at Christmastime. The children sang carols around the family's battered piano. At night they went from door to door, singing. They carried papier-mâché medallions made from baker's sieves, each hoisted on the end of a staff and decorated with mirrors and stars. This was forbidden, but because they were just small children they could get away with it.

At the center of the largest medallion was an icon of the nativity they kept stored all year in the attic. Going into the attic to recover the Christmas decorations was an adventure in itself. They found old clothes of wealthy relatives and fashioned them into costumes for plays. They found photographs of opulent weddings — of women with bare shoulders in taffeta dresses, men in epaulets and monocles standing in glittering ballrooms.

Once in the attic they discovered an old cookbook that had been in the family for generations. It was enormous and black, and it smelled of dried dust and paper. Inside they discovered notes from their great-grandparents stuck between the yellowed leaves, directing servants what was to be served at banquets at the turn of the century: exotic cakes and roasts such as honey turkey or piglet. The notes even contained instructions for slaughtering and carving the animals. The cakes included *scutece*, or god's linen. There were lemon cookies with nuts and four kinds of biscuits, each flavored with raisins, jams, cocoa, poppy seeds, honey, or walnuts from the tree in the garden.

Manea was a master chef trained at the monastery where the family spent the summers. She had beautiful green eyes and wore a black velvet cap like a pillbox with her black habit. At home she directed the children's religious instruction, as well as holiday cooking. For Christmas they ate cow's tongue seasoned with olives in a brown onion sauce, *mîncare rece de iepure* or cold rabbit stew, and Ioan's favorite — turkey with raisins, grapes, and tomato.

Christmas Eve was the one time the children were allowed in the kitchen to decorate their own special cakes. The house filled with the scent of black currant jam and nuts and apples baking. It was a ritual to prepare the dough into its own special shapes, using the family's clay cookie cutters. They iced the cookies with their own sayings. No one else could look as the confections went into the oven, covered with linen towels.

The family did not have money, though. They had lost everything. Ioan's mother and sister spent hours at night carefully resewing the runs in their single pairs of nylon stockings. Like most people, his parents lived in fear, and at the holidays no one was allowed to visit much, because observing traditions was grounds for punishment. But they had *knowledge* of the traditions. Ioan and Tess learned that everything had a sacred meaning, a second level of love or superseding form from a profound hidden world. The cooking and holiday celebration trained them to see that life's sustenance was not simply a matter of being fed.

They knew what they were told in school was false. The school-

· · · · · ·

master, for instance, called Father Christmas "Father Cold," and his picture was a frightening nonreligious symbol. The schoolmaster dissuaded the children from keeping up the traditions. But some teachers protected them. Everyone lived on more than one level.

At night Manea read them stories from Aesop's fables, the *Book of Alexander*—a fictionalized, lurid account of Alexander the Great's conquests—and *The Lives of the Saints*. Listening with his sister, Nene embellished the stories. He made up saints, like one who hung from a tree so his feet would never touch the ground. Tess mocked the pure young girls who hid in mountain caves, casting spells to ward off the lusting Turks. Undaunted by their giggles, Manea told them of a girl seduced by a demon who stroked her with his long cold tail. Slowly they stopped laughing as she described the girl's banishment to the mountains with her demon-child, the two left to wander the windswept hills like animals. Manea's enthralled voice rose in the darkness, coloring their dreams.

❋   ❋   ❋

In one room of the house lay an uncle, an accomplished mathematician bedridden in a cot, slowly dying of gas inhalation suffered during the Second World War. His sole pleasure in life was a devoted Labrador retriever, Dag, who sat at his feet all day. The family wrote medical experts about his illness: it was a hopeless case. Completely lucid, he wasted away in front of Ioan, who brought him math problems sent from his uncle's colleagues and held books over his face so he could read. Ioan took particular care of Dag, walking and feeding him, waking each morning to brush his hair. One day a tenant decided Dag had harmed one of his chickens. He pulled out a shotgun and, in front of the boy, fired at the dog's head, killing him.

Tess and Ioan witnessed the murder of a world. Their father suffered a physical breakdown. As he grew older he depended more and more on the son who came to visit him alone in his small house. Dying in 1964, he bequeathed to Ioan a set of notebooks containing the mathematical formulas he had scribbled in his attempt to understand the universe.

Like the gnostic heretics Ioan Culianu later relished as a scholar, his family seemed to be the losers of history, and their tradition most like that of the House of Usher. Yet they made of their suffering a will to prevail. The potbellied stove and crude wooden floors, the cramped dusty side rooms, the long winding balustrade, and the sometimes frightening tenants all made the house a realm conducive for study, thought, and reading in the labyrinthine traditions of Borges and Poe. The air of threat made Ioan's childhood a time of closeness most children never know. "We learned there are only very few real values in life," said his cousin and best friend, Miron Bodgan. "Very few."

* * *

As Culianu devoured the stories of Dumas and Poe, he came to feel that chance events offered answers to life's most fundamental questions. "He was the most connected young boy I have ever known, and it was evident from the age of twelve or thirteen he was evolving in a much different way than other children," observed Miron. This connection to a second level of existence came most clearly from summers spent at a mountain monastery, where Ioan began keeping elaborate astrological and astronomical notebooks.

Founded in 1808, Văratic Monastery, exclusively for women, was unusual because it both participated in a village's daily life and took in families on holiday. Set near a ridge in the Neamţ foothills among other monasteries dating back to the thirteenth century, the three churches and prayer huts of Văratic looked Mediterranean, with their gleaming white walls, pressed tin roofs, and neatly arched windows. In summer the grounds smelled of rosewater and incense. Vacationing families stayed in the nuns' pale blue homes spread over a hillside, their glassed-in balconies seemingly supported by stacks of firewood jammed in underneath.

The family had been coming to Văratic since Petru Bogdan first vacationed there in 1908. To reach it they woke early in the morning in Iaşi, taking a steam train to the town of Tîrgu Neamţ, with its muddy main street named Eternity. There they switched to a bus or *cursa*, ending this journey at a roadside turnoff by climbing onto a *carutsa*, a peasant's rickety horsedrawn wagon that ferried them the final few miles into the mountains.

Miron and Nene spent their summer days wandering in the mountains, locating the caves of Manea's saints, including the tranquil spot where her namesake, Sfînta or Saint Teodora, hid five hundred years earlier behind rock outcroppings from invading Turkish armies. They learned the landscape by heart, memorizing the flowers like Queen Anne's lace, *conduraşi* or "shoes of the princess," and phlox, as well as the stones, rocks, juniper bushes, pine trees, and deer they startled. Deep in the forest they found tiny, ancient monasteries and hermits. Sometimes they tried, like Renaissance magicians, to communicate their thoughts to each other by telepathy. At fourteen they felt total freedom and irresponsibility. Nothing could disturb this closeness, not even the menace that tormented the grown-ups.

In the evening they talked with the adults, who offered a connection to history through discussion. Many were distinguished professors; some were still active, while others had been forced out of their university positions. They invited the children to join them in intellectual dialogue. In these discussions Miron and Nene learned the chiaroscuro of life under communism. Their aunt Ana and an uncle, both medical doctors, together directed their summer outings. Their aunt was a persecuted dissident, while their other uncle was a high-placed Communist official, later the personal physician to Nicolae Ceauşescu. Yet at Văratic the two packed lunches together, assigned bunk beds, and put aside their different chosen paths.

At the monastery one summer, Ioan's mother and aunt warned a sixteen-year-old second cousin that she had to be quiet. "Nene is sleeping during the day and working all night." At breakfast he noticed her and began pursuing her. He talked of astrology and magic as they walked the paths lined with pine and fir trees, and of Renaissance philosophers who understood the ways in which the mind could be manipulated. In the evenings they sat on the balcony of a nun's cottage, watching the sun set and smoke rise from the cooking of the evening's dinners. Between puffs on his cigarette, he told her his dream and secret ambition. Someday, he said, I'm going to be a famous professor in the West, with a house and a little red sports car. Someday.

Graduating from the lycée with the highest grade, he dreamed of escape.

1967 was a good year for the Beatles, Michel Foucault,

for me and even for Ceauşescu.

—*I. P. Culianu, "Euforisme," Lumea Liberă, 1990*

UNIVERSITY DAYS, 1967–1971

Culianu escaped Iaşi in 1967 to the University of Bucharest, where he enrolled in the Faculty of Romanian Literature and Language. It was an odd choice of "faculty" or major subject for him, coming from a family steeped in the sciences. Romanian literature seemed a minor field (except in Romania), one for student malcontents or those marking time. Yet it was largely from this group of 103 students that Ioan Culianu drew his closest friends, each of whom went on to a prominent intellectual career.

In Bucharest his family had many connections, and his relatives still lived in prominent homes in some of the best districts. His cousin and closest friend, Miron, had grown up there. Yet as much as he wanted to escape Iaşi, Culianu found the move to Bucharest exceedingly difficult. Iaşi was a provincial town in which, despite all the family's suffering, the Culianu and Bogdan names carried a weight of prestige and connection. In Bucharest he was one in a crowd. An Oriental city, as close geographically and culturally to Istanbul as to Paris, Bucharest was dirty, raucous, corrupt, blisteringly hot in summer, and icy and wet in winter.

He lived first in the student dorms at Grozăveşti, several train stops from the main campus. A complex of monolithic Stalinist towers, the buildings resembled most of all a Bronx housing project. Light came from a bare bulb suspended by wires from the ceiling. Hot water ran for only an hour a day, and the hour kept changing. As in the London of Sherlock Holmes, the pollution and dampness of the city caused a deep rolling fog that descended on the already unlit city without warning, so that a person could not see even two yards ahead. Years later Culianu recalled his sense of isolation: "The only way in which I can explain to myself how I later managed to succeed very rapidly, confronting foreign and strange environments, constantly learning difficult unknown languages, is by the trauma I suffered at 17 when I moved from Iaşi to Bucharest. This experience was more difficult than all the others . . . ."* He would later experience wrenching loneliness in true exile, and it is remarkable he felt so alone in a city that was only a six-hour train ride from home.

At the university he was insular and driven, a "fanatic of work," his cousin Miron said. On his door he hung a "Do Not Disturb" sign when he stayed up all night studying. His friends learned to respect it. In part he was fulfilling a family tradition, in part rebelling against the family pursuit of sciences, but mainly he was driven by a grandiose dream.

In an introductory course he met two students sitting across from him, who responded with smiles when he grimaced at the third-rate lectures. Silviu Angelescu was an older, baby-faced, self-assured rival. Şerban Anghelescu was more relaxed and easygoing; they

* Ioan Culianu, "Euforisme," *Lumea Liberă*, September 16, 1990, p. 13.

nicknamed him Bula for the clown of Communist urban folklore. At first both found the thin, intense Culianu foreboding and isolated. In the end their friendships were forged in heated arguments over new European writers whose texts they smuggled into class. In pirated photocopied editions, they read the subversive works of anthropologist Claude Lévi-Strauss, historian and critic Michel Foucault, and psychologist Carl Gustav Jung. They were lucky to be studying during a time of relative freedom when such books could be found. Encouraged by a few teachers, they pursued new trends in European thought like hermeneutics or the art of interpretation, new literary theories and the psychoanalysis of myth, challenging the shabby Communist version of reality.

More important, they uncovered the hidden previous generation of Romanian artists and writers like Mircea Eliade, Eugène Ionesco, and Constantin Brâncuşi. With their "terrifying will to create," these thinkers had worked in the forefront of the European avant-garde in the 1920s and 1930s. They became role models, offering reassurance that Romania had an important world role in challenging both Eastern mysticism and Western rationalism. Of all the radicals of that generation, though, it was the young, handsome, adventurous, bearded Mircea Eliade who captivated them most.

Eliade spent a lifetime exploring modern humanity's lost sense of place in the cosmos and seeking the unconscious symbols or patterns in human behavior. But it was the sheer adventure of his life — his youth as a popular science writer, travels in India seeking the secrets of yoga and eroticism, his work as a cultural attaché in Lisbon, a writer in Paris, and, finally, a renowned religion scholar in Chicago — that most inspired Ioan Culianu.

Culianu and his friends read Eliade in a period when his books could be found in French editions in small bookstores. The available texts included the journal he edited, *Zalmoxis*, and religion studies like *Aspects of Myth and Mythology* and *Myth of the Eternal Return*. Such books hit Culianu like Salinger's *Catcher in the Rye* or Kerouac's *On the Road* swept up a similar generation of young Americans. Eliade was not only one of the most accomplished and boldest intellectuals of the Romanian diaspora, he was also pursuing exactly those questions that most excited his younger follower: What is religion, exactly? Is there a deeper logic in worldwide myths like resurrection, or the eternal soul? Culianu shared other interests with Eliade—Renaissance thought, fantasy fiction, Indian religions, even the patterns in animal behavior. Most of all, though, the young student revered him as a man who lived his ideas; Eliade did not merely study Hindu mystics, for instance, he virtually *became* one. Culianu found in Eliade the only guide who could teach him what he wanted, and more: "His image of what a man should be came from Eliade's books," his former wife, Carmen Georgescu, later said. "A visionary, a hero of special destiny who sees the symbols we cannot see. He modeled his life as an Eliade fictional hero."

As a college junior, pressured by his father's failure and his grandiose self-conception, he vacillated between the humanities and the sciences. Reading Eliade helped him through his "identity crisis," he later explained to an interviewer, describing his decision to pursue the history of religions even though the field was banned in Romania. "I am tied to Mircea Eliade, I would say, by my whole existence."*

* * *

Culianu was probably the best student at the university in fifty years, teachers said, and for that reason he was allowed to make an unusual switch in his second year from Romanian literature to Italian and Renaissance religion studies, Eliade's subject, after passing a full-day examination. By then he led a group of prominent students, including Miron, Şerban, Silviu, as well as Dumitru Radu Popa, his small, quick-minded second cousin whose grandfather had been dean of the medical school, and the tormented Victor Ivanovici, who rivaled Culianu as the group's best thinker. Rounding out their entourage was a thin, self-taught rock-and-roll mystic, Dorin Zaharia. Though Zaharia never took a class, the other boys turned to him, along with Nene Culianu, to direct their Socratic discussions of God, the afterlife, Indian philosophy, and Zen that dissolved into laughter late in the night.

* Ioan Culianu, interview by Andrei Oişteanu, in "Ioan Petru Culianu—A Traveller to the World Beyond," *Romanian Review* (Bucharest), nos. 9–10 (1994): 137, translated and adapted from "Ioan Petru Culianu: Reconstituiri in domeniul mitologiei româneşti," *Revista de Istorie si Teorie Literară* (Bucharest) 3 (1985).

The world to them was a gnostic game, run by incompetent party hack professors. At Culianu's urging they all took on false names: the critical Radu became Rhetoricus Ethicus, and Dorin Zaharia became Chubby, for Chubby Checker. Celebrating his Greek roots, Culianu took the name Brother Ellis, for Hellas. They formed a literary group called Atlantida (Atlantis) and played pranks on their professors by inventing elaborately false bibliographic citations in papers, or challenging them in class to comment on new texts on deconstruction or hermeneutics. One day a professor took Culianu up on his challenge. "I do not know this book by Lévi-Strauss," he said. "Would you tell me and the class what it is about?" His name was Ion Coja. His seeming candor endeared him to the group, as did the support of a few other young professors. They were invited to join, sometimes, in the parties.

The group would meet in the hall or the student bar, talking and joking, reading their papers, poems, and short stories to each other. They exchanged books — a great rarity because it was very difficult to get books by foreign authors. They learned that no regime, no matter how powerful, could prevent you from *thinking.* They participated in seminars and panels, careful not to challenge each other for the same prizes. When one of them won a prize, he had to sponsor a huge celebration that would last well into the morning.

Of all of them, Culianu was the moodiest. He would go three or four days in isolation, eating only honey and milk as part of his Hindu asceticism, working on what would become his three-hundred-page thesis, and eventually his book *Eros and Magic in the Renaissance.* He moved frequently. After his first year he moved to a family home at 23 Bulevardul Dacia. He lived next at his cousin Miron's house, and then an aunt's ornate home that she had kept from being nationalized. Finally he found the perfect place in his friend Silviu's mother's house, a tiny attic room with its own entrance on a pleasant old back street, Strada Turda. He kept it so cold in winter that his breath fogged. He had few possessions except for a cot, stacked with books, and his typewriter. He slept on the floor and practiced yoga for hours a day. He refused to kill any animal, so the room became a sanctuary for mice and ants.

He began studying Sanskrit with Professor Prabadh Vidyasagar. He found in every detail of his life a hidden meaning and felt it critical that Vidyasagar—the only Hindu professor in all of Romania—had studied at the very same Himalayan monastery as Eliade. "It *can't* be a coincidence," he told his sister.

* * *

In the reading room at the University of Bucharest, with its impressive and stately high windows and cold dirty floorboards, Ioan Culianu studied the Renaissance philosophers and magicians Marsilio Ficino (*The Book of Life*) and Giordano Bruno (*The Art of Memory*) in books not yet banned by the government. To call them magicians and philosophers was misleading, because they knew no boundaries between such disciplines and those of modern psychology or hard science. Here he found the possibility of meaningful rebellion for him—not outward, but inward. Ficino and Bruno were famous men in the Renaissance, sought by kings but persecuted by the church, and since that time mostly forgotten. Bruno's ideas on imagery would shape the symbolic pageantry of the court of Queen Elizabeth I, and even the architecture of Shakespeare's Globe theater.

They wrote about an individual's power to perceive the rules of the natural world and to bend those rules to his will. They paved the way for science's assault on the world of faith. This was a new, revolutionary power of the individual in history, as their fellow philosopher Pico della Mirandola wrote: "Thou . . . constrained by no limits, in accordance with thy own free will, shalt supersede for thyself the limits of nature." Finishing his work late at night, Ioan would walk the city streets, his pulse racing, seeing figures move in the shadows, trying to understand how to command a metaphysical world that history had long forgotten.

Back in his tiny room, with its single lamp, small attic fan, and window overlooking a towering elm, he would experiment with Bruno's memory systems, building in his mind a complex structure of astrological symbols and charging them with erotic powers. He talked about such endeavors with humor and irony but took them very seriously. Passing his room at three or four in the morning, his friend Silviu would often notice the light still burning.

Culianu's interest in magic was not only a subversion of Communist reality; it provided an avenue of escape. Like James Joyce, who had felt the same fascination with Bruno and Pico della Mirandola, Culianu found in magic a potential release from all forms of power, even the limit of time or identity. Fighting for a scholarship to study the traditions of the Kabbalah in Israel, Culianu began the work on *Eros and Magic in the Renaissance* that would eventually lead to an Italian government scholarship.

He tried unsuccessfully to find Eliade's student papers from the 1920s. He needed to get to Eliade — not just intellectually but physically. Summoning his courage, Culianu mailed Eliade his two essays on the Renaissance. One essay, "Giordano Bruno and the Coincidence of Opposites," corresponded with the older scholar's work on dualism and the notion that the universe was determined by binary oppositions like good and evil or light and dark. It seemed a doomed gesture, because in Communist Romania all mail was monitored.

＊　　＊　　＊

Not all of Culianu's time was spent in studies, however. At parties he used his astrology games to woo women. When Miron's girlfriend and later wife met Ioan at a beach house in Constanza, she recalled, "Nene had three different girlfriends. He would say, 'I have no time, no time,' complaining about his girl problems."

He eventually fell in love with an outspoken girl, Sanda Ungureanu, known in the school for wearing no makeup or perfume, going without a bra, and mouthing off. Together they listened to the Beatles on pirated tapes. Their favorite songs included "Yesterday," "Here Comes the Sun," and "Yellow Submarine." He tried to learn to play the guitar. Their other favorite was "The House of the Rising Sun," which they spent hours interpreting and reinterpreting, seeking its hidden meanings.

He sought out mystics and gypsies, of whom many were hidden in Bucharest. These trips took him into the oldest sectors of the city, down cobblestone sidestreets that echoed with 1920s torch songs like "Ionel, Ionelule," telling of too-brief and illusory happiness. Once, walking home late on a winter night, he and Silviu found in the icy slush a sheet of hundred-lei notes — the largest currency note available then. It was a miracle. They argued about what to do with the small fortune. Culianu suggested they should spend half on the city lottery and half on books of ancient religions. But to buy the lottery tickets, he insisted, they must follow the law of a labyrinth: Make only left turns. They wandered late-night Bucharest, stopping to bet at lonely lighted kiosks on darkened sidestreets.

They never won the lottery, but their real prizes were the books that seemed priceless then — Marcel Laurent's *L'art chrétien primitif* (Paris, 1911) and *L'univers, histoire et description: L'Egypte ancienne* (Paris, 1839). Twenty years later the texts occupied a special place on Silviu Angelescu's shelf at the University of Bucharest, in his office as dean of the Faculty on Folklore.

*   *   *

One Christmas Culianu, Radu Popa, and Victor Ivanovici all won large grants. They took the group out to celebrate at the Select Restaurant on Alexandru Street, a nondescript eatery that could still be found on the same spot a quarter century later. The feast started at two in the afternoon, with Nene and Victor proposing cheap champagne toasts over *mititei* sausages and boiled eggs. They followed with salad and *ciorba* cream and beef soup, then sturgeon and *sarmale* and more metal-capped bottles of wine. Drinking and laughing, they did not notice that it had begun snowing heavily. After devouring nearly everything on the menu, they followed with bottles of *tsuica* and more wine. At eleven they ordered more food. Outside the snow came down harder. When they finished, past one in the morning, they stepped outside to see a blizzard drifting to the tops of parked cars. The city lay peacefully under an armistice of snow.

The students began throwing snowballs at their professors, who threw back. Someone started singing a Christmas carol, and soon they all were belting them out as they slipped and skidded down the middle of the deserted boulevard. They stopped in front of the Foreign Ministry building, arms wrapped around each other's snow-dusted shoulders. Flushed and tearing in the cold, their professor Ion Coja began singing at the top of his lungs the prewar nationalist hymn "Desteăptă-te, Române" (Wake Up, Romanian), a forbidden anthem. He urged the rest to join, gesturing at the machine gun–armed guard huddled in his kiosk. It was as if the snow had brought everyone together — students, professors, workers, mothers, factory bosses, police, dissidents, and informers — in a single drunken moment of "hierophany," or revelation. Cautiously they joined in:

Deşteaptă-te Române din somnul cel de moarte
În care te adânciră barbarii de tiranii
    barbarii de tiranii!
Acum ori niciodiată, croişte-ţi altă soartă,
la care să se închine şi cruzii tăi duşmanii
    şi cruzii tăi duşmanii.

Awaken, Romanian, from your deadly sleep
In which they sank you, those barbarian tyrants,
    those barbarian tyrants!
It's now or never: cut yourself a new fate
At which will bow even your cruel enemies,
    your cruel enemies.

Of all of them, the most careful was Nene. The others laughed at his silence, loudly teasing him. Finally he began, looking back over his shoulder the whole time at the military guards watching them, singing the words in Latin.

They began to march down Ana Ipatescu Boulevard to the Ceauşescu palace, singing louder and louder. The avenue was completely deserted, silent, motionless. The streetlights made illuminated stars against the last dusting of snow, and the normally busy street opened wide to them. It was, they each recalled from different parts of the world years later, a euphoric moment.

Then, another miracle: Culianu found in his mailbox a letter with the postmark of the United States. From the University of Chicago Divinity School. It was far more important than any grant. Mircea Eliade was replying to him, enthusiastic and supportive.

* * * * * * * *

"DARK PEOPLE, VERY CLEVER"

Culianu was concerned about surveillance on the night of the Christmas party because he had been approached by the security police. Many other students had been arrested, interrogated, and beaten. As early as the autumn of 1969 Culianu had distinguished himself as the best student in the Faculty of Romance, Classical, and Oriental Languages, specializing in Italian language and literature. One day a department secretary told him that a representative of the security police wanted to speak to him.

Even though 1969 was a more relaxed period than the early days of brute violence, or later years of grinding deprivation, the secret police was an all-powerful body whose activities, real and magnified by popular myth, had destroyed the lives of many innocent people. The brutality of Communist Romania, largely ignored at the time in the West, has been unfavorably compared with that of Orwell's England in *1984*. Children of dissidents could be severely beaten in the street, political prisoners tortured and forced to torture others, and common people subjugated under "total censorship and total control of everyday life by an all-powerful secret police," as Indiana University professor Matei Calinescu wrote. At the same time, the regime attempted to co-opt intellectuals into a pseudo-nationalist rhetoric supporting the government. It was not a surprise that Culianu was singled out: at the time the secret police attempted to recruit top talents in many fields. He was making a name for himself. To be summoned by Securitate, however, evoked dimly understood terrors of his childhood.

He met the agent in an empty classroom. The man introduced himself as Captain Ureche — "Ear" in Romanian — of the Council of State Security. He was short, with thinning hair, wearing a blue suit, not cheap but not expensive. They talked for about twenty minutes about nothing much. Ureche gave Culianu an appointment a few days later outside a private apartment building in the city center, near Lipscani Street.

Meeting Culianu on the street, Ureche ushered him on a long walk. "We took many detours to get to the location," Culianu later wrote, "walking through many alleyways. He wanted to impress me with these detours, so that I would think our clandestine meetings were especially grave." At another apartment, Ureche sat him down and began asking more pointed questions about his publications and his friends. Culianu gave him "extremely vague answers." The captain encouraged him to talk more, to be more open, suggesting that if he cooperated his professional goals could be attained.

A few days later Captain Ureche summoned Culianu's friend Victor Ivanovici, the best student in the Spanish section. Although he warned both of them not to talk to anyone about the encounters, they told each other everything in detail, seeking an escape from the harassment. "He's not going to go away," said Victor. "If we refuse it'll only get worse."

❋   ❋   ❋

The secret police in Romania predated communism, going back to the royal secret police who had harassed Mircea Eliade on suspicion of his being a far rightist in the 1930s, or to the police forces of earlier Ottoman rulers. The Communist version, Securitate, had begun training as early as 1944, when the Soviet Union, sensing victory, recruited enforcers from Romanian prisoners of war. Officially formed in 1948, Securitate formed ranks "that swelled with Soviet agents who had become Romanian generals."* The secret police also recruited from Iron Guardists in exile in Austria, thousands of whom grabbed the opportunity to coerce the same population they had sought to mobilize a generation earlier.

"Repression in Romania may have been harsher than in any other Soviet satellite country in Europe," wrote historian Vlad Georgescu, and Securitate proved a particularly vicious and loyal tool of the Soviet empire. In its early years it bolstered the shaky Communists with all-out physical terror, often against Party members. Tens of thousands of political prisoners died while forced to work on the Danube–Black Sea Canal. From 1956 to 1959 terror flared again in response to the uprising in Poland and Hungary, leading to the jailing of an estimated "several hundred thousand" for political crimes, many of whom died in terrible conditions.

By the late 1960s, however, Securitate methods had become more sophisticated, focusing on psychological control of a peasant population that Ceauşescu moved to factories in the cities. Because the country lacked much of a middle class, intellectuals and writers presented the biggest perceived threat to the government. Such a threat required new tactics.

The new tactics centered on surveillance and manipulation. Ceauşescu's passion for hidden microphones and informers stemmed from their effectiveness in helping him discredit his chief rivals. By the early 1970s Securitate was bugging most telephone

* Vlad Georgescu, *The Romanians* (Columbus: Ohio State University Press, 1991), 237.

conversations in the country and all international calls, opening all international mail, and employing video and listening devices to monitor government officials. Ceauşescu's wife delighted in the graphic videotapes of male and female agents seducing diplomats, foreign embassy guards, and political enemies.

Securitate's special contribution to modern repression was to transform a national passion for mythmaking into vicious, endless cycles of rumor and disinformation. Dissent was not treated as dissent, because under Ceauşescu everyone was supposed to be happy. Instead, dissidents were brought in on trumped-up charges of rape, homosexuality, or drug possession. The secret police "relished such indirect, mysterious means of persuasion," wrote Matei Calinescu, who cited "cases in which the school age children of dissidents were severely beaten in the street." In later years Securitate reportedly used radiation surreptitiously to poison writers it had detained. If you were not being watched, you feared you were. According to former Securitate chief Ion Pacepa, "monitoring the thoughts of the entire Romanian population became Ceauşescu's major domestic policy goal." In this way, the regime specialized in the psychological bonds explored by Culianu's beloved Renaissance magicians.

❋   ❋   ❋

Despite the warning, the students continued their pranks, including founding an institute for the study of a forbidden subject at school — semiotics, or the language of signs. They met a visiting Italian at school, Mario, a wealthy executive's son traveling in Eastern Europe to promote the anarchist movement. Mario became a close friend and dated a girl they knew. He took them driving around the country, flying the anarchist flag from the hood of a rental car. That act led to a summons to the dean's office. "It was very formal," said Victor. "When we got there, the dean was gone. In his chair sat Ureche."

Talking to each of the students separately, Ureche gave them different telephone numbers to report to him the activities of their friends, especially anyone who expressed the intent to leave Romania or criticized its government. "Not wishing to contradict or

. . . . . .

provoke him," Culianu later wrote, "within a few months I called him once, in order to tell him that . . . I had nothing to tell."

Each time they met, the stakes increased. If a proposal was made and you refused, you could be expelled from school. Around that time a friend told Ivanovici that if he joined the Communist Party, Ureche would have to leave him alone. The students read of a new law decreeing that a Party member could not be interrogated by the secret police without authorization from the Party secretary. It was a powerful temptation. Many of their friends joined the Party at this time. To become a member was easy. Ceauşescu had recently announced his independence from Soviet influence, and some professors urged them to try to change the system from within. Yet many other friends did not join. To do so would be to make a pact with the devil that had destroyed their parents' generation.

Weighing the merits, agonizing among themselves, knowing fully the implications of such a move, both Ivanovici and Culianu took the step of enlisting in the Communist Party in January 1970.

They attended Party meetings once a month. Culianu spent the time "studying Sanskrit out of a very large dictionary." Only once did he speak, to defend a girl facing expulsion because she had not declared that her parents were rich landowners before the Second World War. "I was merely a physical addition to the Communist Party," he wrote American authorities in his affidavit to the Immigration and Naturalization Service in 1991, "and made no substantial contribution to it in any way." Like Faust, however, about whom he would later write so much, Culianu seemed willing to sacrifice his ideals in order to succeed.

＊　　＊　　＊

The plan backfired. During the spring of 1970 Ureche appeared again and called Culianu for a third meeting. Culianu told him immediately that he was now a member of the Party and that Ureche needed the secretary's approval to interrogate him. Ureche was not persuaded. He "became very angry and said that it was a trifle. . . . He asked me to wait for him a few days later, *in the evening*, inside of the administration building of the university. . . . He unlocked the door of the administrative personnel office where the personal files of faculty and staff were kept. . . . employees of that personnel office were controlled by the secret police, because that office essentially determined what the job assignments of graduating students would be."

Again Ureche tried to get Culianu to become an informer. This time Culianu declined the offer outright, saying he understood the captain's "good intentions" but that he was too busy with his scholarly work. Ureche urged him to reconsider.

Frightened, Culianu turned to his professor Cicerone Poghirc. The director general of higher education in the Education Ministry, Poghirc arranged for his favorite student a position as a librarian at the Oriental Association, where Poghirc was also the director. Together, he said, they could produce the first ever Sanskrit-Romanian dictionary.

A few days later Culianu received a call from a university secretary saying he would not be contacted by Securitate again. "By the way," the secretary added, "you made a *big* mistake."

❀   ❀   ❀

Beginning in the autumn of 1970, Ioan Culianu's fledgling career collapsed. A scholarly journal that had been publishing his stories and reviews since 1967 stopped accepting his work. In June 1971, after accepting his fantasy short story collection and advertising it in its catalog, the Eminescu publishing house suddenly rejected it with no explanation. Culianu applied for a scholarship sponsored by the Italian Ministry for Foreign Affairs. He was ecstatic in July 1971 when he learned he had placed first among the candidates selected to study in Siena. He wrote happily to his sister and mother that he would not see them that summer at Varatic. He would be in Italy!

To take advantage of his offer, however, he needed an exit visa. For three weeks he visited daily the pleasant Ministry of Education building on a Bucharest back street, close to his aunt's home. Every time he showed up, he was told there was "no reply or action" on his request. He awoke daily with an anguish kindled by hope. He even tried to use some of Marsilio Ficino's talismans to beseech the fates. Look, he said, the world is offering to *pay* for me to come! To Italy, birthplace of the Renaissance arts he had been pursuing for years. Every morning he wondered if it would be his day. Weeks passed. No answer. He did not receive a rejection, just "no answer." The

Siena program started in August without him. Only in mid-August did he get his answer in a form letter: the ministry had "regretfully" turned down his request.

It was not only the rejection of a right a citizen in any free country takes for granted, it was not only missing a once-in-a-lifetime opportunity he had *earned* against all the odds of third-rate professors and Third World conditions, but it was the deliberately casual manner in undercutting his *triumph of will.* He was even willing to share his prestige with the odious regime. He had become a Communist despite all the Party's persecution of his family. "It's nothing less than a nervous breakdown," said Vladimir Tismaneanu, associate professor of political science at the University of Maryland, of his similar experience. "You can't function because of the sheer *absurdity* of the rejection, and this sinking feeling your life closed down on you."

＊　＊　＊

Late that summer Culianu headed to the monastery at Vǎratic. They refused me, he told Tess. Dejected, he began rereading his favorite detective stories collected in Borges's *Ficciones.* Prominent among the characters are Buenos Aires Jews, defenders of a life of the mind against the mindless destructive terror of history. Culianu found solace in a writer who employed Spanish, English, French, and German allusions to concepts of philosophy, physics, archaeology, and literary history. For an ambitious, self-absorbed dreamer, the blind writer who specialized in multiple universes offered powerful tonic.

With his university friends Culianu had analyzed over and over the intricate whodunit "Death and the Compass," which takes place in a Buenos Aires reeking of the totalitarian dread of the 1940s. The story tells of a skilled detective, Erik Lönnrot, who agrees to take one last case before retiring. The case fascinates him, as he realizes the killings are following an esoteric, Talmudic pattern. Cracking the killer's logic, the detective suddenly understands that he is to be the ultimate victim of a long-planned trap of revenge, into which the other murders' pattern has enticed him. Facing Lönnrot, holding the gun, his murderer remarks that both he and the detective have been trapped by the past's inexorable logic. "I sensed that the world was a labyrinth," his murderer remarks, "from which it was impossible to flee."

Culianu wrote a long scholarly essay on the story's symbolism: "The major task of art in Borges' universe is to escape the tyranny of a single mental system and enter into as many others as possible, to derive from their comparison a freedom to perceive the world."

The shadows of reality in the mind are closer to reality

than the shadows of life in the lower world.

— *Giordano Bruno*, Shadows *(De umbris idearum)*

A DREAM OF PARADISE

In June 1971 Nicolae Ceauşescu returned from a state trip to China and North Korea, fascinated by the cults of personality in those countries. The period of relative freedom in Romania ended with his own "cultural revolution" modeled on the terror campaign against artists and writers in China. Surveillance of intellectuals stepped up. Culianu's field, the history of religions, became even more taboo.

From Ioan's childhood his mother had whispered to him of his "special destiny." Now just when he had connected with his idol Mircea Eliade, it seemed he would be shut out in this forgotten country. Gradually he withdrew from his family, planning the most irrevocable step of his life. He retreated again into labyrinthine fictional worlds, this time of Eliade, trying to learn if his favorite fantasy stories of mysterious disappearances, "The Secret of Dr. Honigberger" and "Nights in Serampore," had been based on reality as he suspected. Culianu spent the fall in Braşov and Iaşi, sites of the two stories, searching parish records for the real-life models for the characters. He may have felt that shortly he would lose forever the chance to conduct such research.

Of the two stories, "The Secret of Dr. Honigberger," written in 1938, is the more remarkable. It tells of a young man in Bucharest studying Indian philosophy who is summoned to a beautiful home in a fashionable neighborhood. The mistress explains that Indian mysticism was also a favorite study of her husband, whose monumental work was a biography of Dr. Honigberger, a famous nineteenth-century Saxon researcher on Indian religion. Dr. Honigberger inexplicably disappeared, and so too has Madama Zerlendi's husband. She asks the narrator to search through her husband's laboratory journals to see if he can find a clue to their fates, and their secret discoveries.

She makes it sound as if her husband died twenty-four years earlier, but the narrator learns from her enigmatic daughter that Zerlendi only recently vanished. Spending long afternoons in the well-stocked study, the narrator falls into the doctor's intricate accounts of time shifts and perceptive alterations. Wreathed in cigarette smoke, the doctor's beautiful daughter warns him of impending danger: others who came before him in this quest each came to a tragic end.

The story makes fine popular fiction, but it is also remarkable as an experiment in which Eliade employed the clichés of gothic writing to explore real Indian religious mysteries like levitation and omniscience. Culianu suspected that Eliade had used real historical figures *and* personal experiences to "suggest more, and do it with greater precision, than it would have been possible in strictly scientific description." Searching the Romanian National Archives in Braşov, he learned to his astonishment that there was a real Dr. Honigberger who had lived during the mid-1800s in Braşov and an "unlucky Moldavian assistant" who disappeared around 1867.

As Eliade biographer Mac Linscott Ricketts later noted, it seems in the story that Eliade was writing about personal experiences. For instance, the narrator experiences the omniscient sense allegedly produced by intense Hindu meditation: "This sensation was like that of a man contemplating his whole house from the corner of one room. He doesn't see through the walls, yet he does see everything he knows to be in another room, or in the entire house." When placed side by side with Eliade's personal journals of mystic explorations, the story seems to oscillate between reality and fiction. As the young fictional hero follows the doctor's journals into a trap the doctor seems to have foreseen, so too the reader falls into the story's labyrinth, following a character reading another man's journal.

In Braşov and Iaşi, Culianu never found any more evidence of real-life models. He concluded that his mentor followed the time-honored tradition of embellishing fact to make it more entertaining. But more, Eliade seemed to consider fiction, like yoga, a discipline that could help lead one toward enlightenment. He playfully mimicked the mysteries of the cosmos he sought. In later years Culianu suspected his mentor's stories and scholarly books revealed even deeper ambiguities of perception. At the end of his life Eliade, according to Culianu, "seemed to see the world as a machinery much more complex and deceiving than before. Indeed through all his life he had been confronted with different degrees of illusion, and now he was looking back upon his own monumental oeuvre as a powerful hermeneutical operation that had created its own truth." In his later years Culianu attempted to do the same with his own fiction.

By 1972 Culianu claimed also to have learned by heart the Sanskrit verses of the Samkhayarika while studying the Jewish mystics who had inspired some of his Renaissance philosophers. Such investigations were absorbing and diverting. But he faced a pressing problem. When his holidays ended, he returned to the grimy winter of Bucharest and to the questions he had been putting off for so long.

* * *

Secretly in the winter of 1972 Culianu applied for the scholarship offered by the Italian Foreign Ministry. He told no one, not even his sister or his closest friends.

In the spring he submitted his master's thesis, now entitled "Marsilio Ficino and Platonism during the Renaissance." Comparable in scope to a Ph.D. dissertation or a monograph, it was remarkable because its subject was not taught in Romania. It also closely resembled Eliade's graduate thesis presented forty-four years earlier: "Filosofia italiană de la Marsilio Ficino la Giordano Bruno" (Italian Philosophy from Marsilio Ficino to Giordano Bruno). The younger man had never read his mentor's thesis. "It is certain that Ioan Petru Culianu knew of [Eliade's] paper and probably searched for it, because a few years later he would report it was lost," noted the cultural anthropologist Andrei Oişteanu. Culianu did not know that the manuscript *did* exist in university archives registered under the old Faculty of Letters and Philosophy.

He graduated from the Faculty of Romance Languages in June 1972. He received the department's highest grade, 9.89 out of 10, under Professor Nina Façon, one of the few Paris-trained Jewish intellectuals at the university. Supported by his teacher Cicerone Poghirc, he hoped for a doctoral assistantship in the university's Department of Italian, giving him the opportunity to continue his "clandestine" study of the history of magic. When the time came for the assignment of assistantships, however, Poghirc was out of the country. Culianu was assigned instead an awful job teaching elementary school in a tiny, poor village — a punishment, it seemed, for his lack of cooperation.

Yet he also gained something far more important: another Italian government scholarship, this time in Perugia. At first he told no one. While his friends joked, amusing themselves with the games he had once led, he sought the key to his way out, the document that prevented him from leaving a year earlier — an exit visa. But how to do it?

Having been rejected once, Culianu turned to the university hier-

. . . . . .

archy to assist him this time. Once again he faced the nerve-racking process of application. Now the stakes were higher, not only because he had been turned down once but also because he felt this might be his last chance.

* * *

Securitate had not given up on him. A colonel contacted his teacher Ion Coja, to ask him to report on the activities of the student group called Atlantida. Most of all, the colonel said, he wanted to know about Ioan Culianu.

Culianu applied for his exit visa this time through an Arabic scholar, who wrote him a good reference report. As the new dean of faculty, Cicerone Poghirc reviewed his application. Poghirc held two files — one academic, with glowing reports, the other the negative Securitate surveillance file. Culianu got lucky. In the early 1970s hundreds of students still were allowed to leave each summer, with business passports, under the stewardship of an uncommonly tolerant and sophisticated education minister, Mircea Malița. On the same day he learned of the depressing elementary school teaching assignment, Culianu also learned he had won the most coveted gift of his life — his exit visa.

It seemed a miracle. This time he was not about to let it pass him by. He saw his Italian friend Mario, who was now engaged to his Romanian girlfriend. Culianu gave him a beautiful gold-inlaid Oriental knife from his father, asking Mario to bring it to Rome for him. He was preparing not only to leave on scholarship but to leave forever.

He faced one final, major hurdle. The scholarship would pay for his flight and studies and for his food and lodging for four weeks, but to remain in the West he would need money. The problem was that under the system it was practically impossible to save money. He could not tend bar or wait on tables. He had spent the money his mother sent him on dinners and wine with friends. He had the scholarship and the visa, yet it all would seem a cruel hoax if he could not raise the cash to stay in Italy.

Around that time his friend Radu received a call from their professor Ion Coja. "I know of a student," Coja said. "She was supposed to hand in her final thesis last week, but she couldn't do it because she didn't write one. Her father is supposed to be a driver with the Central Committee of the Party, but he lives in a beautiful villa. I cannot help her because it's too dangerous for me, but I thought that you might be interested. It's a lot of money."

"What's the deadline?"

"Five days."

"Are you crazy? What's the topic?"

"Liviu Rebreanu as seen by the critics."

"How could she take such a comprehensive thing? This is something serious. Do you realize . . ."

"That's why I called you."

"Listen, I can't do this by myself. It's not only that we have to write the thing, but I have to work with the girl and make her understand, so she can pass the orals. Who is her master's adviser?"

Coja told him.

"Oh God." A famous literary critic, the adviser specialized in the writer Liviu Rebreanu. "Look, this is serious business. I have to . . . I have to find a partner."

Hanging up, Radu called his friend and future brother-in-law, Şerban Anghelescu. A few days earlier Şerban had said to him, "You know, I'm twenty-six, and I have never seen the Black Sea. We never had the money." So Radu woke his friend at eight in the morning. "Listen, Bula, wake up. I'll be at your place in ten minutes."

At his friend's apartment Radu laid out the story. "I'll take a couple of books and go home and work up the general structure, even though I don't know what to put in it. You go to the library and read and bring everything at about six o'clock and we'll start."

"But I can't type."

"That's OK. We'll interweave the research and talk, and something will come up. I'll type it, and in the morning I'll try to pour all of these things into her head."

By the evening Radu felt exhausted. Around 6:30 Şerban strolled into his apartment with Nene Culianu. They had two bottles of wine and smelled of liquor. "What's going on?" Radu asked.

"I ran into Nene at the library and told him what we were doing. And he said he already had a paper on Rebreanu! He said he'd give it

• • • • • •

to us. So we went to a restaurant. We went to a movie, and then we grabbed the paper, and here we are."

"But what is the meaning of this?" Radu turned to his friend.

"Don't be angry," Culianu said. "It was my idea. My paper's done, so that might be the main part of the thesis. I only need five hundred lei to buy my stuff for Italy."

Over Şerban's objections, Radu insisted they split the money equally in three. They began working. Nene and Radu wrote quickly, first with Nene typing and Radu compiling, then with Nene compiling and Radu typing. They took shifts of two hours each on each assignment. Şerban drank and smoked and offered, sometimes, an observation: "I don't like this word. I would like the other one better." Amazingly, they had fun doing it. It was very good work. By two o'clock in the morning they went to bed.

In the morning Radu went to the girl. She struggled. "This is too hard," she said.

When he realized she wasn't getting it, he said: "Look, when he asks you about this, just mumble something like 'I'm so impressed with you, Professor, that I can't put it better than I put it in writing.'"

In four and a half days they were ready with the text. They waited anxiously as her appointment came to defend her thesis. "This is excellent," the professor told her. "You are really very creative. I'm surprised I didn't notice you in my class."

"Because I'm shy," she said.

"But I am particularly interested in this point related to psycho-analysis. Where did you get the texts?"

"Oh, I am so emotional talking with you that I can't really answer. I can't put it better than it is in writing."

He paused, regarding her over his bifocals. "Well, would you like to clarify this other point?"

"Oh, I don't think so because I'm so . . . I'm really shaking."

"This is not good. You really have to be more confident. Your work is excellent. I think that you will go for a literary career or something."

"Really?"

"Yes. Didn't you know? You scored nine out of ten."

After that the girl's father called Radu, thanking him and inviting him over to receive payment. "This is the first master's degree in our family," he said proudly. "I know that you put great work into this. Tell me, what's your fee?"

* * *

Culianu and Şerban Anghelescu waited for two hours to receive their payment. Smoking cigarettes, pacing the tunneled arch at Piaţa Romană, they watched a little dog chained to a fence that the owner seemed to have forgotten. The circle filled with soot from honking trucks. Ioan inspected every rattling Dacia sedan as it passed. It was two o'clock. The sky was a heated cruel blue above him. What if she forgot? All that work, all his dreaming! How could he think he would beat this system so stacked against him?

Hunched lower and lower, fists jammed in pockets, throat raw from cigarettes, Culianu smelled a manure cart as it moved slowly across the square. He was a thin, intense twenty-two-year-old, with a scar on his left brow; he had recently walked through a glass door in his intense frustration at his publisher's office in Bucharest. His plane was due to leave first thing the next morning, and he had no suitcase or decent clothes.

He saw a couple of young soldiers armed with Kalashnikov rifles. He was to serve in the army next year. Suddenly he heard Şerban shout. There was Radu, cutting through the soldiers, across five lanes of traffic, carrying a big suitcase. Radu wore black sunglasses like someone out of a Mafia novel. In spite of himself Ioan laughed. "What happened? What happened?" he and Şerban asked when Radu reached them.

Radu opened the suitcase. All three of them stood for a minute, flabbergasted. Six thousand lei. A fortune. Culianu caught his breath to say he only had two hours to buy clothes for his trip. They called Miron to drive them to the city's largest department store. "Are you sure you want to give Nene two thousand?" Serban said to Radu as they jammed into the tiny Fiat. "He only wanted five hundred."

"You are such a motherfucker. I can't believe it."

"No, no," Ioan said. "Five hundred's all right with me."

"Absolutely not. Two thousand." Radu took the money and divided it so the three could head for different sections of the store and buy Ioan a suit and some shoes, socks, pants, shirts, and a suitcase. They only spent a thousand lei. Ioan left the remaining thousand, saying, "Maybe I'll need this money when I get back."

* * *

That night his sister, Tess, felt an odd sense of foreboding. She called Ioan at her cousin's house. She wanted to talk to her brother. Her uncle got on the phone. "They're out shopping," he said. "Call later." She called later, and he said the same thing. She said she would call in the morning.

She called in the morning and got no answer. She called in the afternoon, and her uncle said: "He is gone." That was all. Her uncle came to Văratic to tell her mother.

Ironically, one day before he left, a friend who had been working hard on his behalf finally managed to land Culianu a plum editorial position at the major arts publication — covering music, literature, and painting — *Secolul 20* (Twentieth Century). By then it was too late.

* * *

At the dusty, cheaply constructed Otopeni airport Ioan reached the security checkpoint. Everyone knew the story of the conductor of the Bucharest Philharmonic, who had safely made it to his seat on the plane when the Securitate agents had come for him. You forgot your key, they had told him. No I didn't, he had said. Oh yes, they said. Come on down and get it. He never got back on.

So many thoughts and feelings raced through his head that he barely noticed the hot dry sun baking the aluminum shell and the woman cursing in front of him. He wore the dark pants and clean shirt he had bought in the Universal department store. He gripped his shabby little suitcase, shoving past surly attendants. He wanted to hear the jet engines roar. He wanted to be on the plane realizing the dream he had so coveted.

At the last checkpoint an Air Tarom attendant insisted that he stow his cheap shoulder bag. He objected; it contained his books of Cioran and Eliade, as well as the family photograph album he had carefully prepared. They insisted. His faculty adviser, accompanying him, told him to be quiet and get on the plane. The jet taxied past the armed soldiers placed every hundred feet, out onto the cracked asphalt. Sitting back, eyes closed, he felt the throb of the engines run through him as they fired the plane down the runway and lifted it into the air. The date was July 4, 1972.

ARRIVISTE, 1972–1986

I am in a quiet, beautiful place. Swallows fly over

my head. In such peaceful moments I cannot believe

Evil does his work in our world.

—*I. P. Culianu to his mother, August 17, 1972*

THE MYTH OF THE WEST:
ITALY, 1972–1975

It was only a two-hour flight, but it vaulted him from a medieval world to the modern, from loving family and friendships to complete isolation, from a place where you worried who was listening to one where you tried to get anyone to listen. Culianu was an angular twenty-two-year-old in black horn-rimmed glasses, dressed inexpensively but neatly in dark pants and a short-sleeved white shirt. His escape seemed only slightly less miraculous than the sixteenth-century revelations he studied.

As the Air Tarom jet hurtled above the Adriatic toward Rome, he turned to his friend and faculty adviser sitting next to him, a woman named Anca Giurescu. "I can't believe I'm on this plane," he said. "I can't believe I'll be in Italy in two hours."

He was lucky, she told him. The only year the Italian scholarships made it to deserving students in Romania was 1972. This was her third trip to Italy, and the government made her go without her husband and children so she would not defect. She knew and liked Ioan Culianu from classes, and as he peppered her with questions, she tried to answer as best she could. For the next ninety minutes they talked nonstop, switching from formal titles to first names. At thirty-three she was accomplished and strikingly attractive, with short dark hair and a figure that caught the eyes of Italian men on the plane returning from suspect business trips. He pressed her about life in the West. When she answered more cautiously, he asked her for more.

"Listen," she said finally, looking at the students, businessmen, and some suspiciously well-dressed travelers around them. "Don't ask so much here. We'll have plenty of time in Italy."

❊   ❊   ❊

By the time the plane set down in the blistering Roman heat, Ioan was already a different individual from the student who had casually cowritten a thesis for money a day earlier. Here he was at last, in the place he had dreamed of all his life. His eyes moved over the terminal advertisements, the sleek motorized luggage carts, and the well-stocked airport snack bars and restaurants, drinking in every detail.

At the beginning of the two-and-a-half-hour train ride to Perugia, he rode through Rome's outskirts, passing enormous billboards like ancient Egyptian city symbols, madly honking cars, and the lights of an X-rated movie marquee. Against the backdrop of Red Brigade terror and the later kidnapping of Aldo Moro, the graduate student Ioan Culianu arrived in the West.

❊   ❊   ❊

Set high on a cliff, the walled university town of Perugia featured winding cobblestone alleys, a well-endowed library, and architecture inspired by the Renaissance's attention to human proportion and eternity's geometry. In a large square at the town center children played in front of a brilliant white church. At the corners of two city walls rose towering circular turrets. With a rich art collection at the Galleria del Arte Umbria and a commanding view of the plains around Assisi, birthplace of St. Francis, Perugia provided an apt introduction to life in Italy and the West.

From July to August 1972, Culianu lived off his Italian scholarship to follow the *corsi di alta cultura* (major in ancient culture). He took day-long advanced courses in literature, philosophy, religions, and art, taught by leading scholars. With Giurescu, for instance, he took a special course on the architecture of Florence, focusing on the geometry of the body reflected in the Renaissance city's buildings. He took another course in Etruscan studies. After class he studied the *real* texts of the Renaissance, etched both on paper and in stone.

Tense about his future, attracted to his former teacher, he spent much of his free time with Giurescu. In the evening they strolled the city, stopping at snack bars or restaurants, buying a bottle of Chianti and resting on the stone parapets to look out over the countryside. He loved to joke and laugh, making up funny stories about St. Francis. As the smells of cut hay and grilled sausage and peppers rose on the evening breeze, they argued about literature and life, drinking, sharing their hopes and dreams in the casual intimacy of researchers on scholarship. Above them Venus would appear as the night's first star.

He wanted desperately to write home, but he could say only that he was sorry for not saying good-bye. He was even more desperate to write Eliade in Paris about his arrival and his thoughts of defecting. Giurescu advised him to wait; all around them in the tour group, eyes were watching. He decided to take a trip to Florence to mail the letter to Eliade.

In his second week he visited the fabled Renaissance center of Florence. He arrived early, a hard roll in his pocket, the light just breaking over the Piazza della Signoria, and he gazed in awe at the facade of the Ufizzi and the statuary of the Loggia dei Lanci. He mailed his letter to Eliade, reporting that he had come to the West and was trying to decide whether to stay. Nervously he awaited a response.

* * *

He worked hard at his university program, knowing that in less than a month his scholarship would end. He wanted to stay and pursue his life's ambition, but he was afraid. Once he defected he would have no papers, no identity, and no status except that as a fugitive from justice. His mother and sister would be punished. They might lose their jobs. In Romania he would be convicted and sentenced in absentia. When his scholarship ran out he would switch from the charmed life of a visiting academic to the grinding poverty of true exile: he would be penniless and isolated, his mail would be monitored, and he would have no hope of seeing his family again. He would have virtually no chance of finding a legitimate job or pursuing the higher degrees he needed in order to teach.

Even though he had received only a few letters from Eliade, he had come to count on the famous scholar's support. If Eliade would come to his aid, he thought, surely then he could manage. If not, then he had better forget it. Better to disappear in anonymity in a forgotten country than to strike out as a refugee among tens of millions dreaming the myth of the West.

On the Italian Festival of August 15, he went with Giurescu's second cousin, a Sorbonne graduate student named Mircea Marghescu, to Florence to witness the national celebrations. Tall, thin, two years older than Culianu, Marghescu looked a little like Lenin with his goatee and tweed cap. He became a friend and competitor. One evening as the two were coming back to their apartment, they saw a huge spider spinning its web over a trellis in a private vineyard. In Romanian and French folklore a spider in the evening was a sign of good luck. They counted its legs. It had only seven, which meant outstanding luck. Marghescu said, "Now we will go, and you will have the letter of Eliade."

At home he found the letter. It was long-winded, filled with explanations and a few addresses. It said in essence: I am glad that you're considering defection. I think you'll make the right choice. Try to make a name for yourself, and we'll be in touch.

To Culianu the response was devastating. He had all but decided to change his entire life largely because of this man's encouragement. Eliade knew his situation, knew what straits he would soon face. Eliade had seemed to lead him on with hints of assistance and words of praise. Why now, when his young acolyte needed him most, did he respond so coldly? Ioan's scholarship program was about to end, and it was the worst possible time for such a turndown.

After a few days of deep depression, he wrote a proposal requesting that his Italian scholarship be extended. Meanwhile his friends prepared to depart. After a week Marghescu left Perugia for Paris. Anca Giurescu prepared to return to Romania with the group. The time approached when he would have to decide whether or not to stay.

If he stayed he would be alone. No friends, no family, soon no money — *nimic*, nothing. On one of their last nights, he and Giurescu sat on their favorite medieval parapet. He had bought sausage, cheese, and grapes. She sliced up a crusty globe of fresh bread as he uncorked a bottle of red wine. They toasted his scholarship extension; the government had renewed his funds for another month — although he had been told that this was as far as the grant could go.

He talked to her of his father, of aristocratic relatives who were no more than funny relics, of his dream. What, he asked, if I make the wrong decision?

"You're young," she said. "If I did not have my husband and children I would do it too. You have your whole life ahead of you. If you go back, the world will never hear of you."

He stared at her. "I'm at such a crossroads. I'm not sure what's right, what's possible. Do you think I can do it without Eliade?"

She paused, watching the darkness thicken in the gnarled branches of the olive trees spread out below them. The scent of dried flowers and dust and wine wafted on the soft evening breeze. "If your career depends so much on someone else, then it's not really your career, is it?"

A long silence followed as the last light slowly drained and the moon bathed them in its pale light.

During their frantic last two days together, he insisted on accompanying her to buy toys for her children, and he went with her to the train station at four in the morning. She was his only friend in the

West, and only the second person in his life to whom he had revealed his deepest ambition. Then she was gone.

*   *   *

He was still officially on scholarship, still a model of the best a Communist or totalitarian education could produce. He lived for four more weeks in his room on Via Cacciatoreal in Perugia. On the program's final exam he scored thirty points out of thirty, winning the university's first prize and the A. Lupatelli Scholarship. He applied for a third grant with the Italian National Endowment for the Humanities. He was approved. So for the time being, his meager finances held up.

He thought often of his family and friends, feeling deeply guilty about leaving without saying good-bye. At the same time, he liked the idea of being freed from the pressures of history and family pretension. He wrote letters asking for news, but they were often delayed, as were the replies. He did not know that Miron fell into a deep depression when he realized Ioan would not return, or that his old girlfriend Sanda Ungureanu began a long losing battle with mental illness. He steeled himself for his coming trial, remembering Eliade's theory that our lives feature repeated, patterned "ordeals of destiny." He wrote Şerban of the challenge in January 1973: "Now I am in the dark abyss of the West. I have a revolver in my pocket to defend myself from friends. I have changed myself a lot, Bombinelli, since we last saw each other. . . . I am cynical and tough because life here is cheap. Surely, even if life is cheap, the temptations are profound. I can hardly manage to survive or save any money."

He moved to Rome, where life became more and more difficult. For ten days he stayed with Mario and his wife, Dana, in their cramped apartment. They were having problems. Because Mario had married a foreigner beneath his class, his wealthy family had cut him off. His Romanian wife had never worked for a living. With only a high school education, struggling with the Italian language, she fought her own depression. Once she had been attracted to Ioan and was thrilled at first to see him in Italy. Now she and Mario had nothing to give him, and he had nothing to give them. Reluctantly Mario asked him to move out.

He still was not sure he would defect. His sister begged him to return. At her insistence the journal *Secolul 20* kept open his editorial position. He finally told her he could never take it because, he said, "I can only come back a winner."

In his desperation he tried to become a monk in an Appian mountain monastery. After three weeks he gave up trying to pursue enlightenment under false pretenses, only seeking political asylum. He walked into a small dirty police station in Rome, where he turned in his Romanian passport. It was an inconspicuous setting for the most significant act of his short life. The young, self-involved boy raised in a Moldavian atmosphere of love, destiny, and intellectual stimulation was, for all practical purposes, now dead.

* ❉ ❉

A citizen without a country, without papers or identity, he turned for help to a professor and acquaintance, Bruno Manzoni. Manzoni put him up for a while in his apartment in Rome. Then Culianu moved in with a dashing young architect and his wife under somewhat mysterious circumstances. It was a very difficult period. He could no longer juggle his fortunes like a gambler who, as his wife later put it, "could bluff God." He was constantly humiliated. In a photograph from 1973 he is a haunted young man in eyeglasses and an ill-fitting, cheap double-breasted suit that hangs loosely on his hollow frame. His eyes are not so much piercing as frightened.

In Italy refugees were detained in internment or concentration camps, where they had to register all their activities with camp police and were treated with a casual, bureaucratic brutality. With all of his scholarship periods up, his money gone, and his friends at a loss, Culianu was forced to enter the refugee camp at Latina.

Near the Tyrrhenian Sea, the Latina internment camp consisted of bleak rows of overcrowded, filthy barracks set in the middle of fallow farmland. Culianu shared his misery with all the unwanted and unwashed — Yugoslavian convicts, Hungarian gypsies, Algerian refugees — all the people with no connections and no network. He could leave camp only during the day, and only to work. He scraped a living tutoring in English and dishwashing, or "diving for pearls," as it was called. He kept himself to a starvation diet. He picked up a baggy sweater at a flea market and stole food by slipping cold cuts under the sweater. At night he placed his few lire under his army pillow while listening to his mates sharpen knives and tell coarse jokes about their hustles with women in camp.

How far he had fallen since the idyllic evening walks with Anca Giurescu in Perugia. He wrote Şerban: "I have neither the demon's mettle in my blood, nor the peace and patience of a man who is searching for the good. . . . I am longing for everybody, but [Chubby] is the one I miss the most. He gave me strength for almost two years. He will disappear normally and quietly, as he emerged. Nobody will realize his disappearance because he didn't sing his presence. Maybe me too." Dorin ("Chubby") Zaharia died prematurely a few years afterward.

Bad news from home fueled Ioan Culianu's depression. In Iaşi he was convicted and sentenced to seven years in prison for the crime of "denigrating the state." Because of his defection, his sister was fired from her job as an assistant professor of literature at the university their family used to run. Their mother retired just before being removed. Family friends were warned not to associate with them. Some became informers. When he heard of the trouble, Ioan wrote Tess in February 1973: "I can't advise you to be submissive. I know you won't be. But think of your career. I am a hard worker, and to the end our faith, cleverness, and goodness will win."

Hungry, cold, and penniless, he lost his ambition. He hardly cared if it was day or night. He lay in bed in a "heroic madness" that Bruno and Plato had made a key point of their aesthetics. Finally, one night, Culianu pulled out the Oriental knife his father had bequeathed to him. He ran the cold blade along his left wrist, pulled it back, and stabbed. With blood pouring down his arm, he switched hands and sliced open his right wrist. According to Mircea Marghescu's account, he then gouged a line up each forearm. "It was terrible. He showed me the scars. He had cut his wrists and the inside of his arms to his elbows, truly deep, long cuts," Marghescu said. "He didn't joke when he did something." Arms covered in blood, Culianu lay in bed and fell asleep. He dreamed of a pretty blond girl in a lush orange grove beckoning to him. Because he had failed to run warm water over the wounds, the blood slowly dried, stanching the flow. He awoke feeling light-headed and calm. For the next ten years, every photograph taken of him in short sleeves showed him wearing sweatbands to hide his wounds. He never forgot his vision of a blond girl.

Culianu spent eight months in the Latina camp before obtaining official recognition as a refugee under the terms of the 1951 Geneva Convention. He spent the last of his money in a shady deal to purchase a Nansen international passport, "pink and slender as a May rose." He found a position on the team researching labor legislation for the European Institute for the Standardization of Labor Law. He switched to a job as a secretary at the University of Rome. There he spotted an advertisement for graduate study and an assistant professorship in the history of religions at Catholic University of the Sacred Heart in Milan. He registered at Catholic University for an equivalency exam covering the field.

He explained to the dour personnel manager that he had no identification papers save for the questionable passport he had purchased. Because he had defected, he had no proof of his academic qualifications. The field of history of religions was outlawed in his home country.

The man shook his head. He had seen others in Culianu's position, trying to make it in the West after the privations of the East. In his experience it was usually futile. "Did you pay the fee already?" he asked.

"Yes."

"*Poveraccio!* Poor fellow. Well, since you paid, you may as well go inside and take the exam."

Two weeks later Culianu received a letter congratulating him and offering him an assistantship and scholarship. He returned to the same manager. "What's going on here? Were you lying to me last time?"

"No."

"But you received the highest grade!"

He had earned perfect scores on the test in five of the six fields in the history of religions. "I still have no papers," he said.

The man thought. "You must tell your story to the *professore*. He is the only one who can help."

The *professore* was Ugo Bianchi, a leading world scholar in the field of gnosticism. "I'm really impressed. The fact that you achieved this command entirely on your own is absolutely incredible. Still, you must have a degree before you can teach."

"I can't get the degree until I have money. I can't earn money until I teach."

Bianchi arranged for Culianu to enter the graduate program while working as a teaching fellow in the Department of Religious Sciences. He arranged a scholarship to cover Culianu's studies for two years in biblical and non-Western theology, including Greek and Hebrew. In many ways Bianchi became the mentor Culianu had hoped to find in Eliade. Under Bianchi he learned the methods and skills of a professional historian of religion in the West. This tutelage was both a blessing and drawback, because Bianchi's approach was becoming outdated, based as it was on amassing esoteric facts with little attention to theory. But Culianu would always be grateful to him and to the university's dean of students, Giuseppe Lazzati, and the head of the Department of Religious Sciences, Raniero Cantalamessa, for their willingness to grant him the opportunity. To him it was a godsend. In the space of a few months he had gone from attempted suicide in a refugee camp to a scholarship leading to an assistant professorship in the West.

*We are all together the characters of a beautiful book. I
will try to write that book sometime, but it won't be the
same. Every one of us will try to write it, but it won't be,
it will never match . . . THE book.*

—*I. P. Culianu to Șerban Anghelescu, October 26, 1973*

. . . .

CHICAGO, PARIS, AND MIRCEA ELIADE

While the fevers of student revolution raged around him,
Culianu began reading in earnest Renaissance philosophers like
Marsilio Ficino, Pico della Mirandola, and Giordano Bruno in the
world's best libraries on the subjects, including that of the Vatican.
Outside the Vatican, in fact, he passed every day the statue erected
on the spot where Bruno was burned at the stake by the church
in 1600. By tradition it had become the meeting place of Rome's
anarchists.

He concentrated on Renaissance magic, smoking cigarettes to keep himself awake through long nights spent with the eerie thought of the thin, reviled, defrocked Dominican monk Giordano Bruno. What a thrill to read again Bruno's treatises, in the original Latin and Italian. Bruno's command of the *mundus imaginalis* — the precise world of metaphysical symbols — made him a charismatic speaker and thinker in the late sixteenth century. He specialized in the "art of memory," the ancient Greek technique for remembering long speeches by associating sections with different rooms in a memorized house. Giving a speech in a time before teleprompters, the orator walked through the rooms in his mind, pulling out the passages associated with each image.

Instead of a house, though, Bruno claimed to have memorized more than a hundred astronomical, astrological, and ancient Egyptian symbols to construct a complex, mystical architecture of memory. The learner of such magic was to Bruno an "adept" or initiate into a higher world. Using such knowledge, he said, a magician could project his will to seduce a lover or even a whole population. The question of *how* was the mystery Culianu explored.

Shunned in Italy, Bruno had influenced English court life and the architecture of Shakespeare's Globe theater. Culianu compared Bruno's magic to that of advertisers, public relations firms, political spin controllers, and propagandists, exploring the psychological underpinnings of the Western media society he was experiencing for the first time. These professionals tried to manipulate the collective unconscious in ways Bruno had studied in depth. Bruno's techniques worked, or people believed they worked, well enough to bring him invitations from the king of France — and to get him executed for reasons not quite clear to this day.

Culianu's encounters with Bruno's world of signs brought him deeper and deeper into the relation of religion and power, the patterns of history and critical dates he saw charted — however crudely — in astrology, and the unconscious ways a populace is manipulated. Writing to Şerban in Bucharest in October 1973, he hinted at his discoveries and newfound "social success — for which I paid the highest price, greater than any man could endure." He continued: "The loneliness that is all around me now, forever and for good, and everywhere, contains within it a dialectical movement of guilt and freedom . . . to give me powers of a fiend to fulfill my existence. I feel despair in the torment of something that appears to be inexplicable . . . a huge knowledge of a huge power that are not mine. This knowledge and power are of an origin that in the Middle Ages would have been called divine or demonic: *demonic* is the most proper word."

Few scholars before him had seen much of value in Bruno's treatises such as *On the Composition of Images, Signs, and Ideas.* Of those who had, the University of London scholar Frances Yates wrote most brilliantly, trying to unravel Bruno's techniques. Culianu's contribution was to apply the arts of magic and psychological "bonds" to the twentieth-century state. He saw the Western state as a Sorcerer State founded on and influenced by the same principles of emotional fulfillment practiced by Bruno. Studying Renaissance magic, Culianu rebelled against any *single* construction of reality, not only Communist but also Western. He examined the techniques of Western commercials that penetrated the imaginative life of the individual. What is a thought? he asked. How do we manipulate our thoughts or those of others? He found valuable answers in a magician and philosopher's obscure five-hundred-year-old texts.

❧   ❧   ❧

In Milan Culianu lived in a boardinghouse on Necchi Street with ten or eleven other graduate assistants with whom he became friendly. They noticed his penetrating stare — and his insecurity and restlessness. He became closest to Gianpaolo Romanato, scion of a wealthy family who had the same birthday as Miron Bogdan and, later, Hillary Wiesner — August 17.

Romanato recalled Culianu's "quick nervous step" and the thin black cloth jacket that served as a winter coat and a suit jacket: "Culianu had the features of a person who had suffered, a pallor of real malnutrition when we met. I have never met anyone in my life who had the tenacity of Culianu and his ability to endure suffering, to internalize it and to make of it a reason of life somehow. It was a determination like his yoga exercises, of mental conditioning. . . . He would study without interruption fifteen or sixteen hours in a day. . . . He didn't need to take notes; his file was in his mind."

From 1973 to 1976 Culianu and Romanato lived together, eating together every day, joking and living a life of graduate school fraternity, both of them studying with grants from the university. Culianu came to be a regular guest at Romanato's Padua home during weekends. He was often invited home by his other Italian friends, who took pity on a poor fellow student who seemed to intimate but never share dark personal burdens. He made a gracious houseguest, who was adept at making people feel almost magically good about their hospitality. He made a weekend into an adventure of self-discovery, marveling at the odd coincidences and jokes that to him signaled deeper clues to a logic in the universe. Yet no one really knew him, or the life he had left behind.

His professor Ugo Bianchi also took a special interest in him. "I recall his rapidity in translating his thought in written words in many languages: in French, in Romanian of course, in Italian," the elder scholar said. "He thought, and in the same moment he was thinking, he wrote. His thought came fluidly, absolutely orderly, logically. I always envied him because I have difficulty in writing." For the rest of his life Culianu unconsciously honored his mentor by speaking with Bianchi's same grandiloquent Italian.

He made many other Italian friends, including graduate assistants Gustavio Casadio and Mario Lombardo, who along with Romanato remembered their friend's sudden mood swings. It was Romanato who said, "He laughed very little, though we were twenty-three years old and little more than boys. On the contrary, I remember hours of silence, of abstraction, even if he were at a bar or café. He would close in himself, head down, slightly inclined on a side. It was a deep sudden sadness, so melancholy . . . so unexpected."

●   ●   ●

Because of his defection, Culianu also felt constantly afraid. "I was experiencing all the symptoms of that paranoia which is peculiar to recent defectors," he later had a character in a Renaissance murder mystery say, "and was routinely hearing the footsteps of secret police agents behind me as I passed the resident pimps and drug vendors along the stazione by Pensione Cavalari."* His friends noticed him turning around every few steps when walking Milan's streets. They teased him: "Giovaninno, you are not so important that Bucharest comes here to kill you!"

They hung out in bars playing pinball, and in museums studying Italian art. On the whole Culianu seemed more at home in the sixteenth century than in the twentieth. His favorite paintings included Leonardo da Vinci's *La Vergine delle Rocce* (about which he wrote for the journal *Aevum*) and Botticelli's famous mural *La Primavera*. He was becoming an expert in medieval and Renaissance devotional art, reveling in codes and mysteries he saw captured in Botticelli's enigmatic figures. The Venus figure in the center of *La Primavera* especially fascinated him because she resembled so closely the figure he saw in his dream the night he slashed his wrists.

In June 1974 Radu Popa came to visit Italy, the first of the old crowd to make it. He found an immensely changed Nene — friendly as ever but now unwilling to give up precious time from his studies. While Radu visited the tourist sites, his second cousin worked in the Vatican library. Even in the heat of summer, Nene wore a black suit and tie. The Vatican librarians called him, respectfully, Professore. It was clear, however, that he was also intensely lonely. He urged Radu to stay. "He wanted me to defect too; he said it was easy. But I noticed his fear, looking back over his shoulder all the time."

❀   ❀   ❀

Late in the summer of 1974 Mircea Marghescu wrote Culianu from Paris, offering to take him to meet Eliade. Like the hero of a chivalric poem, Culianu had undergone his "ordeal by destiny" and had earned the right to see the great thinker. In September, Culianu showed up and telephoned Professor Eliade. He was invited to the apartment on the Place Charles Dullin, where the Eliades had spent their summers since the late 1950s.

Eliade met him cordially, not warmly but with polite interest. He was already an older man, frail and bald, with a beard, thick black horn-rimmed glasses, and a pipe. He bore little resemblance to the

* Ioan Culianu and Hillary S. Wiesner, "The Emerald Game," unpublished manuscript, 1987, p. 2.

dashing, intense young Adonis of his early years in India. He asked about Culianu's studies and writing. At the end of the visit Culianu asked him the most important question of his life: "Professor, may I come to the University of Chicago?"

"Yes, definitely. We will arrange that."

On the way out Culianu stopped at the front door. He looked like a man in a daze. He rocked back and forth, repeating, like a mantra: He is a shaman, he is a shaman, he is a shaman.

"You watch. Eliade always says yes at first," Marghescu said, taunting him. "He won't do anything."

Culianu turned and looked at him blankly, disbelieving, as if his rival was the last of the ignorant people on earth.

*   *   *

After the meeting in Paris, Culianu returned to Milan in a state of elation. After a week he began eagerly opening his mail, again expecting a letter from his mentor that would herald a new era in his life. He had not only met the man who led the world in the journey seeking the deeper meanings in religion and history, but Eliade had *invited* him to the world's premier divinity school to work. Italy was still only a small country with an uncongenial and straitjacketing left wing in academia. The United States was quite another place — energetic, raucous, iconoclastic, free, rich with media influence and money — *his* place in the world.

He was well aware of Marghescu's taunt. But his friend did not know that he had met with Eliade outside the apartment visit. A special spark had been struck. On September 16, 1974, Eliade noted in his journal a dinner with Culianu in a Chinese restaurant in Paris: "We chat until midnight in my office." The older man was seeking a young follower to carry on his work, so the relationship was not entirely one-sided. And the younger man had begun noticing flaws in Eliade's scholarship. Quite often Eliade failed to document the evidence for his grandly eloquent, broad theories, giving them a speculative quality in light of new discoveries. Culianu was beginning to suspect that his mentor was more a popularizer than an original thinker. With his growing command of the history of religions, he felt he could hold his own. "Eliade became a man, a great man Culianu began confronting equally," Gianpaolo Romanato recalled.

For weeks Culianu received no reply. He sent Eliade his own essay titled "Sun and the Moon in Romanian Folklore," as a gentle reminder for the older man to keep his promise. It seemed incomprehensible that someone could make such an offer only to forget it. Culianu's anxiety grew all the stronger because his planned first book, the one to get him tenure at Catholic University, was to be a monograph on Eliade. The project depended on his invitation to Chicago.

❋   ❋   ❋

Several friends reported that for a time Culianu espoused far rightist ideas in exile. He was impressed by Mussolini and by Salazar, the Portuguese dictator Eliade had admired. Culianu's early, totalitarian education had been "suitable only for making heroes," he told Romanato; in rebelling against the suspect heroes of the left, he turned for a time to the right. In Milan he visited, like many Romanians to reach Italy, a national cultural center run by the enigmatic, wealthy figure Iosif Constantin Drăgan. Drăgan was accused in Italy's largest newsweekly, *Panorama*, of having been an Iron Guardist with close ties to the Ceaușescu regime. The Center offered a library of Guardist histories that Culianu studied closely in order to understand a period entirely removed from his Communist education, yet one so close to his family's and his mentor's past.

In Chicago, for his part, Mircea Eliade was focused on the teaching and writing that accounted for his impact on a huge world audience. Among his and his wife's friends and occasional dinner guests was the young Mircea Marghescu, who had come to the university as an assistant professor in comparative literature. Marghescu asked Eliade from time to time when he would invite Culianu. Eliade said he would take care of it. After several weeks Marghescu pointed out that the elder scholar simply did not have the time to attend to the matter, and he offered to arrange Culianu's assignment as a postdoctoral student *pro forma*. Eliade agreed.

Late that fall, Culianu received the letter he had been coveting — an invitation for the winter and spring terms, 1975, to conduct research at the Divinity School at the University of Chicago. It was a stunning turn of events for a young man who had so recently been a penniless and shunned graduate from a small despotic country. Not only was he now almost an assistant professor in Milan, studying the Renaissance in its original texts, but he had been invited by his hero to come to Chicago as a special assistant.

Once again he sped by jet to a new world that he had dreamed of for years, carrying little more than his battered suitcase, a few shirts, and some books. His arrival at O'Hare in February 1975 differed significantly, however, from his arrival in sunny Rome in July 1972. The jet howled down through a blanket of dark clouds, buffeted by the wet, cold Arctic wind. Instead of having a lively conversation with a beautiful professor en route, he was met by a dour Marghescu, who was determined to lord it over the younger man he had helped so critically. Instead of riding a train to a picturesque Italian town, they took Marghescu's rented car to an apartment at Fifty-seventh and Cornell Streets. Instead of relying on a government-sponsored scholarship, he scrimped to save every penny in the alien streets of the South Side of Chicago.

In Italy he had found a familiar Latin openness and warmth, even if people knew little of his homeland. In Chicago he found a cold, self-involved university founded by the Puritan Rockefellers and determined to establish itself as a world leader in expertise and erudition. "It is very tedious," he wrote his friend Romanato. "The University of Chicago is now the very best in the USA. Very high tuition, professors who don't show up, few students and all of them frightened. To tell you the truth, I like it that way." In his first weeks Chicago fell under one of its worst blizzards in history, with snow-drifts of four and five feet cutting off all contact with the outside world.

Still, he was where he had wanted to be all his life: at the door to Eliade's private office in the Meadville Seminary on Fifty-seventh Street. Eliade was a gentle, beloved figure, called Maestro by many who knew him on campus. He eschewed the limousine provided by the university. He dined nightly in the faculty Quadrangle Club because his wife, Christinel, would not cook. When she turned her back, he would mix his Scotch and rye whiskey. He helped almost everyone who came to him, especially young people from his home country. Once a bearded, penniless, dirty young man showed up on the Eliades' doorstep toting a guitar. The future National Public Radio columnist and author Andrei Codrescu was also taken under the maestro's wing.

Such beneficence seemed holy to those who knew it, and it sprang from a lifetime of true spiritual pilgrimage. From his early twenties in India studying the mysteries of yoga to his exile and fame in the United States, Eliade made a career that was "a microcosm of the pilgrimage of this century through extravagant hopes, dreams and terrors," as a *New York Times Book Review* writer once noted. Forced to flee Romania because of the suspicion that he had been a Guardist, Eliade left all that he loved behind him and never had a chance to see his mother and father again. This experience shaped his thought, recorded in some fifty works covering the history of religions, as well as essays, autobiographical works, and fiction.

A flip side to Culianu's good fortune was to be reminded of how small his own accomplishments yet were. In Eliade's published journal of these months Culianu appears only three times in descriptions of dinners with other people. An entry for February 13 explained the difficulties the younger man faced: "[Culianu] would like nothing more than to sit in on my lectures but I don't know if that will be possible." In all of March and April, Eliade mentioned seeing Culianu only twice — once for a group dinner, the other when Culianu was trying "to put some order in my bookshelves." On May 10, 1975, near the end of the younger man's time in Chicago, Eliade took stock: "At one o'clock Culianu is already in the living room in the midst of a fan of files that he has spread out. He has undertaken to file part of my correspondence. I'll see him again in 3 or 4 hours and I hope we'll have time to have a chat. He has come to Chicago intending to work with me. We have already gotten together several times, but have not yet had the opportunity to talk seriously." After three months in Chicago Ioan Culianu still had "not yet had the opportunity to talk seriously" with the man he had come so far to visit. Eliade was not purposefully keeping him at arm's length, but inviting him and then ignoring him must have seemed a cruel game.

Still, Culianu wrote home excitedly to his friend Romanato of life in the United States, reporting "important and interesting experiences unlike any other." He had met "important people," he said, and found Chicago "very different from European cities. They seem like rat holes compared to Chicago. TV with 40 channels, five from Chicago, and the largest library, skyscraper, and toy store in the world, not to mention daily business activity that surpasses anything I could have imagined."

Daily life, however, was difficult. He could not sightsee because he had no money, so he studied, racking up "8–10 hours of reading a day." Desperately poor, he cooked his own meals instead of taking them with Marghescu. He walked an extra fifteen blocks south to a food wholesaler near the famous old meatpacking houses of Chicago, saving a few cents on liver that did not always smell fresh. Marghescu lorded it over his younger friend, who was still struggling with English, and they quarreled frequently over money. One bitter quarrel centered on a quart of orange juice Culianu suspected his friend of stealing. "It should have been funny, but it wasn't," Marghescu recalled. "What we did to each other was terrible." On his last day Culianu got caught in a cloudburst on his way to say good-bye to Christinel Eliade. She told him to remove his wet things, and then she noticed that his socks and shirt had grown threadbare and filthy. She insisted he throw them away, loaning him some of her husband's. He concluded a dejected letter to Gianpaolo Romanato: "I have met few people so far, and so I'll be happy to come back in June, with the 'glory' of having studied with Professor Eliade."

Despite its disappointments, however, he could call his first trip to the United States a success. He returned to Italy with enough material for his first monograph. He had gained access to his mentor's files, if not his innermost thought (which no one ever penetrated), and had ingratiated himself by helping to bring order to the chaos of a prolific writer's work. He improved his English. In comparison with his European friends, he had accomplished much in a short period. Penurious though they were, his travels gave him more key contacts around the world than many other older scholars with far greater resources could claim. For a twenty-five-year-old recent refugee, such triumphs were no mean feat.

In May he returned to Milan. In June he received his first doctorate, a *dottore in lettere* in the history of religions at Catholic University, graduating summa cum laude. Assistant to Ugo Bianchi, he explored a new area in his thesis: "Gnosticismo e pensiero contemporaneo: Hans Jonas." In Jonas, a professor at New York's New School for Social Research, Culianu found another mentor, an iconoclastic but respected elder scholar who sought general applications of a field close to Culianu's heart — the secret, rebellious gnostic sects.

After spending the summer in Milan working on his Eliade book, Culianu traveled in September to the United Kingdom to lecture at the Thirteenth Congress of the International Association of the History of Religions in Lancaster. Now for the first time, he began finding a world audience for his ideas on the patterns of belief.

He also began, with some prompting by his friend Romanato, to speak out on the crackdown on free thought in Romania. In November, for instance, he wrote an essay called "Exile," published in the prominent émigré journal *Limite* in Paris. Satirizing the cowardice of Securitate, he argued that there could be no return to Romania without radical change. This and his other essays were cited in several attacks by a Securitate writer with the pen name of Artur Silvestri. Culianu wrote a 1975 review of a dissident's book subverting and yet published by the Ceauşescu regime. His political criticism, like his scholarly work, was promulgated in complex, suggestive language for a limited audience.

On November 10, 1975, Eliade wrote him warmly on his doctorate and honors: "Most sincere congratulations for the summa cum laude! For me, tonic and comforting to assist, even from afar, a protean and frantic workshop, as it suits you (as any expatriate's workshop should be, especially one from Romania). I rejoice in everything you do and intend to do, in the coming year." The "protean and frantic workshop" included now three main projects — Culianu's monograph on Eliade, an evolving work on gnostic scholar Hans Jonas, and his original text of *Eros and Magic in the Renaissance*.

⁕ ⁕ ⁕

By 1976 Italy had become a place of turmoil for him. The Aldo Moro kidnapping, other mysterious disappearances of journalists and judges that Italians shrugged off as *fantapolitica*, or fantasy politics, frequent student demonstrations, and the rise of a violent left on and off campus all made him uneasy. As his reputation grew, he

. . . . . .

applied for positions abroad. He began to feel he could hold his own as a scholar beside his idol. On March 1, 1976, he was awarded a four-year contract as lecturer at Milan's Catholic University of the Sacred Heart.

At the same time his applications produced two enticing offers: one a high-paying university position in Romanian studies in Groningen, Holland, the other a visiting professorship at an Indian university. Culianu faced a fundamental fork in his life: the choice between East and West. He had the chance to do exactly what his mentor had done — pursue spiritual enlightenment in the land of the mystics. Or he could plunge into the temptations of a profession in the West — money, comfort, security — at a bureaucratic institution in a small, comfortable, dull country.

Two years earlier he would have leaped at the opportunity of a paid sojourn in Eliade's Indian monastery. Now he hesitated. He turned to his adopted father figure for advice. Eliade wrote him on April 16, 1976: "If the Netherlands is *sure*, accept. You will be able to leave later, as soon as you receive a more interesting proposal. (If I were you I would have chosen India, with all the risk of being expelled one day.) What matters is for you not to let yourself be terrorized by the 'historic moment' — and to continue your work. I have the impression that the Italian atmosphere is now 'unbearable' to you. So, if you see that you don't have a choice you have to leave it . . . Holland, India, you name it." Unlike his mentor, Culianu was interested most in what the past could tell about the future, and the future to him lay in Western technology and commercialism. He decided on Holland.

Though he chose the West, he entertained no illusions about it. He was already dissatisfied with its technical approach to his "unhappy discipline," as Eliade once described the history of religions. Culianu wrote Andrei Pleşu, a friend in Romania who became the country's culture minister after the revolution, of his conclusion: "Here in the West, the history of religion . . . is not the result of an evolution toward a philosophical opening such as was the case for us . . . but an archaeological discipline without existential implication. It is useless for seeking more profound knowledge, or opening toward being." He prepared again to move, this time to the northern Calvinist country of the Dutch.

I open the Latin dictionary at the word "precarious"

and learn it means "that which is obtained with

prayer."... Precariousness... is the only way to

recover religion in a secular time.

— *I. P. Culianu to Mario Lombardo, January 1979*

. . . .

HOLLAND: A RISING YOUNG INTELLECTUAL, 1976–1983

Groningen was the third university town of Culianu's life. A northern, rainy provincial town founded in 1040, it lacked the warmth that had nurtured him in both Romania and Italy. Professors and students navigated cobblestone streets on bicycles. A medieval church clock rang out every hour. Poorer students lived on houseboats on the Verbindingskanaal encircling the old town, a canal crossed by five bridges. Life revolved around a five-hundred-year-old university, then a large public institution. At night it was customary to keep one's house curtains wide open, as if to display the family's lighted living room or den for any passerby to affirm its bourgeois respectability. The custom drove Ioan Culianu crazy.

Yet he enjoyed the comfort of life in a country where people shopped for food in neighborhood health food stores or delicatessens and took advantage of one of the world's best national health care systems. Polite and reserved, the Dutch seemed to prize consistency and thoroughness more than creativity or passion. For an ambitious scholar fleeing one country's repression and another's turbulence, Groningen provided a haven where he could quietly produce the work he hoped would bring him world attention.

Culianu's hiring had come from a combination of chance and fate. The man who hired him was Willem Noomen, a specialist in the medieval French fables called *fabliaux*. A tall, striking, white-haired thinker, Noomen had an interest in medieval folklore that took him and his wife to Romania several times in the 1960s and early 1970s. They had fallen in love with the country's spiritual tradition and warm hospitality. In 1976 Noomen had posted a position in Romanian literature at the university. He wrote the Romanian government's Ministry of Culture, listing a few outstanding scholars he wished to approach about hiring. He received no response. He wrote the Romanian ambassador to Holland on the subject on May 1, 1976. This time he received the name of a Communist bureaucrat with little academic background. He declined the suggestion.

Noomen's Paris connections and his Italian friend Ugo Bianchi brought the name of Ioan Culianu to his attention. Culianu was invited from Milan for a campus interview. "Everyone who met him was very positive about his personality," Noomen observed. "He was polite, even . . . a little too polite for Dutch people." Culianu made a good impression, and most people took his elaborate humility as a humorous play on academic power relations. He was offered an assistant professorship in Romanian literature.

Shortly before Culianu began teaching at Groningen in the fall of 1976, Noomen received an angry visitor, the Romanian ambassador, Traian Pop. "You have hired an enemy of the Romanian people!" Pop said. "My government requests you rescind this offer at once."

Noomen responded that he had asked the Romanian government more than once for its assistance. But the request was simply a courtesy gesture. Dutch academia did not follow the dictates of a foreign government in its hiring.

The ambassador threatened to take the matter up with the Dutch National Ministry of Education. Noomen countered that the University of Groningen was an institute of higher education independent of any minister's meddling. Culianu was hired. But Noomen did call his new protégé into his office in September, privately asking him to keep his political writings as quiet as he could.

Culianu obliged for the most part. In fact, he mostly avoided the growing enclave of Romanian dissidents in Europe. Not sure whom to trust, and not always trusted in turn, he remained aloof. In Italy he had only once spoken out publicly on politics. In a 1978 interview conducted by his friend Gianpaolo Romanato for the popular daily *Il Popolo*, he identified two forms of rebellion against totalitarian power — outright dissent and inward retreat. His response was the latter, he said. Writing Romanato afterward, Culianu noted: "I don't look good as a dissident, and I am not a model. Still, the shape you gave the material made it interesting and even surprising to me."

As the years passed and conditions at home worsened, Culianu did contact the most renowned opponents of the Ceauşescu regime and began to write critical articles, although he couched his criticism in extremely veiled terms. His main interests in these years were not political but professional — finding an audience, understanding the West, and advancing his career. He wrote that Romania did not produce great dissidents but great artists, who pursued in the West roughly the same journeys of discovery they followed in the East, only more openly. But almost subconsciously, his scholarly work on ideas and power pulled him toward issues of great discomfort to a totalitarian regime. Perhaps the secret police stationed in capitals around the world read more perceptively than most of his academic readers, or were more prescient about his future direction than even he was. Exploring freely history's underlying patterns, his writing was disquieting to anyone with power and something to hide.

❋   ❋   ❋

The next years were quiet and solitary, marked by teaching, research, and publishing — twenty-six scholarly articles, sixty-four short articles and reviews, and four specialized books on religion. After his rough years of adjustment in Italy, Culianu found personal calm and economic tranquillity, and he wrote the books he had mapped in his mind in Milan. "I am doing well," he wrote Romanato. "But I don't know how long this will last. I only hope it will last long enough for me to finish the books I have planned."

In winter Groningen was lonely, damp, and windy; at eight in the morning it was still dark, and by four in the afternoon it was night again. Culianu lived according to elaborate plans and lists, writing his friend Romanato of a passing affair with a "lady German friend" and his desire for more companionship—not only for its erotic pleasures but also because "having a woman would help a lot with 'public relations' and also with the daily household chores." He practiced yoga and worried about obtaining citizenship, which he lacked even after four years in the West. Teaching the glories of the Romanian national poet Mihai Eminescu, he was shocked when one of his few students fell asleep.

By 1977 he had learned that his doctorate from Milan's Catholic University did not carry the prestige he needed to rise in his career. He wrote his friend Romanato that the Dutch academic community, like those in most Western European countries, leaned so far to the left that he felt "unprotected by anyone, without friends and without a brotherly soul anywhere." He came to despise the West, where "society offers the bland image of a shop where everything is on sale and nothing can be *received* (nor given)." To bolster his professional mobility he enrolled in 1978 at the Sorbonne to pursue a second doctorate, called *docteur de 3ème cycle en sciences religieuses*, in the Department of History and Philosophy, specializing in late antiquity. Buoyed by the stature of Eliade's name, he was able to choose as his adviser Michel Meslin, the Sorbonne's president.

He began giving presentations internationally, lecturing in Rome in 1977 at the Italian Association for the Study of Religions and in 1979 in Amsterdam at the International Conference on Romanian Studies, traveling every summer to Paris to meet Eliade and publishers, publishing articles on gnosticism, demonology, dualism, and magic for specialized publications like *Aevum, Kairos,* and *Neophilologus.* He worked intensively, following the example of Eliade's fictional hero in *The Boy with Eyeglasses,* by establishing a program that included less and less sleep every night. He pursued his research agenda even as he hoped to move beyond academic writing. He told Gianpaolo Romanato, "I work without enthusiasm at the thesis that I hope will become a book about ecstatic experiences. It will be, I think, my first and last book that is entirely scientific."

Feeling increasingly isolated, Culianu wrote such despairing letters to friends in Italy that he prompted Romanato and his wife to visit him for ten days in Groningen at Christmas 1977, after they had come for Easter only nine months earlier. "Frankly . . . it wasn't a particularly attractive place to spend Christmas," Romanato recalled. On New Year's Eve it rained twelve hours straight, and students set off firecrackers until dawn, shattered store windows, and overturned garbage cans. "I went there with my wife exclusively and only to visit my friend because he had written some very desperate letters full of loneliness, and I was worried about him."

⁂ ⁂ ⁂

One person who began helping Culianu more in his academic rise was Mircea Eliade. On November 24, 1977, for instance, the elder scholar wrote enthusiastically about wanting to take Culianu to the prominent French publisher François Jean-Luc Pidoux-Payot: "I can hardly wait 'til we see each other again, but when? Not before May, 1978. . . . Among others I would like to introduce you to Payot, somewhat *officially*, because I think of you to take care of the new editions of *Traité d'histoire des religions* etcetera, when I will not be available." Eliade was beginning to consider Culianu as a protégé to take over some of the projects he no longer had the energy to complete alone. So it seemed that the collaboration Ioan Culianu wished for was finally coming about.

One problem intervened, however: Culianu's monograph on Eliade was due to appear late in 1978 from Italy's Cittadella Editrice. It would be his first book and the first book by a Romanian on the great historian of religions. It concentrated on the materials written by Eliade in his early Romanian years, unknown to Western Eliade scholars. Culianu worried about how to finish it without offending his mentor yet without writing a paean. He hoped also that Eliade would help him to get it published in France, a more prominent market than Italy.

Culianu had a more specific worry. In his close reading both of Eliade and of the histories of the Iron Guard, Culianu uncovered uncomfortable similarities in the scholar's rhetoric and that of the Romanian fascists. Eliade had written of his reverence for a far rightist professor, Nae Ionescu, and of being pursued by the royal secret police, who suspected him of being an Iron Guardist in the late 1930s. Eliade couched these incidents in the nostalgia of youth, using the term *felixculpa* (happy guilt) to describe how suspicions of the royal secret police led him to leave Romania before it fell to Communist rule. Yet there was little "happy" about the Iron Guard, as Culianu learned.

Culianu uncovered in his research that after 1937 the Legion of the Archangel Michael became transformed from an anti-Semitic youth group into an organization of killers. Reports of the 1941 pogrom showed that thousands were slaughtered in Bucharest and almost as many in Iaşi. The American newspaper reporter Robert St. John recalled the Bucharest atrocities in his book *Foreign Correspondent:* "We counted the corpses, we noted the mutilations, we inspected what little was left of the once-beautiful synagogues, we took careful notes . . ." In an uncomfortable exchange, Culianu questioned his mentor directly about an "objective history" of the period. On January 14, 1978, Eliade wrote back:

> I don't think that it is possible to write an objective history of the Legionary Movement nor a portrait of C.Z.C. [Corneliu Zelea Codreanu]. The documents at hand are insufficient; moreover, an "objective" attitude can be fatal for the author.
>
> Today only apologies for a very small number of fanatics (of all nations) or executions (for the majority of European and American readers) are accepted. After Büchenwald and Auschwitz even honest people cannot afford being "objective."

Eliade seemed to suggest that after the discovery of Nazi (and Romanian) concentration camps, one could never write with sympathy for the Iron Guard without succumbing to "fatal" attacks from those who rightfully deplored the suffering. But he could also have been suggesting that an "objective history" of the Iron Guard put one in danger from its adherents as well. He concluded by apologizing: "I am sorry that I let myself go in all these 'considerations,' sketchy and hurried. I am sending you, however, these pages, at least to propose to you the beginning of a long future discussion." As much as Culianu was wooing the older scholar for his support, so too Eliade was wooing his young acolyte. If nothing else, Culianu's book would help spread his ideas.

   ❋   ❋   ❋

A succinct exegesis, Culianu's *Mircea Eliade* suggested that his mentor's work was mapped out almost in its entirety in a French monograph, *La nostalgie des origines*, published in English as *The Quest*. Eliade spent his life working out three or four themes delineated in *The Quest*, the book argued, based on his youth in Romania. Modern man feels lost and insignificant in the modern universe, just as an exile feels lost in a foreign culture, dreaming a "myth of the eternal return." Culianu examined Eliade's fantasy fiction, such as "The Secret of Dr. Honigberger," and his diaries, considering both critical to an understanding of his scholarly ideas.

One example of the book's contribution to scholarship, frequently cited by other academics without credit to Culianu, addressed a Romanian paper written in the 1930s in which Eliade argued there was no continuity between alchemy and chemistry. Chemistry was not a refined version of alchemy, as many historians tried to claim when demonstrating the "progress" of the Western mind; the two were totally different and discontinuous systems of thought. Eliade said that one had to differentiate fundamentally between the methods of modern science and more elastic and inclusive metaphysical systems. "Culianu was the first critic to note the alchemy paper's significance," observed University of Bucharest scholar Sorin Antohi, "and it *was* very important to understanding Eliade's thought."

When he read the book manuscript, which remained silent on the politics of the 1930s, Eliade warmly endorsed it in a letter: "I liked it, I congratulate you, and I am grateful to you . . . (I hope this book will be published in English and French too.) I liked it in the first place because, although I know you are 'Eliadian,' you do not commit the sin of hagiography. . . . I am glad that you already master all the instruments that will allow you to defend and illustrate our unhappy discipline." Eliade applauded Culianu's structural analysis, recognizing himself in the book's pages and encouraging its author to develop further the tools to address the "methodological challenge" facing the history of religions.

Yet after the endorsement Eliade did not recommend the book to his French publisher, preferring another text written by an American, a book "containing very little information," according to Culianu. The younger man was stunned. He wrote his friend Romanato in November 1978 that he "bitterly regretted" having "venerated [his] idol's doctrine." He felt the only reason for the betrayal was his pursuit of Eliade's personal politics and history: "I am guilty (or better yet, truth is guilty). It is because Eliade didn't like my inquiries about his past and Romania's past, and so he did not recommend my book to his publisher (although I did not enclose those inquiries of mine. . . .) You will say that I am a fool to vex Eliade with all my research. I can say: 'Amicus Plato, sed magis amica veritas,' and this is true." Culianu complained that his role "was to be the cretin disciple who faced any kind of risk to meet [Eliade], but without any space for criticism." Angry, frustrated, and hurt, Culianu nevertheless began a calculated conciliation. "I understood how much really depends on him, so I adopted a more careful and obsequious attitude," he wrote to Romanato. In future public statements, he became Eliade's staunchest defender against those who called him a fascist.

While offering a "long future discussion," Eliade seemed much to prefer to leave the past buried. What Culianu did not know at age twenty-eight was why.

By 1978 Culianu was tenured at Groningen as an assistant professor, and he declared himself a "regular bourgeois intellectual." Yet overall in his first years of prosperity in the West he felt a sense of deluded hope. He complained that in the West "the space for the unfolding of the spirit becomes more and more narrowed." Certainly the cultural model of the East was worse, he wrote, "but directly from this comes the dilemma: that I can't see anywhere the minimum hope. I find myself literally thrown in a world that I don't have a hard time understanding, but to appreciate for what it is." His complaint was against modernity, both Eastern and Western.

He adjusted, however, learning to drive and indulging his new obsessions — playing pinball or new video games, watching profes-

sional wrestling on television, and ordering incessantly from cata-
logs. He responded to whatever mail order offers he received, reveling in credit card purchases, free samples, introductory offers, and
all of capitalism's own magic.

It was also in 1978 that his mother first managed to get an exit
visa for the West. She came to Groningen for two months, sharing
with him the large apartment that he had never been able to fill by
himself. In his diary, he would later record his feelings about this
period as "childish ecstasy."

At a friend's house on July 19, 1979, he met an attractive, dark
woman with eyes the color of the ocean at night. Carmen Georgescu was a graduate student in Russian whose father had died early
in her life. Her husband, a researcher in neurology, was so absorbed
in his work that he ignored her and their seven-year-old son, Andrei.
Ioan greeted her with the oldest line in the book. "We've met before," he said.

"Oh yes, right." She laughed.

"You went to a Physics Olympiad in Iaşi in 1967. You wore a blue
dress, with a white embroidered collar. It was very pretty."

Carmen felt her jaw drop. She remembered the dress and the
meeting vividly because it was the first time her mother had bought
her a debutante dress, and the first time she had been allowed to
leave home alone. Because the academic competition focused on
physics, only a few girls came, and she had enjoyed the attention of
several boys. But who was he? When Culianu laughed, she remembered. His high, needling cackle made her think of a skinny boy in
the back of the room with a hanging forelock and passionate eyes.
He had been shy, quiet, gentle, melancholy. She was heckling the
group leader, calling out answers to the questions, saying they were
too easy. She remembered he had asked her at the end of the day if
she wanted him to show her around Iaşi. She had declined.

As she stared at him the experience of her youth flooded back to
her. But how could he remember her dress so quickly, and in such
detail?

They talked late into the night. A week later he sent nineteen
roses to commemorate the date of their meeting. In two weeks they
began seeing each other. Within five weeks she left her husband,
and she and her son moved into Ioan's apartment. He explained to

her that shortly before they first met, his father had died in poverty. By September 16, less than two months after meeting her, Ioan was writing Gianpaolo Romanato that he had "turned his shoulder on the temporary condition of being single, without the least regret." (After devoting a sentence to his marriage plans, he hastened to query about the book he and Romanato had coauthored with Mario Lombardo, *Religione e potere*, or *Religion and Power*: "Has it come out yet?")

For the next few years Carmen and Ioan were soulmates as well as lovers. He made everything in their lives an elaborate ceremony. The night they were engaged, for instance, he wrote out on parchment, in Latin, a pact attaching their souls together forever. He nicked her thumb, and they both signed in blood. "If anyone shall break this pact," he wrote in mock medieval tones, "may he die a swift and humiliating death."

He sent her nineteen roses every July 19. He covered the house with magical talismans and stuffed cats. When she was ill, he made an elaborate show of turning her trial into a performance of love and sacrifice, behaving like an Eliade hero. But for the most part he treated her much as Pygmalion treated his young lover. "He wanted to shape me from his fictional image of a wife," she recalled. "Yet he helped me tremendously. He helped me discover who I was."

Together they explored astrology. He claimed its powers came from the logic of systematic thought. One did not have to believe planetary positions affected personalities to respect an ancient Egyptian art that offered a method of predicting events. He himself was not very good at it, however, "because he always wanted to influence events, not merely to observe them," she recalled. "He had this dark side that motivated his studies of magic, a far more interesting side," she said. "It was this Faustian side that was most responsible for his success."

They had fun, playing cards and giving parties, as she helped him to understand the agendas of sycophants who began to surround him in his rise. He became particularly close to her son. "He was a child himself," Andrei observed many years later. "When we played a game, like Monopoly, he did not draw a line between fantasy and reality. But he was much closer to me than my real father. He was the only one who would go out and kick a soccer ball with me." Their favorite pastime was watching professional wrestling on television. He knew the matches were fixed but reveled in figuring who was going to win, and how. In the melodramatic mock battles of Andrei the Giant and Hulk Hogan he saw a familiar universe, ruled by ignorant powers manipulating events from behind the scenes.

He tried to play a similarly Machiavellian game in his life and career. He learned to footnote the right people in his articles and to subdivide ideas for multiple publications. In January 1980, when he married Carmen in the Russian Orthodox cathedral in Amsterdam, he did not choose Willem Noomen or Gianpaolo Romanato to be the best man. Instead he asked a prominent publisher he was trying to convince to publish his book, the Dutch scholar M. J. Vermaseren. (Learning that Vermaseren and his wife liked stuffed animals, he sent them a stream of teddy bears, kittens, and monkeys.) Vermaseren did not publish Culianu's Ph.D. thesis, *Psychanodia: A Survey of the Evidence Concerning the Ascension of the Soul and Its Relevance*, and when he rejected another manuscript years later, he was surprised and hurt that Culianu dropped him cold. Still, Ioan would express his gratitude to Vermaseren in his preface to *Les Gnoses dualistes*.

Culianu was not terribly good as a Machiavellian. He was too childlike, almost too much a real human being to manipulate people totally, his wife said. Carmen showed him how to use the Dutch system to get his prized citizenship. "That Romanian ambassador did you a great favor," she said. "Now you can claim for citizenship under 'A' status as a political refugee. You'll be approved quickly." So he did, and was. At long last, with the help of his new love, he had his coveted citizenship papers and new legal identity, and a new family.

※ ※ ※

For a few years he was relatively happy with his salary, his ability to buy a nice home and car, and his marriage to a beautiful woman. He earned a second Ph.D. at the Sorbonne, writing a thesis entitled "Experiences of Ecstasy and Ascension under Hellenism and Islam" and receiving a final grade of *très bien*. He decided to seek a final degree, the highest offered in the world, the Sorbonne's *doctorat d'état*. After much discussion, Meslin agreed to take him on.

The decision to seek a third doctorate signaled both deep, over-riding ambition and insecurity. In Holland he was pigeonholed in the minor field of Romanian studies, though he also taught romance linguistics, literary aesthetics, and, for one year, the history of religions. When the History of Religions Department opened a prestigious position, the one once held by the scholar Gerardus van der Leeuw, Culianu's application was rejected. Dutch culture to him seemed smug and stuffy; his colleagues looked down on Romanian literature and would not accept his speculative, philosophical inquiries into the origin and history of world faiths.

He responded by writing scholarly articles on religion at an almost unbelievable pace — seven in 1983, nine in 1984 — in addition to dozens of book reviews each year. Often he stayed up until three or four in the morning and then slept until eleven. Increasingly he was drawn to the gnostics. He took up the subject in lectures in Paris, Rome, and in 1983 on the invitation of the Werner Reimers-Stiftung in Bad Homburg, West Germany. His mentor was a prominent scholar, Hans Jonas, who linked the gnostics' rise to Byzantine social and political apathy and a search for miraculous salvation. Culianu corresponded with Jonas, inviting him to lecture in Groningen, and began working on a book about him. It was the gnostic notion of a universe ruled or fixed by ignorant gods, like a universal professional wrestling match one must constantly subvert, that appealed to Culianu most.

Yet lectures and articles alone were not enough, Eliade wrote him. "Christinel and I hug you both, and we *implore* Carmen to protect you from the temptations of articles and reviews and to force you (with *spells*) to ready the books." He responded to the admonition, publishing first the elegant *Iter in silvis: Saggi scelti sulla gnosi e altri studi*, or *The Road in Silver* (Messina, 1981). He took up the deeper problem of religion's relation to politics in the book co-authored with Romanato and Mario Lombardo, *Religione e potere* (Turin, 1981). He then edited a festschrift dedicated to Willem Noomen, *Libra* (Dordrecht, 1983). These activities, along with his teaching and attendance at conferences, demonstrated an immense and prodigious effort to learn foreign languages and to publish around the world. Culianu's books hinted at his new methodology in the field that Eliade challenged him to devise.

Over and above the struggle for professional recognition came
the pain of separation and exile. In 1982 his sister married a high
school teacher she had met while he was a student at the University
of Iaşi. Dan Petrescu would soon become one of the leading dissidents of the "Iaşi Group," editing and contributing to cultural peri-
odicals despite the regime. Culianu wrote his sister in 1983 of his
tension and isolation: "Be careful and patient with our mother. I'll
do my best to bring her here, maybe for a long time. I try to make
memory a support for me, not a cause for distress." Until his marriage he had preserved a careful private ceremony, in which he made
the anniversary of his father's death a time of memorializing. He
would not leave the house at all that day.

    *   *   *

In 1983 Culianu made two significant moves, switching from his
early scientific texts to fiction and to a prophetic book that also
signaled the course of his later thought. "I am looking for a publisher for a book on eros and magic in the Renaissance," he wrote
Romanato. Having experienced the success of the bourgeois—
precisely what he detested most—he wanted to expand into the
world outside academics. He bubbled over with ideas for a novel, a
book on East European witchcraft, and a book on salvation. He
wrote Romanato of his dissatisfaction: "Now I am not able to withdraw completely in my studies. No religious 'solution' now I have
'arrived' in a material condition without surprise and anyway extremely unsatisfied. I already know the meetings where I will participate. Everything is reduced now to a machine, a game. . . . In short,
I have the impression that life must be *played*, but not seriously."

Feeling in himself the potent allegiance of fate,

he pushed open the door.

— *Leonard Gardner,* Fat City

1484 AND 1984

In 1984 Culianu's career reached a turning point. Bidding to become a major voice in religion and Renaissance scholarship in Europe, he published two major books with important French houses. One book was a technical work covering shamans and the experience of ecstasy: *Expériences de l'extase: Extase, ascension et récit visionnaire, de l'Hellénisme au Moyen-Age* (Ecstatic Experiences: Ecstasy, Ascension and Visionary Accounts, from Hellenism to the Middle Ages). The publisher was Payot. The other offered the world his study of Renaissance magic begun at age nineteen. Published by Flammarion, *Eros et magie à la Renaissance, 1484* (Eros and Magic in the Renaissance — 1484) was unlike almost anything that had come before in the field. Dense, opinionated, erudite, it proposed a new method of understanding the relation among magic, religion, and science, as *Spectrum Review* put it, "examining a period that, like our own, was concerned with redefining human civilization and recovering the power of imagination and eros."

At the age of thirty-four Culianu was fulfilling his goal to move beyond purely academic writing by offering a new theory of how and why world events occur. Historical change occurs by mutation, not evolution, and often through forces hidden to the actors themselves, he suggested in *Eros et magie*. He proposed a quantum vision of history in which cultural stresses build and build without impression until suddenly an entire culture explodes. During such periods of crisis political leaders confuse effects with causes, old definitions such as "right" and "left" flip into their opposites, and institutions act in completely uncharacteristic ways.

His main purpose, however, was to propose a new way of looking at the Renaissance, by suggesting that the origins of modern technology, political institutions, and many neuroses lay in the Reformation, when censorship of the imaginary and separation of conscious from unconscious became church doctrine. His sources included the philosopher Paul Feyerabend (*Against Method*, 1979), German anthropologist Hans Peter Duerr (*Dreamtime*, 1979), and the historian of ideas Stephen Toulmin (*The Return to Cosmology*, 1982).

* * *

Even Culianu's later detractors acknowledged *Eros et magie* to be a "brilliant book," in the words of the University of Chicago's Wendy Doniger. In it Culianu focused on three philosopher-magicians: the misshapen, pedantic Marsilio Ficino (1433–99), his suave, wealthy disciple Pico della Mirandola (1463–94), and the enigmatic, tortured Giordano Bruno (1548–1600). He examined their nearly forgotten texts to uncover their command of unconscious and erotic, imaginative powers. *Magic* to them did not mean hocus-pocus, but rather a deep, thoroughly documented world of the imagination connecting conscious and unconscious, individual and cosmos, in a way lost to modern man. However imperfect their "sciences" were, they seriously attempted to understand the metaphysical operations of the mind. "Culianu made two key contributions," said Smith College professor Carol Zaleski of *Eros et magie* after it was translated into English. "One was in the sheer mass of his erudition. But his main interest was in understanding how the mind invents worlds and makes them so real they, in effect, become real."

To Culianu these philosopher-magicians were early masters of cyberspace — the infinite realm of thoughts that the Renaissance called phantasms. In his book he began by reviewing past journeyers into mental worlds, like Plato and the medieval Muslim thinker al-Kindi, who said that humans were connected to each other and their universe by invisible rays. When Ficino and Pico rediscovered al-Kindi's works and those of Egyptian astrology, it made for a flowering of Renaissance fantasy, mysticism, and mind games. To them the *ideal* world of the imagination seemed as real as the real world, which was a shadow of deeper spiritual forces. Their era presented not the beginning of modern science, as many considered the Renaissance to be, but the last of a rich magical way of looking at the world in which, as Einstein once wrote, "pure thought could grasp reality, as the ancients dreamed."

Culianu had personal bonds with his manuscript and subject. He had written his first version of the book in Romanian in 1969. He later translated it into French, enriching it based on suggestions from other specialists in Paris, and placed it at Flammarion under the renowned poet and critic Yves Bonnefoy. Bonnefoy wanted to use it for a series called Ideas and Research, provided Eliade wrote the preface. Eliade did not often write such prefaces, but he readily agreed for both of Culianu's French books. "It is with *Eros and Magic* . . ." Eliade noted, "that [Culianu's] most important works begin to appear."

Culianu had other personal bonds with his subject. Pico della Mirandola was an awestruck, sometimes resentful disciple to Ficino, a famous elder scholar, just as Culianu was to Eliade. In the book Culianu highlighted the tangled personal relationship between Pico and Ficino. Ficino chose the term *eros* to describe the reason for magic's effects on other people. Pico added a new emphasis, suggesting that eros linked man with god. Both men, Culianu noted, freely denounced their own writings to avoid troubles with the pope.

Not so Bruno, the former Dominican friar who was the book's real focus. Bruno claimed to raise the ancient Greek art of memory to a level of "global emotional control" by creating a mental computer through concentric circles that he could rotate and recombine. Culianu claimed that Bruno's lesser-known text *De vinculis*, or *Of Bonds*, predicted in detail the means by which a modern population could be controlled through imagery. Today, Culianu said, we call this magic psychology, propaganda, corporate public relations, spin control, and advertising. He claimed that today's multi-billion-dollar budgets devoted to understanding consumer psyches do exactly what Bruno did with his astrological symbols charged by the power of eros — concoct public images to create "the total illusion of total satisfaction."

Examining such concepts as a universal spirit, or "pneuma," which philosophers can manipulate, Culianu highlighted the theories by which early thinkers envisioned a much closer relation of inner thoughts to events in the world than we accept today. As a young scholar who learned the power of thought to free him from a modern culture's thought control, he explained that a historian of ideas can only unmask a culture by paying attention to the movements it marginalizes. A scholar must "look in the wings" to see "the hidden threads that link ideas to the invisible will of the time."

Looking into the wings of the Renaissance, Culianu sought to do more than recover the forgotten ideas of obscure magicians, however. He attempted to shift the great turning point in Western history, when civilization moved from a reliance on faith to scientific doubt, out of the Renaissance and into the period of the Reformation. Luther's reforms subjugated the Renaissance imagination, Culianu argued. The Catholic church responded with a Counter-reformation in which the richly magical world of alchemical and metaphysical thought was crushed. Modern science took wing as an *accidental* consequence of this deeper transformation of the collective psyche. Galileo stole his idea of an infinite universe, Culianu argued, from Bruno and the poet Nicholas of Cusa, who came years before him. Yet the Renaissance was still an era dominated by metaphysics, imagination, and religious faith — not yet the birth of modern science.

Culianu's book made a splash in French and Italian scholarly circles as a "must read" for students of the period. The *History of Science* found it "a fascinating attempt to demonstrate that the scientific revolution did not so much expel magic from science as incorporate it." The *Bibliothèque d'Humanisme et Renaissance* suggested that "all students of the Renaissance need to read this book." The *Christian Century* predicted, "You will hear much of Professor Culianu in the years ahead." Others questioned his reworking of original material: "In his hands religion and science have become disembodied yet potent phantasms," one reviewer for *Church History* later complained, "manipulated at will by Culianu the magician."

The writing was difficult, but that was part of Culianu's method. Drawing on the controversial writing of Paul Feyerabend, he suggested that one should subtly subvert academic discourse, and so he placed his most important points in obscure and buried passages. Filled with antiquated knowledge, his book was almost at times a parody of the scholarly method that he in many ways detested. As Mary Winkler of the University of Texas concluded in the *Sixteenth-Century Journal:* "[It] is both dazzling and vexing. It is dazzling because Professor Culianu offers his readers a truly pyrotechnical display of learning and intellectual creativity. It is vexing, perhaps, for the same reason."

By the book's end, Culianu departed from religion scholarship altogether, delving into modern cognitive science to examine the relation of ideas to power. His was a book not only about magic, or history, but also about the relation of thought to the cosmos it reflected. In Romania, the scholar Sorin Antohi called *Eros et magie* "the triumph of an original thinker over the work of an ambitious scholar."

⁕   ⁕   ⁕

Across the ocean, in Chicago, events took shape that would alter several lives. Following his wife's surgery for a hernia, Mircea Eliade began to arrange for the disbursement of his books and papers — to the University of Chicago's Regenstein Library, to the private

Meadville library, and to the Library of the Romanian Academy. It was a monumental and depressing job for an elderly scholar preparing to retire, plunging him into his past and yet filled with clerical work. His arthritis made writing painful, and writing was for him, as his colleague Wendy Doniger pointed out, life.

In his journal Eliade recorded difficulties with his office assistant, Adriana Berger, who rearranged his working library on several occasions and quarreled with the curators at Regenstein. As early as January 28, 1984, he noted that he was "too sad, too depressed, and too tired to record in this notebook the episodes and adventures in the saga" of his library's dispersal. Berger was staying in his office until late at night, filing his books and correspondence. By April 6 Eliade noted, upon finding his office rearranged so that he could not recognize it: "To keep from exploding, I return home . . . I have been laid low by a series of misfortunes." Adding to his anxiety, later that month his friend, former student, and biographer, Mac Linscott Ricketts, began pressing him on the "allusions to my 'Nazism' (anti-Semitism) . . ." he wrote. "I try to explain."

What Eliade did not know was that Adriana Berger would later mount a public attack alleging his Iron Guardist past. By April he wrote only: "I feel tireder than ever, melancholy, depressed." One of his few recorded bright moments came when he received a three-volume festschrift dedicated to him, edited by Culianu's friend Hans Peter Duerr in Germany and including Culianu's spirited, if convoluted, defense of his mentor.

In June, desperately in need of a rest and worried about the completion of the thirteen-volume *Encyclopedia of Religion* he had to edit for Macmillan, Eliade and his wife, Christinel, arrived in Paris, where they were joined in July by Carmen and Ioan Culianu. The day after the younger couple's arrival, the four drove to a party. "Talking all the while, we lost our way several times in that fascinating quarter, Le Marais," Eliade wrote. A few weeks later he finished his preface to Culianu's *Expériences de l'extase*, required by editor Jean-Luc Pidoux-Payot for publication. "I hope that I shall someday have the time to write all that I think about Ioan Culianu. . . . My admiration for [him] is sincere and unlimited," the elder scholar observed in his journal.

This second major book was mostly scientific, setting the stage for Culianu's later study *Out of This World*. In it he focused on the "shaman," the tribal wise man or woman who travels to foreign realms — either through trance, drugs, ecstasy, or magic — and returns to lead the group based on the new knowledge. Building on his previous monograph *Psychanodia*, Culianu compared shamans in different religions by diagramming beliefs as they changed over time, much as a scientist might chart the behavior of subatomic particles — seeking a pattern or formula.

After a trip to Italy, the Eliades went to Groningen in August for a much-needed vacation. With Culianu, Eliade gradually began to feel rejuvenated in the "pure delight of not having a schedule, of not doing anything, of holding conversations on all subjects." He asked the younger man for help on the *Encyclopedia of Religion* and also proposed that they coauthor another contracted project, *The Eliade Guide to World Religions*. Relieved at Culianu's assent, Eliade happily returned to Chicago.

●　●　●

In Groningen in the fall of 1984, Ioan faced his own crisis. The university was confronting budget cutbacks. The small Department of Romanian Literature would likely be axed. He was tenured but still could be fired. In addition, the whole university seemed smaller to him, not so much safe as stultified. He applied for a scholarship to Harvard, while writing Eliade to confirm his visiting lectureship at Chicago. A lectureship would not only help in their collaboration, Culianu thought, but would also give him a chance to check out university life, and publication possibilities, in the United States.

In September his cousin Miron Bogdan managed a short-term exit visa for Western Europe, and he and Ioan arranged to meet for twelve precious hours in Düsseldorf. "I was so hungry to meet him," Miron recalled. "But he had changed. Though he was very accomplished and self-assured, he seemed somehow . . . isolated." Among other things, Culianu had begun to feel constrained and unhappy in his marriage, although he was working so hard that he hardly noticed.

Perhaps the uncanniest aspect of this year of European success was the fact that Culianu hinted about the year 1984 so much in *Eros and Magic.* It would launch one of those quantum-leap periods, he seemed to predict, as had its predecessor by half a millennium, 1484. To understand why, what he meant by anthropologist Clifford Geertz's term *deep history,* one has to look at his book, his life, and world events.

There is a necessity of law and a certain harmony

between the world's elements . . . even in the society

of brigands.

—*Marsilio Ficino,* Tomo Primo delle lettere

ABUSES OF INTERPRETATION

    A menacing backdrop to life in exile was the opposing cur-
rents of the twentieth century, fascism and communism. In 1980
Culianu had published a review of an Iron Guardist poet that
would plunge him unwillingly into the obsessive world of a fascist movement-in-exile. At the same time he felt threatened by the
Communist secret police even though he was courted, as all prominent exiles were, by the new Romanian ambassador in Holland. In
both cases Culianu stumbled into difficulty mainly through mis-

readings of his work. Like his friend Umberto Eco, who had come to hear him lecture in Groningen on Renaissance magic, he reveled in the idea that misreadings could lead to a higher truth than either reader or writer intended. He took this as a humorous play on the power of fiction, but in his life it was no joke.

In the 1940s many Iron Guardists managed to escape Romania to the West. Some settled in Milan, Madrid, and Freiburg, West Germany, but the largest number came to the United States and Canada — some at the behest of American intelligence, which hoped to use them as anti-Communist forces. They concentrated in Chicago, Detroit, Windsor, and Toronto. A series of exposés by the *Windsor Star* found some of these men to be wealthy and influential in politics by the 1980s. In 1984 in Detroit, for instance, the Romanian Orthodox archbishop Viorel Trifa — who had delivered the U.S. Senate prayer during the Nixon Administration — was finally deported after his past activities were revealed by the efforts of a New York dentist, Charlie Kremer.*

Culianu's run-in with the movement began years earlier. In 1977 he was asked to review the work of an elderly Romanian poet for the *Journal of Romanian Studies.* The poet, Horia Stamatu, had been admired by, among others, Eugène Ionesco. Culianu described what followed in two versions of a fictional story — one unpublished and called "Romanian Fears," the other published in the New York magazine *Lumea Liberă* in October 1990 as "A Unique Chance." Both were based on his real-life experience, but he changed the tale slightly each time as if to tease out different meanings.

The published version referred to Stamatu only as "H. S." In it, H. S. told Culianu he had been interned in the concentration camp at Büchenwald, and Culianu mistakenly thought that the poet was Jewish. He resolved to write a positive review of the poems if he could find one good verse in the collections. "Like Diogenes for a true man with a lit candle," however, he could not find a poem he liked. "Fortunately," he wrote of a new scholarly interest he shared with Eco, "semiotics was invented to allow one to survive elegantly such occasions." Culianu wrote a highly abstract review "which no one would read or, if one would, the chance of understanding any-

* See Howard Blum, *Wanted!* (New York: Quadrangle, 1977).

thing would be very remote." Proud of his solution, not realizing that every line dripped with hints of what he truly thought of the poems, Culianu sent copies of the article to the journal and to the poet himself. He moved back to his biography of Eliade: "As I was finding some obscurities in the biography of this man [Eliade] a first letter from [Stamatu] arrived, one in what was going to be an endless series. . . . To my dismay he was furious. He read [my review] as a display of ironies, which was not entirely beyond my intention. Only his reading was in a key of which I had no knowledge whatever: Romanian political history in the '30s and '40s."*

In the story H. S. considered the review, not as an attack on his poetry, but as a clever accusation that he was once an Iron Guardist. He sent letters, "incredibly long, like nightmares, only far more frequent," trying in part to recruit Culianu. For a time Ioan corresponded with him in order to understand the nationalist movement that had begun in his hometown. When he did, he refused Stamatu's advances. Next, the poet began sending diatribes to Eliade, the journal publisher, and other prominent exiles, attacking Culianu. Ironically, Culianu had no intention of charging Stamatu as a member of what he called "the most secret, the most bombastic, the most mystical and bungling fascist organization of pre-War Europe." By the end of the story, however, the poet's detailed diatribes suggested that he had been a member of the fascist organization.**

The realization sent Culianu back into his history books to understand how a fascist could have ended up in Büchenwald. "At the time I did not know anything about Romania's past," he noted wryly, "having been born and educated in Communist Romania." He discovered that Büchenwald had housed some four hundred leading Iron Guardists in a separate section, kept in comfort as Hitler's hedge if the dictator Ion Antonescu should waver in their alliance.

What Culianu also did not know was that Chicago and the North American Midwest became hubs where Iron Guardists still recruited. Corneliu Codreanu's niece, the last family member to see the charismatic leader before his execution in November 1938, settled in Chicago. One of the men involved in the plot to kill Nicolae

---

* Ioan Culianu, "Romanian Fears," unpublished manuscript, p. 5.
** Ibid.

Iorga was said to live in nearby Detroit. In Chicago the most prominent Guardist spokesman in America, Dr. Alexander Ronnett, published a newspaper and authored a book for Loyola University Press
called *Romanian Nationalism: The Legionary Movement* (1974). His
real name was Rachmistriuc. Ronnett tells the story of how he tried
to attack the Romanian prime minister Ion Antonescu during the
January 1941 Iron Guardist bloody uprising which followed the
movement's removal from power.* Ronnett was the personal physician and dentist to Mircea Eliade for some twenty years; he insisted
that his patient was once a prominent Guardist. Eliade remained
silent on the past, though his silence and refusal to condemn his
country's holocaust might have suggested, as his friend Saul Bellow
put it, that "Mircea kept a secret." When Culianu wrote Eliade of a
campaign to discredit him and prevent him from receiving the Nobel Prize in Literature because of his past, Eliade responded in a
letter written on March 24, 1978. He referred only to his far rightist
teacher of the 1930s, Nae Ionescu: "The legend of the Nobel Prize
is simple: I have always declared that if I were to receive this 'distinction' I would immediately fly to Bucharest to proclaim my identity
as a *Romanian writer.* I haven't detailed to anyone what I am going to
do in Bucharest. I tell only you: I will go to Bellu cemetery, and I will
cover the tombs of my father, mother, brother, and Nae Ionesco
with their favorite flowers."

In the end Culianu's poetry review escapade hinted at the dangers
inherent in his writing, especially when it was read at levels he did
not fully intend. From this point on his most personal ideas would
come out in fiction that stressed, humorously, the deadly risks of
literary creation and criticism.

*   *   *

In the 1980s prominent exiles came under increasing surveillance
from the Communist secret police or Departamentul de Informaţii
Externe, the foreign division of Securitate. The DIE had agents
attached to virtually every embassy in the world, and many Romanian scholars abroad worked as informers. Ceauşescu considered

* Personal interview with Alexander Ronnett, Oct. 31, 1995.

Romanian exiles a "fifth column," subject to the same surveillance and recruitment as citizens. For good reason, Culianu mistrusted most countrymen he met around the globe.

Securitate paid closest attention to those whose media commentary could be most damaging. In 1977 the Radio Free Europe commentator Monica Lovinescu, a friend of Culianu's, was beaten savagely outside her Paris apartment by Palestinians hired by Securitate. In Munich in 1981 the DIE tried to assassinate the Radio Free Europe broadcaster Emil Georgescu, who survived despite being stabbed 22 times. The German Interior Ministry's report noted that the assailants "stubbornly refused to give any information on who had hired them. After the failure of the assassination attempt, other persons from the Romanian Intelligence Service are said to have been given the assignment . . ." In his book *Red Horizons*, former Securitate general Ion Mihai Pacepa asserted the traffic death in New York of an anti-Ceauşescu protest organizer was also a Securitate-arranged assassination.

The worsening conditions prompted Culianu to write articles more frequently for émigré magazines such as *Limite* (Paris), *Ethos* (Paris), and *Revista Scriitorilor Români* (Magazine of Romanian Writers, Munich). In 1985 he began a regular column in *Contrapunct* (Counterpoint, Paris) and served as vice president of the Religion Section of the Romanian Cultural Center in Paris, an anti-Communist organization founded in 1949. He was warned about his writing, he told Carmen. In Italy an agent objected to an article that linked refusal to return home under Communist rule with the manliness of an Eliadian hero. "I was writing on a symbolic level," he told his wife, "but they took me literally."

❋   ❋   ❋

Culianu learned more of the deteriorating conditions in Romania when he received another visitor in October 1984, a writer specializing in cultural anthropology named Andrei Oişteanu. Oişteanu had been purposely granted an exit visa too late to attend an American studies conference in Salzburg, Austria, in 1984, but he took the opportunity to visit Germany and France. In October he phoned Culianu in Holland, asking to interview him.

"He was very suspicious," Oişteanu recalled of their meeting.

They discussed Culianu's work and Eliade, about whom little had been written in Romania. At the end Oişteanu asked permission to publish the interview at home. Culianu agreed, saying he thought there was little chance of success.

The next year Ioan succeeded in a long struggle to get his mother out of the country for a second visit. It was a difficult and emotional reunion for a boy who had worshiped his mother. He loved her but at the same time resented her intrusion in his new life, and he left her for several days to attend a conference of the European Association of the History of Religions. "He did not seem to be able to show he loved her," said his stepson. The only time relations between Ioan and his mother softened was when they played canasta and she began to sing ancient Moldavian songs in a high clear voice that evoked all he had left behind.

She told him that Ceauşescu had passed several offensive laws. Consumer products were disappearing from store shelves. Securitate had become not just a repressive apparatus but a method of government. There were rumors that dissidents were being secretly irradiated. His sister's new husband, Dan Petrescu, was by now a known troublemaker. When summoned to the green, hospital-like Securitate building on top of Iaşi's famous Copou Hill, he was made to wait for hours for no reason. Officers questioned him about activities they already knew of. Afterward they bantered with him. Still, Dan's high school students wanted most of all to be security agents. They get paid regularly and well, with the same checks as the Soviet KGB, the boys said.

Most of all Ioan and his mother discussed his career. He showed her pictures of the Eliades' visit. Eliade was arranging for him to come to America, he said. He would check out teaching positions there. "The salaries and the freedom to write are much greater." She wished he would not move so far.

He did not tell his mother of a strange experience he had at the conference. At his lecture at the French Centre de Recherche Imaginaire et Création in May 1985, three self-described witches objected to his work. He, his colecturer, and several audience members became seriously ill. Such lectures, he wrote in his preface to *Eros and Magic*, were "an enterprise from I will desist in the future."

After his mother left, he felt restless. He felt constricted in a mar-

· · · · · ·

riage to someone who, it seemed, was never satisfied. With his international success, he also felt unappreciated in Holland. His life had become sterile and unreal. Once again, he craved freedom.

He invited Carmen to join him in his visiting professorship in Chicago. When she declined, however, he felt relieved. He yearned to arrive in the United States like Botticelli's Venus on the sea, solitary, free of burdens of family, friends, or history.

Still, the events of the year rekindled a feeling of threat that had never left him since he was a small child in Iaşi. His friend Gianpaolo Romanato observed: "He told me, sometimes, a little joking and a little not: 'I will die young.' This premonition explains his fury in working to say everything soon, to write in a hurry and become famous because he knew or was afraid that he wouldn't have a very long life."

Everything is repeated, in a circle. History is a master

because it teaches us that it doesn't exist. It's the

permutations that matter.

— *Umberto Eco*, Foucault's Pendulum

PURSUIT, 1985

In Romania 1985 marked the beginning of the worst years under Nicolae Ceauşescu. In an effort to pay back the country's foreign debt, he forced the population into the most severe hardship it had yet endured. Electric power went out in most towns at 8:00 P.M. Hot water and heat were scarce. Store shelves were stripped of even the smallest comforts, like women's underwear. Married women were forced to bear no fewer than five children, to increase the country's population. In intellectual life, books became increasingly difficult to obtain or publish.

Ever since Culianu's defection, no one in Romania had written about him; nobody quoted from his works. In 1985 the writer Andrei Oişteanu returned to the country and tried to publish his interview with Culianu. He approached three different cultural journals. He received three rejections. While he was trying to publish the piece, he received a strange telephone call. "I'm from the Passport Department," the man said. "I want to talk with you."

Oişteanu had gone to Holland without a visa, and he thought the man was interested in that. "What's the purpose?" he asked. His caller would not give one, suggesting instead that they meet for lunch. Oişteanu refused. Finally they arranged to rendezvous on the street.

The next morning Oişteanu awoke before five, worrying, mulling over the reasons for the meeting.

The man was about thirty-five or forty, dressed in a suit, not a very good one. He had a certain tie, a certain look. He was unmistakably from Securitate. Again he insisted they go to a restaurant, but Oişteanu refused. They went to a coffee shop instead. The front door was locked. The officer knocked. He showed an identification card. "I have to talk to this guy," he said.

They went in, sat down, and ordered. His interrogator asked him about his work in the history of religions. The system had long before switched from Communist rhetoric to the mystical nationalism Culianu studied, promoted by figures like Eminescu. Religion had been one of the most prestigious fields of study before the advent of communism, in a country where Eastern Orthodoxy and the idea of "nation" had been linked since the nineteenth century. The man started talking about Eliade. Oişteanu tried to find out what he wanted, but his interrogator kept putting him off. "We're not stupid," he said. "I'm also a university graduate. I've learned philosophy. I know about what you write. I know Eliade's books. They're very interesting." He leaned forward. "In 1983 you wanted to go to a scholarly congress. We said no. In 1984 we said yes, but a week too late. I know you've had problems getting permission to travel. I know how to help you travel. As much as you like. More than you'd like. That means, even if you don't want to travel, you will travel."

"How come?"

"We let you travel, and you give us information about Romanian intellectuals abroad."

"Why don't you do it? It's your job, not mine."

"My gates are closed. I don't know anybody. You do. You know intellectuals. Like Ioan Culianu."

"No, I'm sorry."

"Your brother in New York, he does."

Oişteanu's brother, Valery, was an underground poet in New York's East Village who wrote a monthly arts column called "Wall Patrol" by Valery Gallery. He hated the Communists more than anything. The idea that he could be of interest to them was ridiculous. "No," Oişteanu said. "No, I couldn't."

The man rose to leave. "Sleep on it. I'll call," he said.

Oişteanu turned to leave. Then he thought, no, I cannot leave this matter hanging. He wanted to refuse once and for all. He ran to the door and spotted his inquisitor, who had already crossed the street and was going into a Securitate building.

The man telephoned him about a week later. Oişteanu declined his offer. He kept calling, a few times over the next weeks, many times over the next months. Oişteanu's wife became frightened. She feared they would never travel. They'd never be rid of the man. He hinted that if Oişteanu did not cooperate he would not publish. He would lose his job.

Finally the harassment just stopped. An academic journal accepted the Culianu interview. At the last minute the censors tried to stop it, but the journal editors got around them.

The whole incident with the agent was unremarkable, one of the many strange encounters everyone had in those years. Securitate, a friend once said, they're all mystics. Oişteanu had never believed it.

Mircea Eliade told me that in ten years I was going to

be the best historian of religions alive, and he wasn't

kidding, he knew them all.

— *I. P. Culianu to Hillary Wiesner, October 14, 1986*

THE EMERALD GAME, 1986

Culianu came back to the University of Chicago in March 1986, not as a starving and lonely graduate student but as the term's featured guest lecturer. He must have felt that the "social success for which I have paid the highest price" was beginning to take hold. No longer did he wait like a sorcerer's apprentice on his mentor, Professor Mircea Eliade, who had kept him at arm's length on his first visit a decade earlier. Now he was a visiting professor, invited by the world's preeminent historian of religions to assist him with some of his most important works. This time it was the seventy-nine-year-old Eliade who depended on *him* to handle correspondence, offer support, and provide direction to the unfinished projects of an expiring career.

In the spring of 1986 time to finish these projects was growing short. A hint came in December 1985, when a fire gutted much of Eliade's book collection housed in the Meadville Library on Fifty-seventh Street. Apparently ignited by Eliade's pipe ash, the blaze damaged a lifetime's worth of rare texts from the Orient and India and, more important, Eliade's private editions of his own fifty books, each marked with new notes to deepen his most famous theories. Eliade had foreseen the holocaust in a dream, and to a man who had spent his life understanding the meanings contained in dreams, the fire suggested that "the immortality he had sought on the printed page was subject to material destruction," wrote his colleague Wendy Doniger, "just like the immortality he had once, long ago, sought in his experiments with yoga."

The smoke- and water-damaged books of Eliade's library were still packed in boxes when Culianu arrived from Holland in mid-March. He and Eliade faced three pressing projects, including a new *Guide to World Religions* to be written by Culianu, signed by them both, and published by HarperSanFrancisco. The younger man had also brought several articles for Eliade's mammoth, sixteen-volume *Encyclopedia of Religion*, to be published in 1987 by Macmillan. Eliade entrusted to him subjects in which he considered the younger scholar to be a leading expert, including "Ascension," "Astrology," "Gnosticism: From the Middle Ages to the Present," "Magic in Medieval and Renaissance Europe," "Sexual Rites in Europe," "Sky: The Heavens as Hierophany," and two focusing on Balkan sects cowritten with his former teacher Cicerone Poghirc in Paris.

Eliade had another task for Culianu. Eliade was working on the fourth and culminating volume of his *History of Religious Ideas*, in which he sought to find the underlying, unconscious mind patterns in mythical thought, the universal symbols he saw embedded in religious concepts. In the volume's final two chapters Eliade planned to examine "religious creations (as many as there are) on the entire planet from the Enlightenment to the 'God is dead' theology. A good part of this finale I could write myself," he wrote the thirty-six-year-old Culianu. "Would you take the responsibility for the rest?"

An increasingly extraordinary collaboration deepened between the man credited for revolutionizing the field of the history of religions and a new, ambitious thinker who looked up to him as a father figure. Since their respective college days both men had been inspired by the Renaissance idea of *coincidentia oppositorum*, or the coincidence of opposites. Their collaboration, matching Eliade's ending career with Ioan Culianu's coming-to-life, offered a *coincidentia oppositorum* long hoped for by the younger man.

By then Culianu felt his academic post in Holland was only a stepping-stone "until something better comes along," as Eliade had written him. At the University of Groningen the small department in Romanian studies was slated for demise in budget cutbacks. He was moving beyond that minor field to become an innovative historian of religions, but he was not accepted there. From Chicago he wrote his wife daily about the opportunities he saw in the United States. His fourteen-year-old stepson, Andrei, foresaw the result: "He always talked about America, always drinking Coke and taking me to Hollywood movies; he wanted to *be* American."

What a source of tension and excitement then to arrive at O'Hare airport, knowing that the Divinity School needed to replace Eliade soon and that Eliade had proposed *his* name to Dean Chris Gamwell. Culianu taught two classes, Gnosticism and Manichaeanism as well as Renaissance Magic for Beginners. No teacher quite like him had ever entered the classrooms of Swift Hall. Ioan Culianu, who had counted on Eliade for so much of his professional life, had come to make his mark.

❦   ❦   ❦

In the spring of 1986 graduate student Hillary Wiesner was entering her second term in the Committee on the Ancient Mediterranean World at the University of Chicago. A Radcliffe College honors graduate, she specialized in late pagan civilization. At twenty-two she was new to the Midwest, having grown up in the small Upstate New York town of Slingerlands.

Blond and waiflike, Hillary looked like the Madonna figure in Botticelli's *Primavera* — aloof, mysterious, with skin the color of mother of pearl. Her father was Jewish and, like Culianu's father, had died early, when he was fifty-five and she was eighteen. His death at an early age heightened her natural solitude. Her friends said she was brilliant but naive, a little scared of men. "She judged everything and everyone," said Erika Schluntz, a friend from Radcliffe. "I think she thought I partied too much. When I borrowed her notes for a course I was skipping, I saw she was more organized than the professor. Still, she had covered the pages with cartoon pictures."

In Wiesner's judgment the Divinity School did not measure up. Winter in Chicago seemed to last forever, marked by a wet wind that seeped under her fingernails. Professors took little interest in their students. The modern gothic campus, sequestered on the city's South Side, weighed her down. The workload was pointlessly heavy, she thought. Thinking about returning to Cambridge, as some of her former professors urged her, Wiesner prepared to participate in the Harvard archaeological dig at Sardis in Turkey for her second summer.

She did make a few good friends on campus at Chicago. One noted professor, Hans Dieter Betz, suggested that she talk to Professor Culianu about her work. She could not take either of his courses, but she audited them from time to time and slowly became intrigued.

Culianu was different from anyone else at Chicago. With his European-styled shirts and Inspector Clouseau accent, he offered such startling insights about magic that she jotted notes more furiously in his class than in any other. He was attractive, with a puckish face and eyes that seemed to look beyond you, but it was his ideas she remembered. He said that a scholar, like a great scientist, needed a capacity for gentle humility to understand a world on its own terms. When you studied medieval miracles, you had to suspend your disbelief and seek in even the oddest and most inexplicable events a hidden pattern or logic. This passion for entering the mind processes of a subject he likened to eros. *Eros*, the ancient Greek word for love, or embrace-of-the-world, gave us words like *erotic*

and *heroic*. He saw eros as a real force that could unlock the mysteries of the universe, whether scientific or religious.

He was especially interested in the Renaissance mind games that
reached their height with the philosophers Marsilio Ficino and
Giordano Bruno. Bruno's power came, Culianu suggested, because
he charged his magical images with the power of love, or eros. "That
was his secret side we have never truly understood," he said. Culianu
compared Bruno's magic with that of modern advertisers, public
relations firms, and political spin controllers, and with the mind
control of the regimes of the late twentieth century.

The trouble was, Culianu suggested, we are metaphysical illiter-
ates today, our imaginations repressed by the triumph of science and
technology. The Reformation and the church crackdown on magic
accounted for the triumph of reason and many of our modern neuroses. Culianu brought to his subject "boldness, linguistic command
and discipline," as a reviewer wrote, and an encyclopedic knowledge
built up during his years of exile in Italy. He also brought something
else: an obsession for using the past to understand the present and
the many hidden ways he said *our* minds could be manipulated.

Intrigued, Hillary Wiesner went to the library and looked up
Culianu's book *Psychanodia*, published by Brill in 1983 in Holland. It
attacked the traditional diffusionist histories of religions that said
cultures "influenced" each other through the opening of new trade
routes. After showing how such theories could not explain myths as
widespread as reincarnation, Culianu hinted at his own theory: Underlying processes or games of the collective mind, following laws of
logic beneath the day-to-day events of history, shaped human events
at a deeper level than we knew. His idea that history was somehow
ordered, revelatory, even predictable struck some scholars as bizarre, yet it drew in part from Wittgenstein's game theory and the
new science of complexity. It kept Hillary up late into the night,
thinking.

She was working on an ancient Mesopotamian civilization, the
Sabeans of Harran, people she thought responsible for preserving
the ancient sources of Renaissance thought. They, along with their
Hermetic philosophers, astrologers, and planetary temples, had
been swallowed up by history — they had simply disappeared from

the face of the earth — and she wanted to know why. She decided to ask Culianu.

*   *   *

Ioan Culianu lived in the dormitory known as McGiffert House. He wrote his wife, Carmen, of his loneliness, reporting that he had found few friends among the faculty. His days were consumed by teaching, preparing the two guest lectures he was to deliver, and polishing his English. With Eliade's assistance he was revising his *Eros et magie à la Renaissance* for translation by the University of Chicago Press. He hoped its appearance in the United States might lead to a faculty appointment. But this was a sore subject: Carmen was happy in Holland. To assuage her concerns he wrote of the disappointing economics of an American university career; he had realized just how small a house a professor could afford.

It was partly out of financial need, and mainly out of deep desire, that he also wrote fiction. His collection of stories was soon to be accepted by a scholarly publisher in Italy, Jaca Book, the publisher of Eliade. Eco wrote a positive review of the Italian version of *Eros et magie*. He and Culianu were now corresponding regularly, in part about Culianu's fiction. Culianu began dictating into a tape recorder a thriller based on a medieval myth with great significance to him. It told the story of a young man who dies three ritual deaths, saved by a woman each time, and in so doing ascends into three higher states of being to find his true self. The plot was immature, filled with murders and unbelievable conspiracies. One problem was that of all exiles: he had no language yet to call his own. Another problem was that he had to learn to write better fiction.

As for so much else, Eliade presented him the model for this dual career. For them the link between fiction and scholarship went deeper than simply the requisites of writing; it was about the relation of fantasy to life. Like the Eastern mystics and poets, they saw life as a story whose deepest meaning could be read in its smallest details and coincidences. Coming from an oft-conquered people who told stories to survive, both knew the power of an individual's fictionalized or "felt" history to give hope, even to perform miracles. It was only a small step from a storyteller's manipulation of an audience to Bruno's claims of magical manipulation of a populace.

Evaluating Culianu's academic writing, critics had commented on his confusion of a scholar's distanced stance and the practitioner's involvement in a subject. In his life, friends knew why: he did not merely study Bruno; he wanted to *be* Bruno. If you were inclined to believe in such matters, then yes, Ioan was good at magic and divination. It made for a good party game. If not, well, then, he was ridiculous and annoying. Was this wavering between scholarship and practice a form of split personality or simply a hobbyist's enthusiasm that enhanced research? Once Eliade responded to the question in a lecture delivered at the University of Chicago. "Some of my literary creations contributed to a more profound understanding of certain religious structures," he said. "Sometimes . . . my literary imagination used materials or meaning I had studied as a historian of religions."

＊　＊　＊

On April 14, 1986, the fears of many seemed to come to a head: Mircea Eliade suffered a stroke and was rushed by ambulance to Bernard Mitchell Hospital. Ioan Culianu stayed by his side at the hospital, recording in a diary turbulent emotions and international calls of support from friends and colleagues going back seventy years. For a few days it seemed Eliade might recover. He requested books (earlier he had noted in his journal how carefully he would select the stories to read on his deathbed). Then he lapsed into a coma. Many prominent friends gathered outside his room, including Edward Levi, former U.S. attorney general; Nathan Scott, considered a candidate for archbishop of Canterbury; Chris Gamwell, the Divinity School dean, who stood for seven hours in the hall without telling anyone for fear of creating a disturbance; and several others. "Defying all the rules of the Intensive Care Unit, to the despair of the staff," Culianu later wrote, Eliade's friends offered support. On April 22, 1986, at the age of seventy-nine, Eliade died in their presence.

While the larger world mourned, and people including Saul Bellow packed the memorial service at Rockefeller Chapel, Culianu assisted Christinel Eliade in all the tasks for the funeral and burial. When the will was read, he learned that Eliade had left him one last task. He wanted Culianu to be literary executor for his unpublished scholarly papers. This accolade added to a growing turmoil for Culianu, about his post in Holland, his books, and his marriage, and it touched on the deepest secret the two men had shared.

* * *

A week later, on April 30, Hillary Wiesner walked into Culianu's office. She found him in something like a state of shock. His tie was askew, his face ashen. He stared at her as if he couldn't remember who he was. He looked completely exhausted.

"Should I come another time?" she asked.

"No, no," he said. "What is it?"

She explained her research. The city of Harran was the last holdout of paganism in the Western world. From the dawn of history in their remote corner of northern Mesopotamia, Harran's residents had practiced an astral religion based on the moon goddess. Planet worship had continued in the city until its eleventh-century destruction. She thought their religion, recorded in the hermetic texts that were rediscovered in the Renaissance, had played a major role in Christianity and Islam as each developed. What did he think?

Yes, he said, she had a good line of research, and he suggested some texts on the history of Greek and Near Eastern astrology. There was something, well, *different* about him, she thought. The books turned out to be helpful.

* * *

In the midst of the tasks of teaching and working on the Eliade estate, Culianu gave his two scheduled guest lectures, dedicating them to the man who had "changed his life." Culianu talked about the European witch crazes of the sixteenth and seventeenth centuries, attacking the conventional wisdom that crazes died out because civilization had "progressed." In fact, he pointed out, witches were still burned in the relatively advanced country of Germany until the end of the eighteenth century. Why, then, did the crazes stop? To answer that one had to ask why they had started. Why, in the hysteria, did people *admit* to being witches?

To answer those questions he explored the new method of studying history called complexity by French theorist Edgar Morin. Whereas traditional scholarship worked backward, weighing the various versions of an event and then proposing one "truth," complexity worked *forward* in what anthropologist Clifford Geertz called "thick description," examining all the players and institutions — church, government, judiciary, medicine, folklore, and literature — following all the possible versions of an event and holding them all, in a sense, to be true at once.

Informed by his study of Bruno, Culianu said that we have to understand the power of mind and memory, both individual and collective, over perception. He dug up examples of people confessing to crimes they had not committed. He did not find the evidence he was seeking, partly because in 1986 the topic of "recovered memory" had not yet come into vogue. Culianu's view of the witch crazes was ambiguous: he offered both the possibility that perhaps witchcraft did work as well as the traditional idea that the crazes were a case of collective invention.

At the end of the term Ioan Culianu held a party for his classes in his two tiny rooms attached to the Chicago Theological Seminary. Hillary Wiesner hardly ever went to parties, but she tagged along with a friend. He cooked spaghetti carbonara for them. Late that evening everyone began reciting birthdays. When she gave hers, August 17, 1963, he spun around and looked at her for such a long time that she felt truly unsettled.

They ended up that night sitting together as he read Tarot cards for a student who was unsure whether she wanted to stay in graduate school. He gave Hillary a pillow to sit on. Another student was wearing a Deadhead T-shirt and an embroidered denim jacket. Ioan asked her to explain the Grateful Dead phenomenon. "I don't see the skulls," he said. "Look at his jacket," she whispered. That night she wrote in her journal, "What an evening! Tarot cards and talk. But I was too shy and very sorry to leave." She lay down but couldn't sleep. She picked up her journal again: "2 A.M.: What is wrong with me? He told me something, but is it a self-fulfilling prophecy? He is explaining the maze of my life to me, while at the same time planting it like a seed."

The next morning he called to ask if she wanted to tour downtown Chicago. She could not understand why she said yes. She rolled over in bed and looked at the clock. It was 8:00 A.M.

Over breakfast he told her that his two closest friends, his cousin in Romania and his best friend who was a historian in Italy, each had the same birthday as she. Whatever else one thought of his Renaissance magic study, he lived by its precepts. He wore black chinos, a dark green shirt, and a sallow leather jacket. He kept grimacing as if he had a nervous tic. He smoked Marlboro cigarettes. They talked about Weber and Marx's insights into religion. He said individuals lacked free will, that people were all programmed like robots, that she was brainwashed. She doodled a picture of a character with a black cloud hanging over his head. The meal agitated her; his cigarettes gave her a headache.

He suggested they visit the Sears Tower. She was tempted to refuse, but despite his cynicism he sounded so sweet and funny, and interesting, that she agreed. In the glass observation deck, staring out over the radiating spokes of dismal bungalow neighborhoods, she felt suddenly, violently ill. Her palms turned cold; her stomach churned. He helped her down, holding her, and ran into a Walgreens drug store to get some medicine. She had never before had a fear of heights, and later she would notice it only happened when she was with him.

In another long coffee shop talk the next night she asked him about something he had said in class: "Because Renaissance magic is a means of control over the masses based on a deep knowledge of personal and collective erotic impulses, it's possible to say there is no such thing as a self, or individual conscious, only parts of a universal unconscious." He said that whoever controlled your imagination controlled your fate. She said that was nonsense. No one could control your imagination. She wrote in her journal: "He's a walking Encyclopedia of Religions, but someone who knows everything but the truth."

She thought he was clinically depressed. But she kept *Psychanodia* out past the due hour even though it was on reserve. She wrote in her diary: "May 14, 1986: Poor Culianu with his skepticism. Smoking and drinking, telling me I have problems. But I liked his book. His book is brilliant: *he's* crazy."

They met again a few days later at a coffee shop. She told him she had decided to return to the Sardis archaeological dig as an epigraphist, or interpreter of inscriptions. When he said archaeology was too mundane for her, she pointed out the window. "Don't you think that all this too will someday be rubble?" That appealed to him. He wrote into his preface for the English translation of *Eros and Magic in the Renaissance* the "question of a young archaeologist when we were admiring the magnificent buildings of Chicago," suggesting that the edifice of science would one day be reduced to rubble or, at least, transformed, just as magic gave way to the enlightened sciences following Reformation. He also wrote that he had tried some of Bruno's techniques and found that they worked.

He was brilliant, maybe, but the most tortured and bitter person she had ever met. She had few close friends. She was a world traveler, already having visited Turkey and Greece, where she was enthralled by the Parthenon and other famous ruins. She read Syriac, Coptic, Greek, and Latin. At Chicago she studied Babylonian Akkadian. She was as smart as anyone on that rarefied campus, but her friends and fellow students found her daunting.

This friendship with Culianu was interesting, even engrossing, but she knew it could not go far. She would be leaving Chicago soon. Gradually, though, it became harder to know exactly what she was feeling. She went with him to see the movie *Brazil*. It disturbed her so much she couldn't stop shaking. He put his arm around her. She moved away. Then she felt perhaps it was all in her mind. He was . . . so motherly. But he was *married*. "Foreigners," she wrote in her journal. "Like Aunt Mary Ann said, always avoid resident aliens." Her aunt Mary Ann had married a Ukrainian who left her after six weeks with his citizenship papers.

"We're all programmed," he said later that evening. Why did he start in on that again? she thought. "You're programmed," he said. This time she got angry, and they argued. It escalated into a fight that showed, perhaps more than anything else, how close they were getting. In a way, she decided as she climbed the stairs to her apartment, she was relieved. She wrote in her diary: "May 18, 1986: All right, I did my duty. I tried, but I was reprimanded. Now I'm off the hook. I don't have to try and help this person any more."

She unplugged her telephone.

* * *

Mircea Eliade's final request for Ioan Culianu to be the executor of his uncollected scholarly work took a heavy toll. The collection numbered thousands of pages of documents, dating from the 1950s to the present; they had to be cataloged and translated. Many were valuable as potential publications. But there was a deep problem: researchers, mostly in Italy, were now openly claiming that Eliade had kept a secret. In the 1930s Eliade wrote a series of fascist articles supporting the Iron Guard. Now, in 1986, Culianu once again had to confront the possibility his adopted father figure might have been one of them.

He wrote up to thirty letters a day responding to routine requests and queries about the Eliade estate. He met Mac Linscott Ricketts, Eliade's biographer and former student, who had explored in depth Eliade's original articles. How far did their mentor's secret go? This was a man so revered that a memorial had been proposed in his honor in Israel. Saul Bellow had read at his funeral. Andrei Codrescu, who was Jewish, had shown up unannounced at Eliade's doorstep and been taken in. Later Culianu wrote Ricketts: "Finally I am in possession of the whole coveted file concerning Eliade's political sympathies in 1938–40. I was too upset to remember what we discussed about this . . . that [one article] was not written by him. My position is still the same: Mr. Eliade has never been an anti-Semite, a *member* of the Iron Guard, or a pro-Nazi. But I understand anyway that he was closer to the IG than I liked to think."

Culianu later suggested, in his review of Ricketts's *Mircea Eliade: The Romanian Roots, 1907–1945* (1987), that their mentor's case illustrated two of the most disputed questions of literary criticism: to what extent is writing a product of its time, and to what extent is any act of reading a result of misreading, through a lens of our own time? Such a neat summary was impossible in 1986, as he struggled with documents that involved all the terror of searching through a father's secret life. And it may not have been true. A scholar who specialized in history's "bitter furies of complexity" was being drawn into what one Eliade interviewer called an "ordeal by labyrinth."

At the same time he was caring for Eliade's widow, cooking and shopping for her when her housekeeper had the day off. He was making his way as a scholar into a position he had dreamed of since he first found Eliade's books as a teenager. And he had found a young woman to be the object of his mystical chivalry, a figure he was certain he had seen before. It all had started as a game. The trouble was that, increasingly, he could not be sure what was real and what was a game.

*   *   *

The last argument had been so intense that Hillary Wiesner kept her phone disconnected. Even her mother could not reach her. She studied for final exams and prepared to leave Chicago for good. She did not see Ioan Culianu for a week and felt immensely relieved. Yet she recorded her thoughts in her journal: "May 20, 1986: Phone still disconnected. I don't want any more trauma. But what a strange universe he's let me in. It's like entering another world. . . . I felt like I was in contact with someone from another planet, a whole other universe. He has no place in our language, and no place in this time." She could think of nothing else to say. The next day she wrote: "Now I'm bored. I feel like I've fallen off the edge of the earth. But after life on the edge, everything else is pretty dull."

Two days later she plugged her phone in. Culianu called her at eight the next morning. "You can't just cut yourself off," he said. They met, and he taught her to read palms by the lines of Mars and the Sun between the third and fourth fingers. Her palm showed her to be an ascetic, he said. He suggested they get together at the end of September in Paris. She declined. He called to ask if they could meet once more before she left. She hung up and wrote: "I've been sitting in my room, watching the seconds tick away. Really I'd been wishing he would call. I wonder if his wife knows how unhappy he is."

Some weird things happened in her dreams. They became much more vivid, for one. Several times she awoke in the middle of the night, her heart pounding. She told no one yet because it made no sense. It wasn't that she *believed* in Renaissance magic. But he said Eliade had always told him that nothing happened by chance. If the mind created its own reality, then the occult, or ideology, or even the idea of "chance," was an equally powerful metaphor by which people explained their lives.

In the last week of May she prepared to leave for the Sardis project. On one of her last days in town they visited Chicago's Field Museum. In the magnificent, airy lobby dominated by the famous

Brontosaurus skeleton and brace of mammoths, he said everyday objects had meanings that extended into other ways of looking at the world, opening new interpretations in an infinite sequence. Archaeology barely touched the surface. At the dioramas he pointed out the funny shapes and colors of the animals—gazelles, zebras, giraffes, parrots—decorated as if by an eccentric artist who streaked them with colors and shaped them in odd configurations. It was as if they were all recombining similar elements. He talked about a favorite theory he had read, by the Scottish zoologist D'Arcy Wentworth Thompson, who demonstrated that by mathematical transformations one could change one animal into another—say, a fox's skull to a rhino's skull—with just a few steps. "Why those colors?" he asked. "Why are the animals positioned in such strange, funny ways? It's as if an artist was playing a joke."

They paused in front of the emeralds in the gem case. The four stones shimmered. She told him that emeralds were the most important image in her life. Since she was a child she had had a recurring dream about emeralds. He took a great interest in this, though he did not explain why.

They agreed to meet one final time at a Polynesian restaurant called House of Tiki, a kitsch landmark in Hyde Park. Hanging from the ceiling, spiny blowfish lit up by bulbs in their bellies stared at you as you ate. The decor was all beads and bamboo, and the drinks came in glasses featuring naked Hawaiian girls. He gave her a box and asked her not to open it until she left.

"Last night I dreamed of a magician pouring something into a chalice for me," he said. "He gave it to me, and I drank it."

"I wonder what it means."

"Well, I've seen this figure before, only at important moments in my life. Whatever it is, it's significant."

From O'Hare airport Hillary mailed him the inscription from the fortune cookie she had gotten at dinner: "A new chapter in your life is being written." She didn't have to be an epigraphist to figure out *something* was going on.

* * * * * * *

THE BOOK OF LIFE

Just before leaving for Turkey, Hillary Wiesner called one close Radcliffe friend, Erika Schluntz, and told her about this new relationship. "There's this man," she said. "Who?" Erika asked, excited. But her friend was very cagey, as if afraid to admit what had been going on, or of appearing foolish, or of jinxing it.

After an exhausting transatlantic flight and a day-long bus ride, she arrived at the dusty, remote Turkish plain, site of the ancient Lydian city that had been the capital of Croesus. Perched in the green foothills along the Pactolus River in the "breadbasket of Turkey," ancient Sardis seemed a thousand miles from nowhere, cut off from telephones and television. The excavation site featured a whitewashed stone compound that looked out over lush vineyards and tobacco fields. Perfect, she felt, for finding herself in the calm of simple routine. She unloaded her clothes in her room. Before meeting the members of her group, she opened the box Ioan had given her. It contained a collection of stories by Jorge Luis Borges, *Ficciones*, and a box of Fannie Mae candies.

She spent her days digging up and toothbrushing tiny pieces of clay urns and pots on the slope of the ancient city's acropolis. She worked on her Turkish and checked her *Fodor's Guide* for good restaurants in Istanbul, an overnight bus ride or short plane trip away. At night the ancient plain seemed to breathe beneath stars that shimmered like shadows of ideas, as Renaissance philosophers believed. To experience what scholars called the "sacred," Ioan had said, all you needed to do was look into a night sky. The Milky Way spread like a shroud above the ruins of the Artemis Temple, torn by shooting stars. Staring up at night, Hillary felt like a small person with small problems, in a small country, on a small planet on the edge of a small, unremarkable galaxy among millions. Ioan's ideas had affected her all right, even if he was a suspect character.

On the dig she met new people, but none particularly interested her. The accommodations were rustic, the traditions straight out of the days of the British Raj: high tea at four, cocktails at eight. The compound had a cool dark drawing room that smelled of eucalyptus from the old books in the library. They had cooks, houseboys, and village women to do their washing. Scorpions occasionally lurked in the shower.

When she received her first letter from Culianu, she ran to a chair on the veranda to open it. "Dear Emerald Goddess," it said. "I realized in the Field Museum that you are different from everyone else. Now, I know that you are that apparition I hoped you were."

Her pulse quickened. She put the letter in her pocket, then in her drawer; she did everything she could to avoid thinking about it. He was . . . crazy. For a while she hung out with the young people at the dig. She tried to participate in their activities. But on a trip to a bar in town, she remembered that it was the day Ioan was leaving Chicago to return to his wife. For a distraction she picked up an *International Herald Tribune;* the front page said that Jorge Luis Borges had died.

Until then her collection had remained unopened. The gift had annoyed her, like something out of a Woody Allen film — something of an older male professor educating a younger female student. Now, though, lying in bed in soft light, she slowly fell under the spell of the intricate stories. In them she found direct hints of Culianu's scholarly theories. In the story "Tlön, Uqbar, Orbis Tertius," for instance, the narrator comes across a bizarre entry in a reprint of the 1902 edition of the *Encyclopedia Britannica.* The entry described a fictional planet devised in what must have been a huge joke. "The men of that planet conceive of the universe as a series of mental processes," the narrator observes, "whose unfolding is to be understood only as a time sequence." This was Culianu's idea of the history of religions. In another story, "Death and the Compass," a detective in Buenos Aires tracks a series of murders related in a way that he desperately tries to figure out. When he finally uncovers the truth, it is in time only to understand that he is the final victim.

A few days later Hillary received an emerald ring in the mail. She sent it back, enclosing an angry reply: You're a married man who hates the world and deserves whatever he gets. A person has to have some kind of ideals.

There followed an argument-by-mail that lasted for weeks. Gradually a deep foreboding began to weigh on her. Some nights she felt a sense of doom so strong it became a hostile consciousness just behind and ahead of her. She left the architectural dig when it ended in August and flew with a friend to Istanbul. In the church of Aghia Sofia, the center of Eastern Orthodox Christianity, later turned into a mosque, she realized she had never felt so strange before in her life, as if in a daze. She wandered the city half in tears, hardly seeing the tourist sites or the medieval bazaar. At each site she could barely do more than lie down. You're ruining my vacation, her friend complained. But no matter what she tried, she felt lost, as if she had turned him into an enemy, that he was now out to get her. She felt that she was a complete failure as a human being. She jotted a line from an Elvis Costello song: "I was a fine idea at the time, but now I'm just a brilliant mistake."

She left for a break with friends in Munich. She sent him the name of the couple she was visiting.

*   *   *

For Ioan Culianu the weeks after his return to Holland were hellish. Wearing a University of Chicago sweatshirt, he returned to his cramped Groningen home completely unlike himself, not even looking like himself. His face had puffed up; he hardly recognized the small rooms of his own home. He left his boxes stacked in the living room without unpacking. Carmen realized something was wrong, but when she asked him about it, he never replied. She wondered if it was Eliade's death.

After three weeks she could not take it anymore. In a kind of despair, she began fooling around with his computer. On her first try she got into a program. She found a note beginning "Dear Hillary." He had written, "I understand that for the last thirteen years, I have betrayed that light within me, the light I used to cherish for all adverse occasions. If I am now returning to that kind of life I tried to lead when I was just a little bit younger than you, before I left home, it is because of you." He was trying to equate his political exile with some sweet young child he had impressed in class. When Carmen confronted him, his first response was one of anger: how could she have broken the secret code he used in his computer? She could have damaged his files. Next he pleaded with her, explaining that he had never sent the note, that nothing had happened between him and Hillary, that in his loneliness he had made a mistake. But there was a tone in his pleading not of love but of fear. He was afraid of Carmen, even though he suspected her of having an affair. She gave him a day to leave the house.

What bothered her most was that all those years he had worked without a vacation, plotting each career move, traveling to conferences and lecturing, he thought he could manipulate the world. "He kept each part of his life in a separate room, as if he was trying to be a Giordano Bruno," she said. "It wasn't that he lacked love or felt no remorse; it's just he wouldn't allow himself to [feel love or remorse] if those emotions got in his way." He lived his life as a story, she felt, that he could rewrite when it suited him. In the United States, for instance, he had never spoken to anyone, even his closest friends, about his past life in Romania even though he came from a prominent, close extended family who suffered *because of* his defection. No one, not in Holland or Italy or France or America, really knew what he had sacrificed to his dream. Her question was, did he know himself?

Ioan Culianu phoned Hillary Wiesner in Munich. He asked if he could visit, just one last time, saying he could stop in town. Other events came swiftly to a head. His sister, Tess, was due in Holland, expecting his help to escape Romania, even to get their mother out. But in 1986 her husband, Dan Petrescu, had come to government attention as a prominent dissident; he had been beaten savagely several times in Securitate's Iaşi headquarters. The government forced Tess to leave the country alone, so that if she defected he and her mother would have to remain. Culianu was unable to help her scheme a way out. At the same time he seemed to resent her. Even when his mother had visited two years earlier he had resented her, an enmity that surprised his stepson. "It was like she represented something to him, something he hated. . . . He really did not seem to allow himself much love for her."

He met Hillary in Munich in August, claiming that he had asked his wife for a divorce. He stood in the apartment's living room, his elbow resting on the mantel, and tried to affect a casual air. He almost knocked a clock over. She reached, and in a few moments she was more confused by him than ever. They did not say much more, but it was clear to her that she was falling in, well, if not love then something that *felt* like it.

Through the fall he wrote her letters every day, sometimes two or three times a day: "Together we can be a tremendous force, more powerful than you can think." He added that his career, so ascendant a month earlier, was now rapidly dissolving. His Dutch position was going to be eradicated. "But with you I know all things are possible."

He spent the fall at the prestigious Netherlands Institute for Advanced Studies in Waasenaar, in a long-planned leave of absence. He felt free, frightened, and lonelier than at any time since he had been a refugee and defector in Italy. He turned his turmoil into scholarly production, writing in eight weeks the French prototype of *The Tree of Gnosis: Gnostic Mythology from Early Christianity to*

Modern Nihilism. In it he set out to prove, with historical evidence, his concept that universal mind processes shaped human events. His evidence came from the development of gnostic sects from the ancient Manichaeans to nineteenth-century nihilists. "Gnosis" offered a parallel set of Judaeo-Christian beliefs: some of the stories were the same as those in the Bible but were told with different interpretations . . . such as the story of Adam and Eve told by the serpent, or an interpretation of a Christ who had never been crucified because he had never been corporeal.

Many gnostics believed in a dualistic universe in which good and evil were equally powerful. Others felt the forces of darkness equaled those of light only because of human ignorance. To a man who had been able to divide his own self, the idea that the universe was fundamentally split was attractive. *Gnosis* itself means "insight" or "knowledge." To know oneself, gnostic heretics claimed, was to know human nature and destiny.

The gnostics appealed to Culianu precisely because they never held power. The history of their ideas was therefore "pure," unadulterated by political wrangling, war, or any other distortion. They offered a perfect opportunity to examine a doctrine unfolding over twenty centuries. Branching over time, their beliefs resembled a tree when diagrammed, Culianu argued. Any religion, or science, would do so. More important than the content of the religion was the binary *process* of forking and branching; this pattern presented the most basic force of history. His work was a crucial, transitional book for a career moving already beyond the history of religions. The manuscript drew heavily from his seminars, garnered a rave from Umberto Eco, and had much less to do with gnosticism than with a new approach to history.

He wrote his friend Gianpaolo Romanato of the events of his last few months. It had been a "year of trial and death" — death of Eliade, of his old position, of his old self. Now he had entered a period of rebirth and rejuvenation, he wrote. As part of his trial, he admitted, he had lost sight of that which the gnostics held dear: "Unfortunately, one forgets everything and what is important to fulfill your tasks and . . . survive. . . . In this life without any stops, without any pauses one ends up being foreign even to oneself."

He met friends in Paris, who noticed he was smoking less and wearing more brightly colored shirts. They walked together along the Tuileries at night, circling the Louvre. Ioan mentioned his new romance. "For the first time," he said, "I can feel that I've not been cheated by life." He still had the habit of checking behind himself every few steps, as if afraid he was being followed. Now at least he made jokes about it.

* * *

Back in Cambridge, Hillary Wiesner spoke only a little with her friends about her new relationship. They could not believe it. Erika was dying of curiosity. He was married? Who *was* this man, the only one her closest friend had ever taken seriously? What were his motivations? Did he understand how special she was? Well, yes, I think so, she said.

Each day she received letters from him: "I love you, every bit of you, the visible and invisible you. . . . Believe that I approach you with awe and reverence, fearing that I might destroy this apparition. All in the world is mystery again." In her mailbox every day she would find letters covered with funny stickers and written in the style of adorational Renaissance poetry. He was creating a religion based on her, but he had a strangely morbid sense: "I am going to prepare that place where death cannot part us. This place exists, and we can create it. It is an island and it is very beautiful. There is not much time to lose though." He rarely put in a closing, which was too final. Usually he ended conversations with "Hello." He wrote her of his new research into modern physics and the theoretical notion that time does not exist, that we are living in what Borges called a "vague memory or dim reflection, doubtless false and fragmented, of an irrevocable process."

They met in Cambridge in November and again in Paris at Christmas, a little later but just as he had first proposed back in May—what seemed a lifetime before to both of them. It rained every afternoon in Paris, but they ran from awning to awning, taking cover in a café just before a cloudburst, where they sat and watched the streetlights glisten in pools in the cobblestones. She loved the rolled carpets Parisians put out to direct the water runoff as they had since medieval times. He covered their apartment with talismans of stuffed animals and cards. She found a note: "The goddess invites you to the emerald game" and, with it, another emerald ring.

They decided to take a drive to Florence to see Botticelli's *Primavera* and the many sites that had enthralled and saved him when he was a refugee back in 1972. They paused on New Year's Eve in a small hotel in Zurich. In the middle of dinner she looked up to see him staring at her with such darkness that she stopped eating.

"What?" she asked. "What is it?"

"There are things you need to know about me."

"What?"

He told her about an intelligent man crushed, almost from within. This was the only time he ever talked to her about his father, who died when he was fourteen. He never even mentioned his name, nor the names of his mother and sister. The talk continued long after they headed up the red-carpeted main staircase to their room. When he died, Ioan said, his father left him a collection of notebooks. They contained a baffling legacy of mathematical formulas from a brilliant man's lost life. For a year it had completely oppressed him, he said. "Finally I broke with it." He smiled at her. "I said, 'No more, I want my own life.' I threw them out."

He talked about his mother's sometimes funny, sometimes sad stories of nobility and wealth and the feeling of safety even in the few rooms to which the Communists relegated them in their home. He told her about summers at a monastery where the mysteries of the universe opened up to him, even while he knew fear in the night when a relative was taken to prison. Hillary didn't know what to make of it. "He had undergone systematic abuse and alienation," she said, "like a person who had been run over again and again." It began to dawn on her that his interest in gnosticism and Renaissance magic were not simply the chosen vocations of an ambitious career; the topics chose him.

For her part, she was gradually giving in to whatever was happening to them, something bigger than themselves, she felt. She was on a magic ride indeed, a thrilling vertigo of ideas like nothing she had ever experienced, as if she was a child on a swing soaring high up into the sky. Eros, Bruno had written, eros is all. And it was only beginning.

Photographs from the Culianu and Bogdan family albums in Iaşi

*Left to right, Ioan Culianu's father, Sergiu Culianu; his mother, Elena Bogdan
(in the passport photograph); and his aunt Dr. Ana Bogdan*

*Ioan Culianu
and
Hillary Wiesner
in Italy, 1989*

Ioan Culianu playing the board game Talisman with Erika Schluntz

*Ioan Culianu with Mircea Eliade at Culianu's house
in Groningen, August 1984*

*FBI composite
sketch of the man
seen by Judy
Lawrence in the
elevator and third
floor hallway of
Swift Hall shortly
before the murder
on May 21, 1991*

Ioan Culianu, right, with King Michael, center, at the
University of Chicago's Divinity School, April 12, 1991

Ioan Culianu at his typewriter in Groningen, ca. 1980.

IV

• • • • • • • • •

"LIKE BEING FAMOUS,"

1987–1991

These days many things become clear to me though I

could not explain them to others, or to myself. This has

to do with the future, which I have contemplated . . .

and you are in it to such an extent that I do not know

any more who you are or who I am.

—*I. P. Culianu to Hillary Wiesner, October 27, 1986*

"ALL IN THE WORLD IS MYSTERY AGAIN," 1987

Hillary Wiesner and Ioan Culianu spent two weeks in Florence, taking in the city's many wonders. During the days they joined the tourists paying homage to Michelangelo's *David* in the Accademia, Raphael's *Madonna* in the Pitti, and the luminous facade of the Church of Santa Maria Novella. In the Church of Santa Croce they visited the tombs of Michelangelo, Machiavelli, and Galileo. He proudly showed her the humanistic plan of the city as he had learned it fifteen years earlier in his first experience of the West. She showed him the excitement of a new mind encountering Old World riches. At night they picked restaurants and wines to sample before heading home to the wonders of time together in their *pensione*.

For Culianu the trip offered much needed respite from pressures — some self-inflicted, like abandoning his marriage, home, and former life, and some beyond his control, like losing his position and his mentor. Visiting Florence reminded him of how far he had come in the fifteen years since his defection. The city also embodied many important paradoxes for him. In this most powerful center of the Renaissance, he had noted in *Eros et magie*, our image of the artist as the tortured hero questing after truth took shape. Yet Florentine artists also played power politics — bestowing honor on the ruling Medici family, whose names remain well known largely because of the paeans of their grant recipients. During the twentieth century, it was in Florence that Europe's modern nationalism and fascism took root. As Christopher Duggan noted in the *New York Times Book Review:* "A curious paradox of the city's history is that this great crucible of culture should time and again have been home to acts of appalling savagery."

To Culianu, Florence was, most of all, the city of Sandro Botticelli — the artist whose sculptures and paintings celebrated the power of the goddess. Ioan and Hillary returned again and again to the Uffizi to see Botticelli's often analyzed painting *La Primavera*. Completed in the mid-1470s, the dreamlike, intricate picture seems to tell a story that has never yielded its full meaning, despite the efforts of numerous art historians who have been pulled under its spell.

A ten-foot-long, horizontal mural, *La Primavera* was meant to hang over a daybed or *lettucio*. In it, nine semimythical figures gather in a grove of orange trees. The action seems to move from right to left. At the right an angry flying zephyr urges a reluctant, seminaked girl forward into the verdant foreground. In the middle a Venus or Madonna figure smiles enigmatically, head tilted to one side, eyes following the viewer. To her right three beautiful maidens, also barely clothed, gather in a circle. These "Three Graces" signified in astrology the Sun, Venus, and Jupiter, Ioan said. One of them casts an adoring glance at a handsome Mercury in the corner even as she is about to be shot by Cupid's arrow. Mercury turns his back on her, however, reaching with a caduceus toward a wisp of cloud or smoke in the sky.

Though many have tried, no one has ever come up with a completely satisfactory explanation of the painting. Was it meant as a paean to Marsilio Ficino and the neo-Platonists' Academy of Botticelli's time, as some thought, or as a warning to the artist's patron, the young Lorenzo, il Magnifico, for not wedding the girl of his dreams, who died the year after the work was finished? Could it signify an alchemical formula, as some suggested? The fact that the answer is not clear is one of the painting's main appeals. What is clear is that it offers a disturbing, enchanted vision of the power of eros in the human universe.

Culianu shared Botticelli's obsession with the goddess figure because he felt such a figure triggered his own creativity and had saved him in his moment of attempted suicide. Hillary resembled Botticelli's Venus, and he became convinced she was the blond woman he had seen in his vision. He also noted in *Eros et magie* that Botticelli's use of mythological subjects allowed the artist to make "incredibly bold studies of the female nude."

To everyone who has marveled at its erotic qualities, the painting seems designed to invite speculation. Hillary and Ioan saw in it a *ludibrium*, or high riddle, that, like the Rosicrucian hoax, offered a key to understanding the world. They decided it would make an excellent subject for a Renaissance murder mystery in the style of Ioan's friend Umberto Eco. It could be Ioan's key to fame. They would cowrite it that summer, renting a villa in a village they had admired on their drive from Paris. But first they both had to return to pressing and, for him, distasteful loose ends.

＊　＊　＊

She returned to her studies at Harvard, he to a makeshift apartment in Groningen. He had submitted his third and final thesis to the Sorbonne, and on January 10 he went to Paris to defend it. His adviser, Sorbonne president Michel Meslin, admired the work but had reservations. "Culianu truly had an encyclopedic knowledge — an interest in everything. His thesis was a huge scholarly work." Meslin could not find the conclusions or significant points, however, intuiting the fact that Culianu either purposely hid what he was thinking or worked at times without conviction in the plodding methods of scholarship. "It seemed he was collecting notes . . . and then, like a computer, he pushed a button and everything came out."

Despite Meslin's reservations, Culianu defended the thesis successfully. Back in Groningen he began turning the text into the book *Les Gnoses dualistes d'Occident* for Plon. In it he compared gnostic beliefs over time, charting the patterns in their development. Whereas his European and American colleagues were either doing comparative work or tracing the evolution of a particular religious tradition, he worked on both. His unique, if questionable, methodology made him something like a comparative encyclopedist.*

He was doing more, however, than charting and comparing the beliefs of widely different movements, from eighth-century Manichaeans to nineteenth-century nihilists. He was also seeking the universal basis for patterns in religion and history. He thought he found it in a form of chaos theory applied to human events, and in the spring of 1987 he began reading widely on the new science of fractal equations then gaining popularity. Fractals worked on strings of binary choices like forks in the road, built in a complex architecture like one of Bruno's mental systems. With them scientists tried to predict weather patterns, earthquakes, and the shape of tree branches. If one could discern patterns in such intricate creations of nature, he reasoned, then it seemed possible to do the same with human creations like religions or revolutions.

Unlike Eliade, Culianu was not seeking escape from history. Rather, he sought to incorporate it by mapping it, and by mapping it to master it. Like Ficino and Bruno, he defined a thought as a shape or pattern *in time;* like Einstein, he suggested that scientific measurements should chart patterns as they changed over time. All of these thinkers agreed on one thing: historical time is malleable. Marsilio Ficino tried to prove this with magic potions and talismans, Albert Einstein with his equations that showed time sped up and slowed down. Culianu linked the two by connecting science, which predicted the future, with imagination, which altered the present, with memory, which altered the past.

In his bare Groningen apartment he arranged his family photographs in doppelgänger pairs, placing side by side pictures of his

* Lee Smith, "Mind Games," *Lingua Franca* (September–October 1992): 24.

mother and his nanny Manea as young women and old. The photo pairs illustrated to him that the logic of character transcended time. He fashioned a shrine to Hillary above his desk, placing her graduation photo beside a close-up of the Madonna from *La Primavera*. Juxtaposed, they indeed looked like dead ringers.

To most people such a resemblance was mostly coincidence. But Culianu wanted to know if "coincidence" itself was a reflection of deeper patterns he located in the mind. He explored cognitive science to understand the way the mind perceived and created the world. Theorists like the mathematician Rudy Rucker were reviving Plato's notion that our universe was merely a shadow of eternal mental or mathematical processes. Culianu began reading Rucker's book *Mind Tools*, which begins: "Mathematics is the study of pure pattern, and everything in the cosmos is a kind of pattern." Rucker noted the close relation between early religion and mathematics, showing how the Arabs, for instance, expressed God with the symbol for zero or infinity. He noted Jung's cultural archetypes, built on fourfold figures he called "tetrads" or "quaternities," like the four seasons, four directions, or four stages of knowledge: seeing, thinking, feeling, and intuiting. Rucker suggested that even individual subjectivity could be assigned a mathematical formula. In such studies Ioan Culianu linked for the first time his personal and professional life, joining his spiritual childhood and his father's specialty in higher mathematics with his scholarly studies of religion.

In the spring he found a much larger audience for his thought on cognition than that offered by his books' readers. Through a broadcaster he met at a conference, he was placed under contract by BBC World Service in London to broadcast talks on history, science, and religion into Eastern Europe. If the scholarly world was unprepared for what Harvard's Lawrence Sullivan later termed Culianu's "startling juxtapositions," it was hard to imagine how his former countrymen, suffering under the century's most complex censorship, would react.

❋   ❋   ❋

In the spring Culianu also came back to the University of Chicago Divinity School, where he taught and gave two guest lectures. His friend Anthony Yu could not believe the change from 1975, when they had first been introduced: "When I met him in the Eliades' apartment, his English was virtually nonexistent. Now he was speaking well, even joking. He was a well-established public scholar, one whose books I had read and admired in French. The way that he juxtaposed materials, not only those that were religious, but also cultural and literary, showed a range that was very exciting for me. He had wit too, not something I could attribute that easily to Eliade's writing." Forced by exile to make international contacts and learn new languages, Culianu now offered better linguistic skills and international academic connections than most American scholars his age. "He was a very charming, highly ambitious European intellectual on the rise," said his University of Chicago Press editor David Brent, who noted that Culianu's working method came from an older era when a scholar could go into a secondhand book shop, read everything on a subject, and then write something better. "His learning was so prodigious that he was kind of intimidating." Following Eliade's suggestion, Brent was about to publish Culianu in the United States for the first time; *Eros and Magic in the Renaissance* was due in November 1987. Culianu's painful years of voluntary exile began to pay off.

He lectured in Hyde Park on one of his favorite topics, the Faust legend. Reviewing versions of the myth from ancient times to the present, Culianu claimed that only after the Reformation did storytellers impose a moral punishment on the man who worked with the devil to achieve his desires. Earlier variants applauded his daring quest to pursue his lover. The story resembled, Culianu might have added, his own myth of his life.

In the spring he worked on the *Dictionnaire des religions* project he had promised to Eliade. To check himself, Culianu asked colleagues to scan some of the entries. Yu reviewed his summary of Chinese Taoism. "The distillation was delightful," Yu said. "He could not read the primary texts in Chinese, but he offered a very competent review of the European scholarship on the subject."

Culianu was also attending to the Eliade papers, going for walks with Eliade's widow, Christinel, and cooking for her when she entertained friends like Saul Bellow and his wife. "He was charming," Bellow recalled, "very gracious and funny. Like Mircea, he treated everything as if it were a game." Most of all, Culianu was looking for job openings in the United States. Staying once again in McGiffert House, he met Alexander Arguelles, a first-year graduate student from California. They discovered they both used the same obsolete European word processor. When Arguelles's printer shorted out, Culianu let him use his. "He wore this red paisley robe," Arguelles recalled. "I thought he was a student at first. He said that America was where the action was in scholarship and art."

Ioan Culianu had come full circle from the dreaming, ambitious boy bragging to his second cousin on the balcony of a nun's cottage in a Romanian monastery. In May, the same cousin invited him to speak on Eliade at Indiana University, where she was now a lecturer. Speeding down the streets of Bloomington, he looked exactly like what he had predicted he would be eighteen years earlier — a successful professor in the West with a shiny red sports car. Laughing, she commented on his success.

The lecture, however, was a disappointment. He was unprepared and superficial. He read from a news article and offered few insights into his mentor's work and significance. Afterward he explained he was "tired of all that Eliade stuff." He breezed out of town, back to the prestige of his visiting professorship at the University of Chicago Divinity School. His red sports car, he might have added, was rented.

❀ ❀ ❀

In June in Paris he prepared for the grave presentation ceremony for the Sorbonne's *Doctorat d'Etat es Lettres et Sciences Humaines*. It was indeed "the highest academic degree in the world," as he liked to say. A formal reception accompanied its bestowal. He brought Hillary to the reception but did not introduce her to most of his friends. He seemed to fear the impolitic appearance of a girlfriend at a critical time when most colleagues thought he was still married.

His relation with Meslin was also becoming strained. "He was very complex, very secret, almost tortured," Meslin recalled. "He was a go-getter with the instincts of an *arriviste*." When he did reveal his divorce to friends, he maintained that his traveling, or Carmen's unwillingness to move to the United States, had been the cause. He had written Romanato in April 1987: "I apologize that blind natural selection has kept me from writing. Last year I left in March, came back in June, left again in August, now I am going back to the USA. The result was almost natural for the circumstances. Divorce . . . I could no longer take the responsibility for two and of being a protection for someone who is always unsatisfied." It was the last letter he ever wrote to his closest friend.

Following his graduation, the Sorbonne and the Romanian-American Academy cosponsored an international conference celebrating what would have been Eliade's eightieth birthday. The conference was critical to Culianu because so many University of Chicago faculty would be there, including former dean Jerry Brauer, the Catholic theologian David Tracy, and Indologist Wendy Doniger. He knew they were likely to be searching for a new colleague shortly. He wanted to put on the performance of his life. He spoke in several sessions, including one called "Hommage à Mircea Eliade," and participated in a panel discussing "the history of religions after Mircea Eliade." He also arranged to edit a collection of the conference papers for the *Journal of the Romanian-American Academy.*

In Paris, however, a relative appeared, as if to disrupt his performance. His sister's husband, Dan Petrescu, won an exit visa to attend the conference because he was writing a doctoral thesis on Eliade's fiction. At home, the lives of the family members had grown increasingly tense. In 1986 Petrescu's list of dissidents was intercepted at the border; the family's Iaşi home was ransacked in retaliation. In punishment another room was taken from the few to which the family was relegated.

The Paris meeting of Petrescu and Culianu was not a happy one. Culianu frequently abandoned his brother-in-law, canceling dinner appointments at the last second as he raced from publisher to publisher. He seemed to see his relative by marriage as something of a parasite.

With a sense of the absurd honed as a dissident, Petrescu felt the slight without revealing it. He also felt a deep disappointment in the West. At the conference, for instance, he stood up to object to the scripted parade of academic paeans to Eliade. He was cut off. "I experienced more censorship in Paris than in Bucharest!" he complained to Carmen.

*   *   *

By late June the public performances were finished, the dickering over his divorce settlement concluded. Ioan finished the *Dictionnaire des religions*, inserting in the introduction hints of his theory that all religions were a map of the human mind. While he insisted that Eliade had reviewed the *Dictionnaire* entries until his death, it was clear that Culianu had changed the work a great deal. "It was a usurpation," complained Meslin. Nonetheless, the book was destined for popular success, even a Great Book of the Month Award in France.

In July 1987 Culianu gave the first of two broadcasts for the BBC World Service focusing on the growing controversy about Eliade's past. During the spring, he said, he had heard from Professor Vittorio Lanternari at the University of Rome, who claimed Eliade extolled the Iron Guard in a far rightist newspaper called *Buna Vestire* in 1938. Lanternari claimed a manuscript had arrived from Romania documenting Eliade's anti-Semitism. It was the diary of Eliade's friend, a Jewish novelist with the pen name Mihail Sebastian. Culianu responded angrily that Sebastian's work was biased. Then he wrote Mac Linscott Ricketts for copies of Eliade's incriminating 1930s articles that Ricketts had unearthed in the Romanian national archives.

In his first broadcast Culianu blamed the controversy on Eliade's reverence for his university teacher, Nae Ionescu, who had "functioned toward Eliade as a Mephistopheles, drawing him into a political adventure with very grave consequences." Culianu claimed that Eliade had never been an anti-Semite but admitted his mentor may have been an Iron Guard sympathizer. With a novelist's instinct, Culianu ended his talk with a cliffhanger: "What happened later, as Nae Ionescu slid more and more toward the Legionary Movement? What happened, in particular, during the electoral campaign of 1937 . . . ? Is it true that Eliade was pro-Nazi? We shall try, soon, to return to these questions at length."

●　　　●　　　●

Not until late July did Ioan and Hillary finally escape on their long-coveted journey to Courmayeur, a mountain village in northern Italy favored by Nietzsche. They turned to their long-discussed murder mystery, titled *The Emerald Game*. Opening with a preface by a young man who, like Culianu, had left Romania in 1972 "under pressing circumstances" to come to Italy, the book tells of a mysterious Renaissance manuscript he finds stuck in his bag. Translating

• • • • • •

it at night, he noticed he is being watched, then followed. One night the manuscript is stolen, leaving only his translation — the novel.

"I leave here a great and unsuspected secret of an extraordinary time," begins the text's narrator, Thomas Anglicus. An Englishman who came to Florence in 1494, Anglicus is swept up in a series of bloody murders linked to Botticelli's *La Primavera*. "Was the crime which haunts me relentlessly," Anglicus asks himself, "the fruit of my own will or of my destiny?" His adventures feature Renaissance figures like Marsilio Ficino, Pico della Mirandola, Sandro Botticelli, even the mapmaker Amerigo Vespucci. Exploring Renaissance beliefs about the arts of divination, astrology, and memory, the novel takes Anglicus through a dark and contradictory Florence ruled by a complex web of relations and secret power networks, which can only be comprehended through metaphor, that is, his manuscript, or magic. Observing anti-Semitic mobs, masochistic sects, and the luminous members of Ficino's Academy, Anglicus becomes both a murder suspect and an amateur sleuth, assisted by a gentle Dr. Altavilla and a beautiful lady friend. Using Altavilla's arcane knowledge, they begin to predict when new victims are to be killed. The plot's climactic murder takes place on Tuesday, Mars's Day (Culianu himself was murdered on a Tuesday). Though the motive appears to be that of sending a message to others, Thomas observes to his beloved Vittoria: "The immediate agents of the murder . . . are scarcely important. All that matters is the crazy puppeteer."

Culianu and Wiesner wrote the book in alternating chapters over five idyllic, exhilarating summer weeks. Each morning they rose and typed — one in the front room, the other on a sunny balcony overlooking snowcapped Mont Blanc. When Thomas observes the unique harmony of the natural world, he probably reflects his authors' sense of calm and joy in their first summer together.

The novel also dangerously blurs the line between reality and fiction. In his investigations Thomas encounters several characters modeled on University of Chicago professors. The kindly Dr. Altavilla, for instance, is based on David Tracy, the sinister security police colonel on the late Allan Bloom. A number of other Chicago faculty seem to appear in unflattering portraits. For a scholar angling for a position at the exclusive institution, his fictional exercise seemed a potentially self-destructive or talismanic game at a time he was playing the perfect friend and colleague.

Though the book names a murderer, the ultimate motive involves magic and science at a level deeper than even the murderer understands. The crime's solution can only be arrived at through magic, so the wisdom in arcane practices mastered along the path of the investigation becomes the story's ultimate reward. It does not matter that the stated motive turns out to be largely unintelligible or that the *Primavera* turns out to be a forgery meant to convey a deadly alchemical formula by the positioning of its figures. "The concept of forgery and authenticity was a relatively new one in the Renaissance," Culianu later observed, "and not entirely applicable to our needs."

After further editing, Culianu and Wiesner submitted the book to a literary agent. They wanted more time with it, but Hillary's mother was to remarry, and they were called back to Amherst.

* * *

They returned to the United States at the end of August for the wedding of Dorothy Wiesner to Kurt Hertzfeld, the widowed treasurer of Amherst College. It was one of the few times Ioan had met many of Hillary's best friends, and he came under close scrutiny. "He seemed, well, smaller than I imagined," noted Erika Schluntz. "After hearing all this stuff about this wonderful man, it seemed so much love could not be stuffed into such a small body." Ioan loved ceremonial occasions, in which he could excel as the director of a play he was performing. On the sunny lawn outside the Victorian home in Amherst he was a big hit. "He had more family feeling than I did," Wiesner recalled. Everyone loved him. "I was happy because Hillary had such high standards we never knew if she was going to find someone," said her sister, Nikki, two years older and more outgoing than she. "They didn't make it too public that he was married when they met." Kurt Hertzfeld came to cherish Ioan as a family member who worked to unite his children with those of his wife.

In the fall of 1987 Culianu again taught two courses at Chicago as a visiting professor. Now the stakes escalated dramatically. The Divinity School officially posted an opening for a tenure-track professor. It was the position for which Ioan Culianu had lived his life.

He had already begun to build a student following. His more

· · · · · ·

creative colleagues, like Lawrence Sullivan, enthusiastically recommended his courses and his book *Eros and Magic*. Because his work was scattered in so many languages and subjects, the search committee asked him for six recommendation letters rather than the traditional four. He pulled together impressive support, from Umberto Eco, Michel Meslin, Hans Jonas, and the Divinity School's Joseph Kitagawa and Lawrence Sullivan. "The Europeans praised him sky high," recalled Anthony Yu. He submitted a letter from a Romanian professor in comparative literature at Indiana University, Matei Calinescu: "I am now reporting a thought that Eliade himself expressed in several conversations we had during the last years of his life — that Professor Culianu has become the major continuator and emulator . . . of Eliade's distinctive hermeneutic approach to religion." Culianu's sixteen-page résumé listed eleven books and translations in four languages, published or under contract. The list of articles and reviews was similarly staggering in quantity for a thirty-seven-year-old thinker.

The faculty split roughly between an old guard who saw in Culianu not only a reminder of the school's grand Eliade tradition but also a productive and creative new voice. Some newer faculty questioned whether the school *wanted* another Eliadian and whether Culianu really was strictly a historian of religion at all. "The objections had not so much to do with his specific competence," recalled Anthony Yu, "but rather, is this the kind of person we want right now?" Of the ten teaching interests Culianu was listing on his vita by 1990, for instance, only one covered the history of religions or Christianity. How well would he do with the survey courses required for students to pass their master's exams? (He disliked teaching the courses and did poorly at first.) Some objections masked deeper reservations about the quality of his numerous publications. "No one really knew him, and you could not say that of anyone else in the faculty," said Wendy Doniger.

In the end the yes votes prevailed. On an icy cold January 5, 1989, Ioan's birthday, the telephone rang at Hillary's cramped Cambridge apartment. It was Dean Chris Gamwell. He was calling to offer Ioan an associate professorship with assured tenure. "I express to you the enthusiasm of the faculty here . . . and our profound hope you will accept this invitation," Gamwell said.

Culianu accepted, thanked him, hung up, and leaped around the apartment in joy. He had done it! Despite all that the world threw against him, all the weight of terror, hard work, hunger, and vicious infighting, he had won! All those languages he had learned, all those nights of anguished reading until his eyes teared, all that indifference and contempt. He had done it! They telephoned Hillary's mother in Amherst and danced around and shouted for joy. Hillary broke open a bottle of champagne to celebrate.

Later that evening she went out. He closeted himself in the spare room. He crossed his legs in yoga meditation, contemplating all that this meant to him. He had done what his father could not do, he thought. And he was only just *starting*.

Wearing his paisley robe, he felt a stab of fear. He never before had anything, like this position or Hillary, so valuable that he could not stand to lose them.

People like us, who believe in physics, know that the distinction between past, present and future is only a stubbornly persistent illusion.

—*Albert Einstein*

* * * * * * * *

RELIGION AND SCIENCE:
THE FOURTH DIMENSION, 1988

Dean Chris Gamwell had offered Culianu the possibility of beginning full-time in the spring or the fall of 1988. When Hillary received a grant to do research in Spain, Egypt, and Israel, he took the opportunity to join her. He felt he was a new man. Yet if his opponents from Paris or Groningen could have seen him, they might not have believed he had so completely shed his trickier Manichaean side.

In 1988 he became increasingly interested in the tricks and veils of the universe. After concluding his second BBC broadcast on Eliade with a rousing defense of his mentor, Culianu switched from political topics to those of theoretical science, with commentaries entitled "The Fourth Dimension," "Schrödinger's Cat," "The Fifth Dimension," and others. Scientists were the shamans of our age, and he wanted to explore the "growing acknowledgment among physicists worldwide, including several Nobel laureates, that the universe may actually exist in multidimensional space." He read the new theories of "hyperspace" in popular books and science journals, reporting the new discoveries about inward escape to a receptive audience, his former countrymen.

Conditions in Romania in 1988 went from deprived to unbearable. The few items left on store shelves disappeared. Everything from milk, meat, and butter to tampons and nylons could not be found. Light and heat went out after dark. Yet a troop of official poets extolled the virtues of the Great Sage of the Carpathians, Nicolae Ceauşescu, in terms that would have made Stalin blush. Once proud of its reputation for independence, the country fell into a black hole of mutual spying, eavesdropping, and mindless, personal betrayal.

As Ceauşescu became more unpopular, he had to rely more and more on his security police to prop up his dictatorship. Since 1986 Dan Petrescu had been routinely summoned by Securitate and threatened, but by 1987 he was being questioned regularly in the Iaşi headquarters. Early in 1988 Petrescu had given an interview to *Libération* in Paris, attacking the Communist regime. The interview was published in France on Ceauşescu's birthday, January 28. After the interview, Petrescu began to write articles for French newspapers attacking, for example, Ceauşescu propaganda's attempt to latch on to Romanian nationalism. In its last years the regime turned to the darkly lyrical rhetoric of mystical nationalism to bolster its appeal. A movement called protochronism, for instance, sought to claim Romanian primacy in world fields ranging from the sciences to literature.* Anti-Western, antirational, it appealed to the most primitive instincts of a national unconscious.

If love and success had indeed made Ioan Culianu a new man, then now was a moment to step forward. His vow of self-censorship

* Mircea Eliade had urged some scholars to push the "protochronist" movement. Norman Manea, "Happy Guilt," *New Republic*, August 5, 1991, p. 35.

to Willem Noomen had expired. A year earlier he had greeted by telephone one of the most prominent dissidents to escape to the United States, the poet and Voice of America broadcaster Dorin Tudoran. Tudoran invited Culianu to serve on the editorial board and write commentary for his new, influential international journal *Agora*, funded by the Foreign Policy Research Institute in Washington. In 1987 Culianu contributed an article entitled "Sin against Spirit" ("Păcatul împotriva spiritului"), linking religious imagery with an attack on his homeland's government—a hallmark of his later political writing. "Daring to form an idea leads to life," he wrote his fellow Romanians. "Have the courage to say no, and you will rise on the third day. . . . There is no death but the spirit of death and no other resurrection but the river of ideas."

But in all he remained silent on the pain at home.

· · ·

In the spring of 1988 he joined Hillary and met her childhood friend Cathy O'Leary in Chicago. Culianu booked a kitchenette suite for a week in the Flamingo-on-the-Lake Apartments, which catered to retirees and which the women dubbed the "Flaming O." One night he created a memorable dinner using vitamins, a plastic spoon and fork utensil from the neighborhood deli, and paper plates. He added a piece of bread, some bacon dip, and a bottle of Asti Spumante. "Now," he said, "we haven't even gotten to the main dish yet!" In the pool Hillary and Ioan spun around and around, trying to achieve a shaman's altered consciousness on a log roll. Evenings they stood together on the fire escape overlooking Lake Michigan.

Ioan wrote a final letter to Carmen indicating his remorse over their failed marriage, after he had given her the house: "I see now that I have ruined your life, and don't you think that it fills me with sorrow? I could not stay on in Holland. I had to move forward in a way I cannot explain to you or myself." He would not admit to it, but he felt a little frightened about the blood pact they had made when he proposed to her in 1979, linking their souls forever under the threat of death.

· · ·

In the summer months before he joined the regular faculty at the Divinity School, Culianu traveled with Hillary to Cairo, Jerusalem, and several cities in Spain — months marked on his calendar with magical talismans for luck and the word "Free!" He attached special significance to the word. His letters to friends were filled with meditations on freedom, occasionally cynical, occasionally lyrical, sometimes humorous. Before getting into bed, he would untuck the sheets, joking, "I have to be free!"

Hillary and Ioan met in Cairo, where they stayed five weeks in a small hotel. He spent his mornings at the library of the American University, reading some five shelves' worth of books on Muslim Spain. Afternoons he sat on the hotel balcony, trying to learn spoken Arabic from a dictionary and a newspaper while Hillary worked on her dissertation on the medieval mystic al-Kindi, the man responsible for preserving much of the magical tradition Ficino and Bruno revived. She began to suspect that al-Kindi was a plagiarist and that some of his most important sources were forgeries. Ioan reveled in her discovery. All that mattered, he said, was that Renaissance magicians *believed* in the authenticity of al-Kindi's texts.

They visited Alexandria, the Pyramids and the Sphinx. Everywhere they went he tried to converse, even pun or joke, in Arabic. He loved the mathematical nature of the language, which worked through permutations of three-letter clusters. In the library at the University of Cairo they dreamed up a story based on a real incident of an academic's forgery that Hillary had heard of in her Egyptology course in Chicago. He and Hillary turned the incident into the short story "The Late Repentance of Horemheb." It explored his growing conviction that forgeries are never merely fakes, but much more consequential attempts to alter the past, and thereby the future.

* * *

They stopped at Hebrew University in Jerusalem to see Ioan's new friend, a Romanian exile and expert in the Jewish mystical Kabbalah, Moshe Idel. The two men had hit it off at their first meeting the previous fall in Chicago. "He was the first Romanian I spoke to in about twenty-seven years of exile," recalled Idel. "We became extraordinarily close quickly. We spent the whole night talking in Romanian and getting nostalgic." Idel came from Tîrgu Neamţ, where as a child Culianu had caught a bus on the way to Văratic Monastery. "Finally we decided not to talk about Romania, nor in Romanian,"

Idel said. "It made us both too sad." For his part, Culianu was deeply taken with a man he saw as his spiritual double. Not only did they come from the same region of the world, but Idel had continued the research he would have pursued had he gone on to Israel instead of Italy. They were both fascinated by the Jewish mystics called Kabbalists and their idea that the universe can be perceived through repeated mystical and mathematical steps. In the Renaissance, Pico della Mirandola had translated the Kabbalists whose works, like al-Kindi's, sparked the theories of Renaissance magicians.

In Nerja, Spain, Ioan marked his calendar with a lion for Hillary's birthday, plotting out various Kabbalist letters for September 1 and 14, adding the word "Idea!" to give it the weight of Jewish mysticism. They took a house on the beach at Nerja, visiting the Islamic ruins in Granada, Córdoba, Valencia, Madrid, and Seville, where he studied the Inquisition, concluding that it was a less destructive crusade than the Communist persecution in his own country.

＊　＊　＊

In September they returned to the United States, where Ioan joined Hillary in Lexington, Massachusetts, with her friends Erika and Cathy at a wedding. Ioan and Cathy O'Leary helped Hillary move into a larger apartment on Harvard Street in Cambridge. One day he went to the Cambridge magic shop called Arsenic and Old Lace. The clerk undercharged him for some dream powder. When he called it to her attention, she became angry and defensive. Walking out, he showed Hillary the new bill.

"Her magic was weaker than mine, and now she has again undercharged me." In her haste the woman had taken some other herbs off the bill by mistake.

Out on the street he hesitated, then suddenly turned back to the store. "If I don't pay," he said to Hillary, "then neither the herbs nor the powder will work."

＊　＊　＊

In the fall of 1988 he came back in triumph to the University of Chicago as an associate professor, guaranteed tenure once his immigration proceedings were completed. He taught two courses on subjects he was exploring for books under contract to mainstream

American publishers — HarperCollins, HarperSanFrancisco, and Shambhala. One course, Religion as a System, explored his theory of religious history as a long sequence of binary choices. He drew upon its contents for the new introduction of the English version of *The Eliade Guide to World Religions*. But the course that forged his core group of students was his most ambitious to date: Religion and Science: The Fourth Dimension.

The course covered the science of multiple dimensions, seeking in literature and theory explanations of age-old stories of after-death journeys, miracles, and ecstatic experiences. There was nothing new about this approach; even Lenin had addressed it in his *Materialism and Empirio-Criticism* (1908). But Culianu brought to the subject seriousness, boldness, and his command of languages, multiple cultures, and the occult. He also had a great deal at stake. This course would help create the opening chapters of *Out of This World: Other-worldly Journeys from Gilgamesh to Albert Einstein*, a book he hoped would take him to his career's next step — popular success in America.

On the first night of the course he met his ten graduate students at the door, greeting them each by name. He announced that "a small dynasty of human beings had changed the face of the world" and that they would explore their secrets. The class included his closest students: Greg Spinner, son of a Jewish shoe salesman in Tennessee, and Michael Allocca, a Brooklyn native. Nathaniel Deutsch audited the class. Among the others were Margaret Arndt-Caddigan, Stephanie Stamm, Beatrice Briggs, and Julia Dulocq.

Scientific revolutions always defy common sense, he warned them, so they should prepare for some "brain damage." The reading list included Rudy Rucker's *The Fourth Dimension*, Edwin Abbott's *Flatland*, Lewis Carroll's *Through the Looking-Glass*, and books by Einstein, Asimov, Borges, and others. Whereas other scholars thought of "the sacred" or the supernatural as something internal or mystical, he suggested that new understandings could stem from insights into high-energy physics as well as cognitive science. These insights, startling as they were, could simplify and explain many inexplicable or even supernatural events.

In brief, he said, the four dimensions were once understood to be length, height, width, and time, adding that new theories of hyperspace suggested we live in a universe whose dimensions number anywhere from eleven to twenty-three. Theories of hyperspace suggest that we live like fish in a pool, affected by unknown forces in parallel worlds that we understand as dimly as fish do the world above their pond's surface. If hyperspace simplified observations of the physical world, Culianu offered, perhaps one could find in it the sources of metaphysical arts like Renaissance magic, astrology, and mysticism. Whatever metaphor you chose — that of hyperspace or the medievalist's cosmic "ether" — each holds clues one can follow to uncover new mysteries in the cosmos.

At the course's first meeting he read aloud Borges's story "Tlön, Uqbar, Orbis Tertius." It tells of an imaginary country called Uqbar, invented as a mind game by some scholars who included the heading "Uqbar" in a limited edition of the *Encyclopedia Britannica*. All the epics and legends of Uqbar refer to the imaginary places Tlön and Mlejnas. In Tlön *mind* was a "synonym for the cosmos," and the cosmos was a giant riddle working itself out inside the mind of each of Tlön's inhabitants. Although the narrator knows by 1941 that Tlön is a complete fiction, he hears in 1942 of a real object from Poitiers, France, inscribed with one of the Tlön alphabets, found in a princess's apartment. A few months later in South America an unknown metal is discovered in a dead boy's pocket, also from Tlön, and in 1944, forty volumes of the *First Encyclopedia of Tlön* turn up in Memphis, Tennessee.

Culianu said the story presented an intellectual riddle that offered a hidden truth about the power of the mind to create the world. In a tradition practiced by Poe, Borges also offered in his 1941 fantasy story a specific political allegory about the power of fascist propaganda to create imaginary doctrines of hate real enough to motivate the actions of millions.

During the next ten weeks the students planned potluck dinners, gave reports, and went out after class to continue their talks. "We came out of there with our heads reeling," said Spinner. "We didn't want to stop." While the subjects inspired them, the relationship with their teacher made the class unique. Culianu talked with them more than any other professor, supported them more, listened more, joked more, and even remembered their birthdays. They in turn invited him to their parties, teasing him about his accent and his wardrobe, which was still very Italian. He liked to wear a brown and gold-flecked sport jacket, often with a pastel shirt. "His shirt collars were always a little too big," recalled Alexander Arguelles. Occasionally he wore a silk scarf or an M. C. Escher tie that Greg had given him for Christmas. His favorite shoes were soft-soled and geeky brown, but he loved the brand name: Mephisto.

* * *

At Michael Allocca's house on the class's second meeting, Culianu cooked pasta carbonara as they began the first of two discussions of Edwin Abbott Abbott's *Flatland*. First published in England in 1884 under the pseudonym A. Square ("A" for Abbott, squared), the occult political satire became a lasting best-seller. Abbott invented a world of two dimensions — Flatland — where residents can only move sideways, not up and down. If a three-dimensional creature dips a spoon into their world, Flatlanders perceive it as a supernatural cataclysm affecting their universe like an earthquake. In Abbott's novel the lowest on the social scale are women, who are only one-dimensional lines, followed by middle-class men, appropriately called Squares, and then the High Priests, who, as three-dimensional spheres, are able to see the third dimension the others cannot.

When one Square travels accidentally into the third dimension, he comes back preaching revolution. A rebellion begins. The events offer a familiar pattern: Mr. Square is labeled a criminal and is imprisoned and tortured. When rebelling women seem about to win higher status, a rape charge is used to discredit their leader. When other leading rebels get too powerful, the High Priests admit them "at once to the privileged classes," thus turning them "perfectly Regular." The High Priests allow some change but ultimately marginalize the hero, who, abandoned by his followers, is finally left only to write his book for posterity.

The fact that Abbott's odd short classic went into nineteen printings and is still popular today seems to be a result of the plot's insightful exploration of pattern in revolutions throughout history. Culianu emphasized something unusual in the book — the novel's love interests. Could "love" in its Greek sense of *eros*, he asked, be a path to understanding the fourth dimension? This gentle, intuitive approach to the world marked history's great scientists, he said. And the romantics' imagery of rapture and lust offered remarkably similar metaphors to those of near-death and after-death experiences. During the second class on Abbott, someone joked about the *Ghostbusters* sequel that had recently opened in Chicago. The group decided to see it together.

❀   ❀   ❀

In their fourth week Greg Spinner reported on a late nineteenth-century mathematician who also enjoyed popular success, Edward Hinton. Among other items, Hinton invented the modern baseball pitching machine, but he was most significant in history for an early set of toy cubes, similar to Rubik's cube. To solve Hinton's cubes, the player had to imagine moving them through time as well as space. Borges played with the cubes as a child. Frank Lloyd Wright played with similar cubes, leading him to the modular block design of his prairie houses.

Next the class discussed Lewis Carroll's *Through the Looking-Glass*, focusing on Carroll's send-up of the overintellectualizing of his Cambridge colleagues—the models for his Mad Hatter, Tweedledee and Tweedledum, the crazy Queen and her court.

Like Hinton, their sixth week's subject, the Russian mystic and con man P. D. Ouspensky (1878–1947), suggested that ghosts were really apparitions from a fourth dimension. Culianu showed that such theorizing had important political consequences. Lenin waged a vicious campaign against a spiritualist branch of the Bolshevik party that admitted theories of higher dimensions.

The night they discussed Ouspensky, they went out to Jimmy's together. Over pitchers of beer, Ioan Culianu told them how his mother helped his nanny cook the most incredible Christmas holiday dinners despite the deprivations the family endured. His mother hovered over every guest, he said, making sure everyone was happy before eating herself. It was the first time he ever told his students in the United States that he was Romanian.

Hillary came for Thanksgiving at his rooms in McGiffert Hall, joined by her friend Cathy O'Leary, who was studying political science in the graduate school at Chicago. One night afterward Culianu took O'Leary out to see the movie *Colors*. He liked action movies because they cleared his mind of the dense arcana of his research; she liked to escape the stress of graduate studies. Walking home that night, he kept turning around and joking, "Uh oh, we'd better watch out. I think we're being followed." He made a game of the movie's paranoia. He shivered deeply against the cold, but it was his habit never to wear a jacket. Likewise, when he was ill he would ignore any symptoms. "He lived by ideas," said Allocca, "so he wasn't the most streetwise person."

·   ·   ·

The goal of the term, he said in the final meeting of Religion and Science, was to understand how authors create fictional worlds to *unlearn* what this world is supposed to look like. Imagination is a form of perception. It isn't that fantastical realities exist in the mind, but that the real world is fantastical and multidimensional. Our inability to perceive this comes only from the limits of our minds. The course finished with Stephen Toulmin's *The Return to Cosmology* (1982), which argues that modern science is itself in some ways a myth.

At the end, students gave Culianu rave evaluations. But popular as he was in seminars, some of the faculty advised students against working with him. "It wasn't that they disagreed with his methods," said one student. "It was the fact they did it behind his back." In the winter he faced teaching the first half of the survey course on Western religious traditions. He looked forward to finishing his three books under contract and then pursuing his main love, fiction. Through fiction he could discern the currents of the world around him.

. . . .

DIVINATION, 1989

In the winter and summer of 1989 Culianu and Wiesner traveled in Italy, where he lectured at the Universities of Siena and Rome, the Stensen Institute, and elsewhere. Several years in the planning, the two trips were a triumphal return to the country that had seen his darkest moment of transition to the West. He was invited by two leading Italian scholars, Grazia Marchianò and Elémire Zolla. Zolla had first noticed and admired Culianu's review of his book *Archetypes.* He wrote Culianu inviting him to Italy;

Marchianò arranged a visiting professorship. Chair of aesthetics at
the University of Siena-Arezzo, Marchianò ran an international organization called the LORO Group, with the delightful purpose of
"focusing on the vital legacy of Eastern and Western philosophies of
beauty and mind."

In 1989 Eastern Europe's Communist dictatorships began falling
with almost unbelievable ease — in Czechoslovakia and in Hungary
and Poland. Lecturing in Italy in February, Culianu did not know
what lay ahead for Eastern Europe's most odious Communist regime, but he had suspicions. At the time, Ceauşescu's Romania
seemed more comparable to ironclad China or North Korea than to
the other countries of Central Europe. Culianu and Wiesner stayed
in Italy until March 3, and he delivered half a dozen lectures on
subjects ranging from feminism and fashion to magic and gnosis,
from dualistic heresies of the medieval period to Mircea Eliade and
the methodology of the history of religions.

They were frequent visitors to Marchianò and Zolla's eerie, lofty
Rome apartment, where a brilliant crimson hall was covered with
frightening masks from Asia and Africa. Over breakfast Culianu and
the white-haired Zolla read the newspapers at a second level to
decipher the trends behind communism's astonishingly swift fail-
ures. What, Zolla asked him, would become of Romania?

He offered an answer in his first book-length collection of stories, published by Milan's Jaca Book and dedicated to Hillary. Entitled *The Emerald Collection*, it contained a satire of the fall of the
Ceauşescu regime he had written back in 1986.

* * *

Culianu's political farce, "L'intervenzione degli Zorabi en Jormania" (The Intervention of the Zorabis in Jormania), used science
fiction to dissect political truths in much the same way as Abbott's
Flatland. Like Borges's "Tlön, Uqbar, Orbis Tertius," it created
a fictional country, Jormania, ruled by a sultanic dictator named
Gologan. "The distressed and tormented inhabitants dreamed of
getting rid of him, but nobody had the strength and courage to
arrange a coordinated movement of rebellion." The Maculist, or
Soviet, empire and its secret police, BDKR or Bedeker, finally decide to undermine Gologan because his unpopularity threatens

· · · · · ·

their control of the region. The BDKR develops two housecats that metamorphose into tigerlike "Zorabis," who not only annihilate their targets instantly but also procreate at an exponential rate.

The Maculist plan begins well when the cats quickly dispatch the dictator and his wife. A revolution ensues. Popular riots break out, are crushed, then break out again. Leaders of the ruling party grab state-owned factories at bargain rates. Responding, the Maculist-controlled secret police attempt to occupy the television center as planned: "Their script predicted their own failure, but instead nobody resisted. So, changing plan, they took possession of the center to communicate to the population that they represented an armed group of *Im*maculists with the purpose of freeing Jormania from Maculist influence." The demonstrations widen when some government leaders flee the country with money secreted in Swiss bank accounts. The energy minister is said to commit suicide, but he is actually murdered. Against all odds Jormania implements real free-market reform, causing "for the first time . . . more or less authentic smiles on the salesmen's faces."

In the end a second series of Maculist-supported crackdowns, camouflaged as responses to threats against "democracy," leads to a new regime run by former insiders. The regime allows some freedom of the press, including "the authorization to start indigenous pornographic magazines, a development that seemed to enormously stimulate everyone's spirits." Jormania ends up run by corrupt and scheming groups propped up by death squads.

The satire offered several clues to events that were about to occur. But more important, it left a disquieting impression that its author was only hinting at deeper ideas that he planned to disclose later. After a small book tour for the same publisher's Italian translation of his work on gnosis, Culianu arranged to return to Italy in June.

❀   ❀   ❀

In the spring he came back to Chicago, discussing with Wendy Doniger the preparation of a book of Eliade's 1930s articles, accompanied by the full historical context and an explanation. He hoped the text would address fully the lingering doubts about his mentor.

He discussed the project with Dorin Tudoran, who was eager to publish such a book. Because of Christinel Eliade's strident objections, however, Culiano ultimately dropped the project.

Spring term began in late March 1989. Students pestered Culianu to learn what he was going to cover in his course Religion and System: Fashion. All he told them was that it would focus on the high heel. The course examined clothing styles as symbols of deeper power structures, and it recruited more students to his inner group. In the syllabus he explained his methods, saying he would cover "historical knowledge, 'facts,' and theories that do not form the object of the ordinary curriculum. We will focus on . . . religion from a rather peculiar angle." The course covered everything from Chinese foot binding to the plunging bodices of Renaissance fashion. He told his students of his friend Hans Peter Duerr's theory of the witch's broomstick — that hallucinogenic herbs had been rubbed on the vagina as a means of inducing ecstasy among early matriarchal European tribes. Only later did church propaganda twist these practices into the figure of the old, ugly, crazed witch.

If there was a single thread to his courses, it was the desire to cast a net as widely as possible in seeking the underlying forms or structures embedded in religion. He assumed that events always had a hidden subtext. "That course," said Liz Wilson, who became a specialist in religion and gender studies at Miami University of Ohio, "shaped me my career."

*   *   *

With Hillary, Ioan traveled to Italy again in the summer, delivering talks on a variety of subjects. Again he went on a whirlwind lecture tour, delivering seven talks in ten days. Over lunch Zolla and Culianu discussed every conspiracy theory in history, from the Rosicrucians and the Freemasons to the kidnapping and murder of Aldo Moro. Culianu took a particular interest in the case of Georgi Markov, the Bulgarian diplomat assassinated with a poisoned umbrella tip while waiting for a bus in London in 1986. Markov had been receiving death threats for his political writing, but the case was never solved. The first U.S. edition of his book, *The Truth That Killed*, had been published in 1984.

For Hillary's birthday Ioan took her out with Zolla and Marchianò for a sumptuous feast on a patio overlooking the Tuscan plains.
Between the antipasti and the salad they polished off two bottles of
wine. Ioan directed the twelve-course meal, during which they
tricked Hillary into eating boar. Having proposed marriage, Ioan
vowed his undying love. The next day Ioan and Hillary prepared to
depart for Rome, and then the United States.

*   *   *

Back in Chicago shortly before fall term, Culianu ran into Michael
Allocca and Greg Spinner. Allocca took a deep breath. "Greg and I
were wondering," he asked, "if you would consider giving us a special course in divination." They knew that normally professors did
not give reading courses; it added extra work for no additional pay.
But they would accept any conditions Culianu might set.

He would teach the course, he said, but on one condition. As
their final exam they had to predict the future. He would judge them
not so much on whether they were right — because he would have
no way of knowing — but on the quality of their readings. They
could pick the art: geomancy, Kabbalism, Tarot, or astrology, or any
other practice they studied. But they would have to figure out the
question he was asking as well as its answer.

"He was adamant that you could not merely study these arts, you
had to practice them," said Allocca. "He was also the only person I
have ever seen who required you to figure out the question as well as
the answer."

Allocca and Spinner met Culianu weekly in the reading rooms at
Regenstein Library, spending their off time seeking the obscure
books, manuscripts, and forgotten texts that covered the lost or hidden arts. Their first lesson, Culianu said, was to learn that such
systems were not about the occult or evil. Rather, in physical steps
comparable to those of an analog computer, each art sought to create a transparent logic, perfectly mastered and followed through to
the last consequence, that did not offer predictions so much as permutations. Each was a self-enclosed system that worked by quan-
tifying possible outcomes of any situation and then choosing the
most likely.

In October Culianu attended the beginning-of-term party where

he practiced geomancy for several students with Allocca and Spinner watching him. Allocca already knew Tarot and found the reading course subjects easier to master than Spinner did. Unwilling to
suspend his disbelief, Spinner struggled. Week by week they delved
deeper into hidden practices, digging up more and more obscure
texts, making frequent pilgrimages to Chicago's Occult Bookstore
near the intersection of Clark Street and Belmont Avenue. Culianu
did not differentiate between high and low magic, as long as the
system was true to its own logic. Still, much of the relevant material was available only in Latin in original medieval editions located either in Chicago's Newberry Library or in the humidity-
controlled, air-cooled Special Collections Room at the Regenstein.

One night Allocca and Spinner suggested that Culianu come to a
student Halloween party. He declined. But the following week after
class Allocca handed him a black plastic cape and fangs. "You're
going as Dracula," he said.

So Culianu went, unwillingly, to an event recorded in dozens of
photographs. He danced like a Peanuts character. "We were both
dressed as vampires," said another student and friend, Karen de
Leon Jones. "He was going around and telling everyone in his Romanian accent that he was going to suck their blood." He read Tarot
cards for a number of partygoers. He predicted that Jones, a daughter of a Panamanian general who wore her curly hair tied back in a
crimson scarf, "would shortly meet a tall blond man you will almost
marry." The striking, dark Jones, sought by many men but not with
good results, was skeptical.

"Well, you know," she recalled later, in her perfect Oxfordian
accent, "that was exactly what happened."

*   *   *

Far from the library reading room and Hyde Park parties in the fall
of 1989, however, Culianu's world and past life suddenly erupted. In
November 1989 Nicolae Ceauşescu was elected General Secretary
for the fourth consecutive term by the fourteenth Communist Party
Congress. Seventy-one years old, he had led the Romanian Communist Party for twenty-five years. Before the Congress, Culianu's
brother-in-law, Dan Petrescu, had gathered hundreds of signatures
to a letter protesting the election. Afterward, in the family home in

Iaşi, Petrescu began a hunger strike protesting the president's reinstatement. On October 9 Petrescu gave telephone interviews for Radio Free Europe and the French newspaper *Libération*. After that, Securitate cars remained parked in the narrow street outside the house. The telephone worked perhaps one time out of a hundred tries. Nobody could see them. Nobody could enter the house.

Still, Petrescu managed to conduct a second telephone interview with Radio Free Europe. An Italian woman phoned Ioan Culianu in Chicago, giving him a number to another apartment where he could reach his sister. He telephoned on the tenth of October, Tess's birthday. Dan asked him to tell their friends to start telephoning them from all over the world. Many called, but on the third night, as the Petrescus moved through darkened Iaşi streets to the apartment, they were followed. From October 13 to December 22 Dan was under house arrest. The house was ransacked, the telephone removed. Suddenly the games were over.

Guards flanked Tess Petrescu whenever she went out to work or to shop for food, her only permitted activities. She could not see friends. A Securitate commander, wearing combat fatigues, spent hours beating with a night stick the walnut tree Ioan had loved as a child. When one friend tried to pass a message to Tess in the town's open-air market, he was threatened and shoved away by Securitate men.

From Hyde Park, Ioan Culianu circulated a petition internationally for his family's release. He asked the Wiesner and Hertzfeld families to start a campaign sending postcards to the family home. He called Dorin Tudoran, who eventually testified to Congress about the situation and the growing general unrest in Romania.

One night after the weekly meeting of the divination course, Michael noticed how preoccupied Ioan looked. He asked if something was wrong. Ioan told his two students what was going on with his family. "I'm not sure even if Dan and Tess are still alive," he said. He asked Michael and Greg to sign an open letter to the *New York Times* or the *New York Review of Books*.

On November 5, 1989, he traveled to New York to hear Umberto Eco and Moshe Idel lecture on *Foucault's Pendulum* at the American Academy of Science. Hearing that Culianu was in the audience, Eco invited him onstage to speak about the novel. Culianu explained his friend's idea that misinterpretation becomes a reality more real than truth when enough people believe in it. "Nothing reveals this principle more than the Holocaust," he said. "When crazed minds are in synchrony they create an alternative reality; *they kill for invented reasons;* they find reasons to act by making of themselves a fixed point in the universe."*

From New York he flew with Hillary to the annual American Academy of Religion conference in Los Angeles, visiting Disneyland and the Getty Museum in Malibu. When he returned after the eight-day break, he found his Chicago apartment door pulled off its hinges. The rooms were a shambles. He had only moved into the apartment on Sixtieth Street and Woodlawn Avenue a few weeks before. The police report showed that his television, computer, printer, disks, a silver cross, and three bottles of wine had been stolen. It was an insecure building, police said. It seemed an inner-city crime. Culianu complained bitterly to Allocca and Spinner that the university had not warned him that there had been other similar break-ins in the building.

Yet the robbery came at the height of Dan Petrescu's house arrest, just as Culianu was trying to publish his petition. He never mentioned his suspicions to most of his friends, but he received a strange letter mailed from Romania: "Do not let yourself be maneuvered . . . into political matters that rob you of precious time. Do not act in a way that shadows you personally."** The letter accused his brother-in-law of carrying on affairs, living off of food parcels sent by Ioan, and refusing to work to support his sister. It inspired Culianu to write his first article for *Lumea Liberă* (Free World), a New York-based émigré newspaper. In it he predicted the imminent fall of communism in Romania — not a staggering prediction at the time. But he predicted it would happen within "a few months at most" and said that his brother-in-law and his old university friend Andrei Pleşu would soon be ministers. Those *were* unthinkable developments in December 1989.

He also mentioned the apartment break-in to Notre Dame

* Ioan Culianu, "Umberto Eco and the Library of Alexandria, I," *Lumea Liberă*, October 20, 1990, p. 6.
** Ioan Culianu, "Scrisoare deschisă către Ungureanu Fl[orica]," *Lumea Liberă*, December 9, 1989, p. 9.

scholar John Collins. "These were not ordinary thieves," Collins recalled. "He thought someone was trying to scare him." Culianu told Greg and Michael he felt that the intruders had come to steal his work on his computer. They scoffed at the idea.

To Dorin Tudoran in Washington, he was more specific. "They were interested in my diskettes," he said. "They checked everything and yet left the academic research."

"Why don't you tell the police your suspicion?"

"The police won't believe me."

"It's worth it to put it on record."

"I didn't trust the policeman who took the report."

· · ·

Strange things had always happened to him, however, and he maintained to Hillary that the break-in was nothing more than a common inner-city incident. Once he had received a check for twenty thousand dollars from his Dutch insurance company for a minor bike accident. At a Dutch department store a clerk once emptied her register and gave him the cash. (He returned the money on both occasions.) As for his predictions, he seemed best at convincing his listeners of their accuracy. "Ioan just had what I call a Weirdness Magnet," concluded Greg Spinner.

In early December in the divination reading course, it came time for the final exam. Spinner blew it, ending up with a B+. Then it was Allocca's turn. Michael chose to practice geomancy. Carefully he drew out the lines and circles on a sheet of paper, just as Culianu had taught him. He connected the dots, then drew his circles, followed by triangles. He took the results and began again.

"You're going on a trip, and you want to know something about it," he said.

"Good," said Culianu, leaning forward.

"You want to know if it's going to be a success."

"Very good."

Allocca started the process again. He stopped this time, dead cold. "For the most part, yes, it will be a success. You may have some troubles, but it will be a good trip."

"I don't believe you. You're right on everything but the outcome." Allocca got an A.

The night of the final exam, Culianu and the two students went out for dinner at the Thai Twin on Fifty-third Street. Culianu told them he was growing more worried about his sister and brother-in-law's situation. "Ioan, why don't you bring the petition to the Christmas party at Stephanie's?" they suggested. "You'll get tons more signatures."

He reluctantly agreed to take a break from his packing and preparation to teach again in Italy. On December 18, 1989, Culianu attended Stephanie Stamm's Christmas party in Hyde Park. He brought the petition and got his signatures, and once again he read Tarot cards for several guests. At the party Ioan told Michael and Greg to watch events in Romania. (He may well have seen news reports two days earlier that demonstrations had erupted into violence in the western city of Timișoara.) "Something is about to happen there," he said.

* * *

A few nights later, home before Christmas, Michael sat in his parents' living room in Brooklyn, eating yogurt and watching the local television news. He saw the map of Romania come up behind the news announcer's head. He lunged to flip up the volume. "Unexplained fighting in Bucharest," she said. "Airport closed . . . Ceaușescu missing . . ." Michael's breath caught.

Ioan must know a lot more than I thought, he decided.

Only when apparently chaotic structures multiply is it

possible to understand their hidden structure, the

computational "logic" that secretly organizes them.

—*I. P. Culianu and H. S. Wiesner, introduction to*

The Eliade Guide to World Religions

"REVOLUTION," CHRISTMAS 1989

The spark came in mid-December in the city of Timişoara, where a popular priest named László Tökes refused an order transferring him to a smaller parish. After allowing students to recite defiant poems in a church service, he had been harassed for months and was told to leave his hometown. A crowd formed outside his home to protest. When Tökes, obviously under pressure, appeared on his porch asking the people to disperse, the first cries of "Down with Ceauşescu!" were heard in the country.

Fueled by anger and desperation, the rebellion spread. Some army troops fired on demonstrators, but with notable exceptions and little conviction, and within a few days rebels held most of Timişoara. Ceauşescu ordered his more loyal Securitate forces to massacre the rioters — not all of them, just enough to send a message. He then made the blunder of his life. He left the country for two days on a previously scheduled trip to Tehran.

By the time he returned he faced a spreading national uprising, stoked by courage and army ambivalence about shedding blood to save an unpopular dictator. Too late to engage in his usual tactics of subversion, Ceauşescu arranged a "spontaneous" celebration of support on December 21, 1989, outside the stone balcony at his official office in Bucharest. Accounts differ as to how the trouble began. Some said an accidentally toppled lamppost caused a woman in the crowd to scream, spreading cries that Securitate was shooting at them. Others concluded that the shouts of opposition were arranged by a faction within Securitate that wanted to oust Ceauşescu. Instead of cheers, people began yelling "Remember Timişoara!" and "Down with the Tyrant!" If the first shouts were heroic and genuine, Culianu later wrote in his short story "Free Jormania," the sudden appearance of anti-Ceauşescu placards and the switching of stereo speakers, normally used to augment the crowd's cheers, to augment their jeers seemed as planned as the speech itself. No one disagrees that the most unforgettable image of the revolution remains the stunned, wooden smile on Ceauşescu's face as he waved at a crowd turning angrily against him. His wife, Elena, finally pulled him back from the balcony. They fled to the building's roof, barely escaping by helicopter the rushing crowd.

In living rooms across the nation, the television screens went blank for three minutes. A producer quickly put on some patriotic music, but the damage was done. The dictator had been proved vulnerable. With a furious populace, the examples of the overthrows of other East European dictators, and a group of insider opponents, history's first televised revolution began.

At the Culianu home in Iaşi on December 22 no one knew about the events in Bucharest, except what little could be gleaned from the radio. Around ten in the morning, Tess Petrescu heard someone pound on the front door. Two guards, holding paper bags as if about to deliver groceries, ordered her to leave. She refused. They reached into the bags. She felt a terrible sensation, like seasickness, convinced they were going to die.

Then she and her husband heard a noise outside the house unlike anything they had ever heard before. It was a dull rumble, like a fight in a bar. A raggedy crowd marched to the house, chanting, "Ceauşescu is gone, free Dan Petrescu!" The Ceauşescus, the crowd shouted, had fled.

Their would-be assassins disappeared into the crowd as Dan Petrescu emerged in his sandals and baggy pants to be swept up into the city mayor's office and, one week later, into a post as vice minister of culture in the new government. All around them, the country erupted in joyous violence.

＊　＊　＊

Much of what followed echoed Ioan Culianu's fictional account written in 1986. Ceauşescu's defense minister committed "suicide" after being accused of arranging the "provocations" around the country. Protests grew. The dictator and his wife were caught and hastily brought before an Ionesco-like tribunal set up by several men, including a general, Victor Stănculescu, and a bearded "occultist," Gelu Voiculescu. Aside from the accused, the attorneys, and three judges, "Stănculescu, Voiculescu, and their aides were the only independent witnesses to the alleged trial," noted Edward Behr in his book *Kiss the Hand You Cannot Bite*. In a series of articles in the newspaper *Dimineaţă*, Stănculescu and Voiculescu claimed that the trial's hasty ending in execution (in less than an hour) was motivated by the participants' fear of pro-Ceauşescu forces massing around the country. Yet the brutality and similarity to a Stalinesque show trial was condemned by other countries' leaders and news media. Around the country, people marched, demonstrated, fought, or simply bore witness to the increasingly surreal events. Many innocent victims died in battles between factions within Securitate and army forces around the television station, the Communist Central Committee headquarters, and elsewhere, although the station and the CC building themselves were never damaged, much as Culianu's story had outlined.

Inside the old Communist Party headquarters on December 22,

another strange meeting was preserved on videotape by a student
angered to find high officials plotting a new government. Among
the group, as Culianu's story predicted, were former Communist
ministers like Ion Iliescu and the newly named defense minister,
General Nicolae Militaru. No one selected them as leaders or gave
them the right to pick a cabinet, but the videotape picks up *after*
the point when their leadership was settled. (It was reported that
a faction of Securitate refused to assist the rebellion unless the
new government featured old faces.) The group is seeking a name:
"Hey, guys, the National Salvation Front has been in action for six
months, man!" Militaru blurts out in a now-famous quote that opponents claim proved the revolution was mainly a coup.

No other East European overthrow happened so swiftly, killed so
many, or remained so shrouded in swirling rumors. The new leaders
blamed Middle Eastern terrorists for the killings, but no evidence
ever backed that claim. On the contrary, Securitate officials developed the macabre idea to spread corpses from a nearby morgue
around the main square in Timişoara to make it appear as if there
had been *more* fighting than actually took place. The official number
killed — a proof of the fierce fighting between "terrorists" and revo-
lutionaries — mysteriously sank from 60,000 to a total of 996. What
began as a genuine popular uprising seemed to be quickly co-opted
by a faction of Securitate, who decided that Ceauşescu's was the
losing side in this battle.

* * *

At Christmas at the Hertzfeld house in Amherst, Massachusetts,
lights blazed all night as Ioan Culianu sat glued to CNN, calling
friends in Paris, and hastily arranging two BBC broadcasts by telephone to his homeland. He tried to reach his mother in Iaşi, but the
telephones were dead. Racing from room to room, he excitedly
reported news to Dorothy and Kurt Hertzfeld, calling Hillary and
Nikki in to watch television. He made the V for Victory sign, a habit
he kept until his death. "For once," he cried, "I am proud to be
Romanian!"

Despite his joy he remained skeptical of the television images.
"He was excited," recalled Nikki Wiesner, "but he said that some-

one was behind the events, and that what followed might be no improvement on the old."

＊　＊　＊

The Ceauşescus were held for two days before the new government announced their capture; they were dead twenty-four hours before the new government announced their "execution." No one knew exactly what went on inside that "courtroom," even though a partial videotape was shown on Romanian television on Christmas Day 1989. On the tape one could hear the judges' voices but could not see their faces. The complete tapes of the Ceauşescus' "trial" were only released months later, in April 1990, to the French media. Only then did viewers learn who the judges were. At one point on the tape an unseen questioner asks, "Do you know who is holding you?"

"Yes," answers Ceauşescu. "Securitate."

The Ceauşescus' killings occurred not by army firing squad, as announced, but by a single bullet to the back of the head. Based on interviews with other members of the military tribunal, the killers appear to have included "Virgil Magureanu, a philosophy professor at the Securitate Academy, and Gelu Voican-Voiculescu, a geologist and amateur astrologer," wrote Andrei Codrescu.* Eventually Voican-Voiculescu himself told the newspaper *Dimineaţă:* "It was my idea to kill the Ceauşescus. Iliescu called it abominable."** Regardless of whose idea or act the Ceauşescus' murder was, it was clear there was no real trial. Just as the early Communists undermined their credibility by executing Ion Antonescu, so too the early post-Communists in 1989 managed to derail a genuine uprising by hastily concluding what Culianu called a forgery of a trial.

The library of the University of Bucharest mysteriously burned in what appeared a diversion from pitched battles inside the Communist Party headquarters. After Iliescu nominated himself president, his first official act was to call the Soviet embassy. He promised elections but postponed them, and promised and then rescinded reformist laws like preventing Communist Party members from en-

---

* Andrei Codrescu, *The Hole in the Flag* (New York: William Morrow, 1991, p. 47).
** *Dimineaţă*, May 4, 1990.

gaging in politics, assuring restitution for all properties taken under the Communist regimes, and opening secret police files. The uncertainty caused more demonstrations and riots over the next eighteen months, as Culianu's story predicted. In the end, observed former Radio Free Europe director Nestor Ratesh, the events left "the striking paradox of a basically anti-Communist revolution producing a regime dominated by former Communists."

❋   ❋   ❋

In January 1990 Ioan Culianu moved into a new apartment in a high-security, high-rise building at 1700 East Fifty-sixth Street in Chicago. His apartment was a clean, white two-room studio on the ninth floor, lit by glorious sunlight reflected off Lake Michigan. He decorated the walls with a print of his beloved *Primavera*, M. C. Escher and Victor Vasarely optical illusion prints, his pictures of Hillary, and a four-foot-tall wooden medieval crucifix painted in Assisi. He divided the small rooms with tall black and gold Chinese screens and placed his white leather couch against a picture window. Most important to him, the building featured a twenty-four-hour doorman, a security alarm, and steel, locked front doors. "He was really excited because it was a high-security building," said Greg Spinner.

Culianu shared a special friendship with Frances Gamwell, wife of the Divinity School dean Chris Gamwell, and over lunch every six weeks or so he told her about his new projects and concerns about his homeland. She talked to him of her work at the Native American Educational Services College and as a consultant to nonprofit self-help groups based in Chicago. Unknown to her, he quietly contributed large amounts of money to the groups she described. Black, outspoken, and fiercely independent of the stiff academic world of Hyde Park, she found in Culianu a kindred spirit. Early in 1990 he told her that his brother-in-law was wrong to participate in the new Romanian government, which was riddled with the worst elements of the old.

Culianu launched his new international scholarly journal, called *Incognita: International Journal for Cognitive Studies in the Humanities*, taking the title from a beautiful Romanian novel. He asked Nathaniel Deutsch to be the journal's assistant editor and named his secretary, Gwen Barnes, managing editor. At the inaugural reception he told his friends and students: "This journal offers the sum of what I don't know. And so it will run for many issues." The introduction to the inaugural issue explained the journal's philosophy: "History is a sequential interaction of systems which show three characteristics: They derive from a basic set of logical rules. They exist in their own dimension which is not the dimension of history, and they are activated by human minds in an unpredictable sequence." Umberto Eco and Lawrence Sullivan served on the journal's editorial board.

Seeking to unite the "cognitive revolution in science" with the study of the humanities, the journal was "out there on the fringe of scholarship," said one colleague, but was also "something truly exciting in intellectual life." It was yet another activity for a scholar with three books under contract, demonstrating Culianu's ambition to rise above scholarship and influence the world — with books, student followers, and now an international journal dedicated to his new theories.

* * *

In January 1990 the chaos at home prompted Culianu to publish two pieces in the New York émigré newspaper *Lumea Liberă*. The first, "Viitorul României in 11 puncte," outlined the future of Romania in eleven points. It called for removing the secret police, instituting an independent judiciary, privatizing television, and fully recognizing all ethnic minorities as prerequisites to becoming a democratic state. As his countrymen debated which models to follow in reshaping their national institutions (much as his great-grandfather and other Junimea Society members had done more than a century earlier), he stressed American-style democracy: unleashing an aggressive free television and press and a free judiciary. Most of the measures were never adopted.

Culianu also published an open letter he had drafted a month before the revolution at the request of the BBC. In a postscript he challenged his friend Andrei Pleşu and his brother-in-law to resign if the new government did not move swiftly toward real freedom (Petrescu resigned two months later; Pleşu was ousted in a coup eighteen months later). Suggesting that the people "are not as free as the government says," he urged his countrymen to seize and shape their

destiny. He raised disturbing questions about their national character, mixing religious imagery with a condemnation of the recent
past: "Why did we accept so much suffering without saying anything? Why did we permit ourselves to be robbed more than other
people in the world, by a dictator both mediocre and mad? Why
have we merited to be the shame of the world . . . ? This stain is more
difficult to remove than that of original sin." Published on January 27, the piece ranked Culianu as one of the first writers to accuse
the new government of engineering a coup. (Others voiced the same
accusation, but in more muted and garbled terms.) He was the only
writer to mix religious imagery and sweeping condemnation with
that particular insight in his political attacks.

One day later, on January 28, 1990, thousands of miners from the
Jiu Valley arrived by train in Bucharest to assault supporters of opposition parties protesting the slow pace and outright reversal of
many reformist laws. The first of several Securitate-inspired assaults
on its own people brought a sudden halt to talks of reform and
democracy in the country.

This was the great error of our generation,

that . . . we remained outside of political life.

— Mircea Eliade

FREE WORLD, 1990

Early in January, Hillary Wiesner escaped with her sister, Nikki, for a Caribbean trip. They visited Pine Cay in the Turks and Caicos Islands, while at home Hillary's fiancé could not put politics out of his mind. Culianu argued by phone with his sister in Bucharest, calling her naive to think that real democracy was taking shape or that "miners" had acted without provocation. Tess agreed but was too excited to pay him much attention. She, Dan, and their friends were tasting freedom for the first time, staying up all night smoking cigarettes and plotting the future. She urged her brother to return. He declined. He mentioned to her the break-in at his Chicago apartment the previous November, joking about it.

While Romania prepared for its first free parliamentary and presidential elections, miners again attacked demonstrators, newspaper publishers, and opposition party offices on February 18. The government claimed it suspected a coup d'état was about to occur, yet it never named any conspirators or summoned legitimate law enforcement forces.

Ioan Culianu and Hillary Wiesner left for another trip to Italy in February. Grazia Marchianò had arranged for him a three-month contract as visiting professor in the Faculty of Education at the University of Siena, running from March 1 to June 1. He gave lectures on subjects ranging from medieval dualism to myth analysis at the Universities of Siena-Arezzo, Salerno, and Rome. In Italy he was well known; *La Repubblica* called him one of the "maestri del pensiero contemporaneo."

In Italy, Culianu spoke out on Romania and the revolution in the mainstream press, penning an article as early as February 8 for *Panorama*, an Italian news magazine, titled "The King Is Dead. Watch Out for an Heir." Noting that "all events that happen in our poor country are the repetition of some archetypes embedded in our religious history," he analyzed the famous videotape in which the new self-proclaimed leaders tried to come up with a name for their party: "Umberto Eco says that everything depends on what use one makes of symbols. The case of Romania shows that he is right. No sooner had the people forced the bloody dictator to leave the presidential palace than the government that was formed took the name National Salvation Front. They couldn't have chosen a less fortunate label: the name calls to mind a comparison with the fascist National Renascence Front, which was the sole party created by King Carol II in 1938 after he dissolved parliament and proclaimed himself dictator."

Despairing of Romania's fondness for dictators, the article examined the dangers in the "confusion of symbols" represented by the resurgence of Iron Guard symbolism (several new far rightist parties had appropriated Iron Guard rhetoric). Culianu planned to develop a study of the misuse of mystic symbols in a book to be

. . . . . .

coauthored with University of Maryland political scientist Vladimir Tismaneanu.

His prognosis was bleak even at a time when his brother-in-law served as national vice minister of culture. "With a few notable exceptions," he wrote, "Romania has absolutely no intellectual elite who could truly ensure a transition toward a pluralist, normal future. Without the determination to come out of its isolation, Romania will not be able to keep from falling into an abyss even deeper than that from which it has just emerged."

Culianu appeared to be correct. On March 2, 1990, the unedited three-hour videotape of the Ceauşescus' trial was released to French and Romanian television for a profit. On the same day Georgică Popa, the trial's chief judge, committed suicide in Bucharest. This added to a growing list of "suicides" of key figures from the revolution—beginning with one of Ceauşescu's chief generals and followed by that of the dictator's brother, Marin, found hanging in his apartment in Vienna, his private safe cleared out.

●　●　●

Demonstrators now gathered regularly in University Square in Bucharest and elsewhere, demanding an independent television channel, free elections, and the president's resignation. Several far rightist parties sprang up. Of these, the two most important were the Party of Romanian National Unity (PUNR) and Vatra Românească. Serving as the main media outlet of this mix of national communism and the far right was a retooled version of a vicious Communist newspaper, Săptămîna (Weekend), now called România Mare (Greater Romania). One of Ceauşescu's chief propagandists, Corneliu Vadim Tudor, served as the newspaper's editor, making free and frequent use of Securitate files to discredit his opponents.

Vatra Românească, by contrast, declared itself a "cultural movement" politics. Culianu's old teacher Ion Coja served as its "chief ideologue," in the words of political scientist Vladimir Tişmaneanu. According to Coja, "the popularity of Vatra spread like wildfire" after it attacked the Hungarian minority's demands for further development of native language education. In mid-March, however, the cultural movement became embroiled in shady ethnic riots in the city of Tîrgu Mureş, in which armed thugs fomented the sizable Hungarian minority marking a national celebration. The government supported the vigilantes who arrived in trucks to quell the "demonstrators" with the same clubs, pitchforks, and crowbars "used against the demonstrators of Bucharest," observed Andrei Codrescu. Many of the attackers were drunk. The incident led Dan Petrescu to begin writing articles against his own government. As for Vatra Românească, a former Securitate colonel quoted by Norman Manea characterized it as "for all intents and purposes an arm of Securitate."

As early as January 1990 the deputy prime minister, Gelu Voican-Voiculescu, had been placed in charge of a provisional intelligence service. He claimed he had sought to organize the institution into separate departments independent of the influence of Securitate. The Tîrgu Mureş riots, however, provided a pretext for instituting a new security service, under the Defense Ministry, with wide wire-tapping and harassment protections. Securitate was reorganized as the more benign sounding Romanian Information Service (SRI) under the leadership of Virgil Magureanu. Significantly, according to *Jane's Intelligence Review* (January 1995), the reorganization was done secretly, by a presidential decree that was never announced in the government's official bulletin. According to its own reports, it re-enlisted some 6,000 of the hated former institution. It retained its external service or DIE almost completely intact, according to Ion Mihai Pacepa, under the leadership of a master spy of the Ceauşescu regime, Mihai Caraman, who had particularly close ties to the former KGB. As *Nation* reporter Paul Hockenos observed of the fomented riots and government response: "Securitate was back, its plot a grand success."

In Romania in April 1990, after Dan Petrescu began attacking his government, *România Mare* resurrected a story of Petrescu's conviction for rape when he was a high school teacher in Iaşi. Years earlier, Petrescu had been tried and convicted under Ceauşescu's judicial system for a crime that never occurred. In a sequence of events that seemed to come straight out of Abbott's *Flatland*, Petrescu was forced to resign.

Later that month, on April 24, a large crowd of demonstrators in Bucharest marched on the television station. Attacked by police

wielding iron clubs, they retreated to University Square and declared it a "neo-Communist free zone." The demonstrations continued during the next thirty days as the country prepared for national elections. In May the ruling National Salvation Front won
these first "free" elections in the country by an 85 percent margin,
amid charges of widespread harassment, violence, and extensive vot-
ing fraud. The clearly rigged election caused the United States to
withdraw its ambassador.

＊　＊　＊

Ioan spent Easter in London and Canterbury with Hillary, giving
seven BBC broadcasts on world religion directed into Romania. He
spoke at Trinity College in Dublin, at the School of Hebrew and
Biblical and Theological Studies, giving lectures entitled "Religion
between Spiritualism and Quantum Physics" and "Religion as a
System." He was by then well established as a leading international
scholar.

Returning to Italy, Wiesner and Culianu remained until June,
enjoying the sun, the warmth, and the pleasurable company of Marchianò and Zolla. They toured the Italian countryside, tasting the
wine and food of Umbria and spending summer mornings in long
discussions on the veranda of their second apartment. Culianu went
on another whirlwind lecture tour, delivering on May 3 a lecture
titled "Medieval Dualistic Trends" at the University of Salerno, on
May 4 a lecture on fantasy at the Instituto Suor Orsola Benincasa in
Naples, and another on Elemire Zolla's work.

In the Italian newsweekly *Panorama*, in June 1990, Culianu wrote
about the manipulation of his brother-in-law's removal and criticized a government increasingly controlled by old Communists.
He began to receive threats in Italy, but he kept them mostly hidden
from his hosts, mentioning his telephone calls only to Hillary. He
was the subject of a written attack as well, and slowly old fears of
political reprisal came back to him.

He and Wiesner turned to fiction again to understand the multiple realities of past events as they reverberate in the present. The
story they cowrote, called "The Late Repentance of Horemheb,"
was first published in the Massachusetts quarterly called the *Harvard Review*. Based on a true case of archaeological forgery, the story

wove together the threads of their lives, their research, and current events.

In the story an Egyptologist named Professor Doktor Gr. finds an ancient relic to prove his new theory of ancient Egyptian culture. His opponents claim the relic is a forgery. The story's narrator counters: "Our common concept of forgery did not exist before the Renaissance, itself a time of spectacular forgeries. . . . For the first time, the Renaissance established a rigorous sequence of befores and afters. We have lived in that sequence ever since." In a plot twist similar to that of Borges's "Tlön, Uqbar, Orbis Tertius," artifacts begin turning up around the world that confirm the relic as "authentic." Some scholars attribute the new artifacts, however, to Gr. himself, who eventually escapes the mounting suspicions and professional inquiries when he "forge[s] his own suicide by dying in a car accident."

Following Gr.'s research and mysterious fate in obscure academic journals, the story's narrator wonders if the past is still "happening." He mentions such hoaxes as the Malayan Senoi tribe's alleged sophisticated dream interpretations (Michael Allocca showed him research that proved them to be an anthropologist's hoax of the 1930s). The narrator becomes more and more curious, reasoning that Gr. himself may have unwittingly been "manipulated by a plot played out by the past in order to change itself." By the end the narrator speculates that there are alternate universes or dimensions in which history's victims are all victors and the powerful are all victims. He feels increasingly frightened, sensing in his own curiosity an "insidious conspiracy of the past using me for its shadowy purpose, purposes which will continue shifting forever after my illusory disappearance."

❋   ❋   ❋

In June, Culianu returned to Massachusetts with Wiesner to put the finishing touches on *The Eliade Guide to World Religions* for HarperSanFrancisco and *The Tree of Gnosis* for HarperCollins. He was also working on *Other Realms: Other-worldly Journeys from Gilgamesh to Albert Einstein,* based on his courses on the fourth dimension and shamanism. Ioan and Hillary split time between her apartment in Cambridge and the roomy, comfortable Victorian house of her mother and stepfather in Amherst. The former home of Robert Frost, the house had winding wooden hallways and bedrooms that were said to be haunted.

From Washington, Dorin Tudoran encouraged Culianu to contribute regularly to the émigré newspaper *Lumea Liberă*. It was their moment in history, he said, and Romania needed Culianu's perspective if it was to progress rather than spiral backward into the same old conflicts and dangers. Culianu balked.

"It's not the right place for you and me," he said, referring to the newspaper's small circulation.

Yet Culianu published an article in *Lumea Liberă* entitled "O lecție de politică," or "A Lecture in Politics," that explored the challenge posed by current events for exiles like him. It was a review of Andrei Codrescu's book *The Disappearance of the Outside*, in which Codrescu wrote: "The myth of exile was imbedded archetypally in our culture." Culianu explored Codrescu's idea that Romanians were forced to develop an exquisitely rendered and hidden "inside" or inner self, like Blaga's "mioritic space." Codrescu elaborated on the pleasure of the tactic and of the consequences of its loss in the West, where outside and inside disappeared. The trouble was, now that the time came to take charge of their country's destiny, the tactics of subversion became a hindrance rather than a help. To Culianu, Codrescu's words struck deep. "I have lived this experience," he wrote in *Lumea Liberă*.

❋   ❋   ❋

As Culianu explored hidden logics in history, events indeed seemed to spiral backward in his home country. In 1990 "the most crucial obstacle [to democracy] was a crisis in the relation between state and society," suggested the scholars Katherine Verdery and Gail Kligman. "The organs of governance were disrupted by infighting and power struggles, while the populace showed itself to be relatively ungovernable."*

As new institutions like a free press fought for fundamental freedoms, Verdery, Kligman, and others downplayed the notion of a

---

* Katherine Verdery and Gail Kligman, "Romania after Ceaușescu: Post-Communist Communism?" in *Eastern Europe in Revolution*, edited by Ivo Banac (Ithaca, N.Y.: Cornell University Press, 1992), 142.

single controller of the harassment, corruption, and violence. Power struggles continued; no one single force seemed to be in control. Yet to Culianu and many other observers, the former Securitate continued to manipulate events through its influence over the single official television station, pro-government newspapers (opposition journals coped with paper shortages from the country's one supplier), the instigation of the Tîrgu Mureş riots, telephone and mail monitoring, and disinformation. Mario Possamai, in his book *Money on the Run: Canada and How the World's Dirty Profits Are Laundered,* noted of the country: "Phones continue to be tapped, informers recruited, and opponents of the regime threatened and (in some cases) beaten." Reports in publications ranging from *România Liberă* to *Harper's* detailed renewed Securitate intimidation at home and abroad. The French émigré newspaper *Lupta* quoted a former Securitate general bragging that no one "would ever find out what we are doing." In one humorous example of security police activity, the outspoken scholar Vladimir Tismaneanu told of attending a conference in Cluj in 1992. At three in the morning he and his roommate were awakened by their private hotel room conversations being played back loudly at them from a room below.

Culianu saw events following a pattern — but at a deeper level than the players knew. He told Gwen Barnes that those in power were simply carrying on what Ceauşescu would have wanted. He told Hillary Wiesner that the country was sliding into an archetypal situation similar to that of a Central American country, ruled by a corrupt and vicious oligarchy. He told his students that there had been no revolution, only a flexible reaction to changing world events. He saw much more going on as well, but he could uncover these trends only by writing about them.

In a foggy, chilled dawn on June 13, 1990, in Bucharest, the young university demonstrators were about to disperse in disgust. Suddenly thousands of miners and agents attacked them, killing many and destroying the headquarters of the two main opposition parties over the following two days. The hero of the student protests, a bearded, ascetic young man named Marian Munteanu, was beaten, flayed, and then arrested in his hospital bed. When the President thanked the so-called miners "with all my heart" and castigated the protesters in the language of the old Communist regime, calling the students fascists and *golani*, or "hooligans," an international uproar rose.

The uproar included critical articles and editorials in the *New Yorker*, *Newsweek*, *Time*, the *New York Times*, *Washington Post*, *Stern*, *Paris-Match*, and many other leading European publications. The miner's riots seemed to prove once and for all the widespread allegations of a coup in Romania. Why would *miners* care if students demonstrated peacefully at a university hundreds of miles from them? reporters asked. If a legitimate government wanted to act, why would it not use police or the army? If there was nothing to the protesters' accusations, then why attack in the first place? These questions led to other never-answered queries about the revolution: Why were so many young people killed? Who killed them? Who selected Ion Iliescu in the first place? The uproar was devastating to a government desperate for infusions of foreign cash and legitimacy.

In addition to the international uproar, the miners' attack incited Ioan Culianu's "latent explosion," to use author Norman Manea's term for the belated political engagement of the Romanian intellectual exile. The country had one, just this one, chance to join other civilized nations, Culianu realized. Thus far the native opposition at home had been outspent and outmaneuvered. He needed to talk directly to others who understood the world outside of Romania. Banding together, with their know-how, they were the *only* ones who could help support a truly effective opposition.

* * *

First he authored a short story, "Free Jormania," that appeared in Dorin Tudoran's widely circulated magazine *Agora* in July 1990. Using the same characters as in "The Intervention of the Zorabis in Jormania," the story plays on fiction and fact, text and review. It offers a former Securitate colonel named Boba, forced into retirement abroad, publishing a book on the revolution and receiving his first review.* In Jormania, the reviewer recalled from Culianu's 1986 story, most names end in *-an*, just as many of the key insiders of the revolution had names that ended in *-an*.

---

* Ceaușescu's key aide was named Bobu. In the presidential couple's hurried flight from Bucharest by helicopter, Bobu ended up sitting on Ceaușescu's lap.

Boba's book called the revolution a coup, complete with corpses exhumed to simulate battle deaths and prepared placards at the Ceauşescu speech. A guiding hand behind the rebellion in the Soviet Union and the KGB engineered the events. Boba also furnished "the name of the colonel who drew up the plan, as well as a list of his Jormanian participants." Of the new leaders, whose identities were only revealed by the release of the videotape of the dictator's monkey court, "Boba suggested that all eleven of the initial government knew they were supported by Maculburg [Russia], but they did not know the details of the plan. Today, however, those who have not died tragically in confrontation with the masses — and there are just three of them left — know exactly from whom and through whom they received orders." Criticizing the resurgence of the rightist "Wooden Guard" as a convenient cover for old communists, the reviewer tells of Boba's comfortable retirement in the United States with his share of the Ceauşescu fortune (moneys earned by illegal Securitate activities and deposited in Swiss banks) and a lifetime subscription to *Penthouse*. As with Borges's fantasy stories, the reader of Culianu's story feels caught in a loop of "history" and memory that leaves the impression the author knows more than he is saying. "If Boba's hypothesis is correct," the reviewer concludes, "it means that the people were pulled by a string. . . . But isn't this the essential function of the people?"

Months later in Romania, several key conspirators in the National Salvation Front *were* forced into retirement. Nicolae Militaru and Dumitru Mazilu claimed that conspirators had used the spontaneous uprising to engineer a long-planned coup. Former key figures like Silviu Brucan and Mazilu began working on their own books, like Culianu's Boba. Several other real-life government officials seem to have been hinted at in Culianu's fiction. Suggesting insider officials from the revolution were disappearing one by one, the story seems to hint prophetically of events that followed its writing.

At least one key figure in the government, deputy prime minister Gelu Voican,* had taken a keen interest in Culianu's writings for years. "I met Nene Culianu in 1972 when he was finishing his

---

* Voican-Voiculescu was the deputy prime minister's full name as it appeared in civil documents. Socially, he used the shortened name Voican.

· · · · · ·

studies in Bucharest," Voican recalled. Then an editor at the historic literary quarterly *Viata Romania* (Romanian life), Voican accepted Culianu's early submissions and, years later, followed his internationally published work on Eliade. "He was more than a friend or fellow writer," Voican said of their common interest in secret societies. "He was a soulmate." In the tumultuous months of 1990, Voican regretted that his government role, first as security police commander and later as deputy prime minister, forced him to abandon the pursuits of the intellectual to do "things I did not want to do."*

   As Romania lurched toward further violence, Culianu talked with the editors of *Lumea Liberă* about writing a regular column for them. They were delighted.

* Personal interview, by telephone, April 5, 1996.

An ancient Greek term used by Freud for voyeurism,

but which literally means "the pleasure of seeing."

—*I. P. Culianu*, Lumea Liberă

. . . .

SCOPTOPHILIA

Published out of a basement on Alderton Avenue in Queens, the Romanian weekly *Lumea Liberă*, or *Free World,* was in 1990 a leading émigré publication with a circulation of ten thousand. The revolution thrust the newspaper into the world's spotlight, attracting prominent contributors. As one of the best independent sources for news of Romania during 1990 and 1991, *Lumea Liberă* had an influence well beyond its circulation numbers.

Culianu's twenty-seven weekly columns for the paper, entitled

"Scoptophilia," ran for one half of a year, ending on the first anniversary of the revolution. They were parables and arguments drawing on all of his systematic thought, the imagery of Orthodox religion, the unconscious and Renaissance magic, even his distance from Romania, to focus on the forces behind events. Each column was a call for action comparable to rants in today's underground press, or the pamphleteering of Thomas Paine or Giordano Bruno. Culianu's style was "complex, nonlinear, subtle," argued one friend, Mircea Sabau of the University of Chicago. "You must put the pieces together. Then they're devastating." Mac Linscott Ricketts noted their similarity to Eliade's 1930s journalism, finding the style "truly remarkable . . . a mixture of bitter hatred and dark humor." One could not catch Culianu's full meaning on one reading, or by sifting only a few articles.

The series began humorously with "Filme de groază" ("Horror Films"), an article comparing the security police to medieval gargoyles and movie monsters. In Hollywood stories end happily, Culianu wrote: "But in Romania there are so few real humans and those few so vulnerable, that they find themselves easily exterminated. Their only solution is to find each other and organize together. But more important, they must give up their fear."

The first thirteen weeks featured his most blistering attacks on Securitate, including a two-part series called "Dialogue of the Dead." These two pieces used Plato's and Giordano Bruno's form of a dialogue between two opposing viewpoints to reveal a new insight. Like Bruno, who wrote his biting satires in the vernacular Italian, Culianu wrote in a vicious, imagistic Romanian. In "Dialogue of the Dead, Part I," President Iliescu awards Ceauşescu's ghost a "Hero of the Revolution diploma" because his legacy made possible the new government's success. Observing that Ceauşescu's corpse has "a bullet wound where no hole ought to be (in the temple)," the article underscores the dictator's assassination rather than lawful execution. When Iliescu reports that he won the elections, Ceauşescu replies: "I hope you stuffed all the ballot boxes!"

". . . We didn't have to! At the most 30%, maybe 35% . . . but even so, the result was overwhelming; everyone voted for us!"

Iliescu explains that the true subjugation had occurred in the people's *minds*. The miners' attacks demonstrated Ceauşescu was right: the *people* did not want liberty. "The Securitate was there — I don't deny it," Iliescu says, "but under 20%, or perhaps 30%, or maybe even 40%. . . . But at least 60% were miners" who feared disorder and welcomed the government's granting of a rise in wages. The real "genius" of the Ceaușescu regime lay, not in tapping telephones and imprisoning opponents, but in its psychological "bonds," or *vinculi*, that Giordano Bruno had examined five hundred years earlier.

Over the following weeks Culianu discussed themes he had explored his whole life, according to his University of Chicago colleague Mircea Sabau: "How can one find truth? How can one separate good from evil" in a world in which the two come linked so closely? In a column called "The Fourth of July," he told of a chilling dream he had experienced, observing that "dreams always have communicated meanings deeper than those of a waking state."

In the dream he returns home, finding most people in abject poverty, many of them dressed as miners or as police. A friend takes him to the Orthodox church headquarters, to a darkened basement. They meet three "priest-miners" in black robes. The head priest-miner wears a helmet with three lamps arranged vertically; the lesser priests have two lamps or one. The head priest welcomes him, observing that Culianu was a disciple of Eliade, of whom "we think very highly." He wants to offer Culianu the directorship of an institute but faces "objections." Would he consider a token expression of support for them? That night they see only miners on television, intoning against "foreigners who come to rob the country" and invoking "God and the ancestral soil." His friend suggests that he make a public statement holding a miner's lamp in his hand as "a symbol of light."

With its funny, subterranean religious setting, the story evokes the labyrinth of the unconscious. It also helps explain why Culianu kept delaying each time his sister asked him to come home: he saw return as symbolic support of the new government.

Around that time in Cambridge, one night after poring through stacks of notes and articles kept by Eliade and Culianu in preparation for their *Dictionnaire des religions*, Hillary Wiesner dreamed of Mircea Eliade. He was walking toward her, she told Ioan the next morning, holding up his hand in a conciliatory gesture. "He was

· · · · · ·

checking you," Culianu said, "and you were sensitive enough to feel it. He was telling you he was all right, that he was not a bad person. He was not a member of the Iron Guard."

Culianu produced another harsh, two-part series, "Cea mai pro- astă inteligenţă," or "The Most Stupid Intelligence." Satirizing the cultural movement called protochronism, which in the 1980s sought to prove that a variety of important intellectual innova- tions had begun in Romania, Culianu acknowledged one manner in which the small country did lead the world: "It can be stated with- out hesitation: Romania holds first place with respect to the stu- pidity of its intelligence service." He claimed that Securitate con- tinued to manipulate events even after the revolution: "It is clear that under Iliescu, the Securitate feels justified in leading the coun- try on, knowing that it alone played a first-rank role in the over- throw of Ceauşescu."

Using phrases like "brainwashed idiots," "diabolical cretins," and "most imbecilic intelligence service," the article asserted that the result was the hold up of "billions of dollars [in aid], indescribable misery, hunger, cold, and AIDS . . . and a deep shame before the whole world." He advocated setting "fire to the whole Ceauşescu heritage" and beginning to rebuild from zero. "Now, obviously, what is being done is exactly the opposite," he observed. The same bureaucrats who led the Ceauşescu terror now led Romania to an "imminent catastrophic bankruptcy." Most of all he lamented the fact that, though Securitate "retouched" the election results, it ap- peared the people desired old faces.

He took up the future more hopefully in the next week's column, "Dialogue of the Dead, Part II." It described a near-death experi- ence of a girl beaten by miners but saved by a doctor who showed that many in the country are "still normal and good." In her vision, God tells her that the Romanian Orthodox church has allied with his "enemy," untruth: "Evil, Stupidity, and Falsehood — the pro- tochronist trinity that defends the active trinity formed of the Se- curitate, Miners, and Government — are not eternal! They are vul- nerable. You struggle for Truth and are fed up with tyranny and useless victims, with the terror of the Securitate and its tortuous, dark maneuvers, with the blood continually being spilled by it, with its obscure lying power . . . unite! Unite in a minimal program calling for the purification of the governmental leaders and punishment by bullets for liars."

* * *

One hot summer day in her apartment on Harvard Street, Wiesner handed Culianu a letter addressed in Romanian and forwarded from *Lumea Liberă*. He opened and read it. He threw it away, saying nothing to her. Another letter came the following week. This one he simply threw away. "Aren't you going to open it?" she asked him. He shook his head. It was simply one of many events in a busy time, and he did not want to worry her with the responses to his articles. She did not press the issue.

A few nights later they went to see Gérard Depardieu in *Cyrano de Bergerac*. At the end, she noticed Ioan was crying. "What's the matter?" He laughed, embarrassed. But she felt that "in his own mind he *was* Cyrano, on a secret ideal quest to avenge his father and the past in his writing."

He responded to the written threats in another column. President Ion Ilisecu had voiced an oft-used accusation that exiles who had left the homeland in time of trouble had no right to criticize it now. The tactic turned the strength of voluntary exiles, their knowledge of Western ways, into a liability — their "sellout" to foreign powers. Noting that he had discovered one thing in exile, "that it is possible to live normally and well . . . without imbeciles who plan for a dead economy," Culianu wrote back: "You gave me nothing but suffering, misery, stupidity, and pain. You stole twenty years of my life. . . . I pretended for too long that I did not hear you. Now is the time when you must hear me. And I'm going to speak whether you like it or not, often and louder."

* * *

For their vacation Ioan and Hillary spent a week on the beach near Ogunquit, Maine. He preferred big modern impersonal hotels, having had his fill of dirty European *pensions*. They walked on the rocky beaches, enjoying a fog that obliterated all sensation except the sea smell and the sound of the wind in the pines. He loved the hotel ice machines. Evenings they headed to the wooden shacks that served up fresh lobsters, salted in seawater and drenched in butter on paper plates.

When they came back to Boston he found more letters forwarded by *Lumea Liberă*. He called his friend Dorin Tudoran. "The letters were similar to those I received," Tudoran said, "from a group claiming to be the Sons of Avram Iancu." Hatchets, large knives, and dripping blood decorated the page, which promised: "Our arms will hit those who accept wages to profane their nation, and we will put them to sleep in disgrace forever." Securitate often invented fascist groups to threaten exiles, and German journalist Richard Wagner traced "the Sons of Avram Iancu" directly to it. Iancu was a nineteenth-century Transylvanian nationalist.

Others had received the same letters in Paris and Munich, Tudoran said. "Let the police and the FBI know," Tudoran told Culianu. "The more we all report them, the more seriously each of us will be taken."

Culianu declined. "He had the magician's logic," Hillary Wiesner suggested. "He thought, 'If I ritualistically tear up and destroy these papers, the circumstances behind them will be disarmed.'"

* * *

On August 17 they celebrated Hillary's birthday in Cambridge. That summer he met a new friend, the fantasy writer John Crowley, who would invite him to speak at a coming spring conference on magic in the Chicago area. Based in Amherst, Crowley had admired Culianu's book *Eros and Magic in the Renaissance.* Author of *Little, Big,* as well as *Novelty* and *Engine Summer,* Crowley explored notions of magic, multiple universes, and time travel in critically acclaimed books.

Afterward, Culianu wrote a column for *Lumea Liberă* linking magic, cognitive studies, and politics, explaining the reasons for the clairvoyant quality of his work. He proudly cited his past predictions about the revolution and the ministry appointments of his friend Andrei Pleşu and his brother-in-law, Dan Petrescu. He did not "know" more than anyone else, he said; in fact, "after Mircea Eliade's death in 1986 my contacts with Romanians became quite sporadic." To explain his insight, he turned to complexity theory. "I had solved a chess-game problem that the KGB also had solved. The problem admitted of only one solution: the fall of Ceauşescu. The universes multiplied in such a way that a few dissidents were utilized by the computer to 'puff' the rubber puppets like Iliescu. . . . Knowing them well already, my mind foresaw, probably, that Pleşu and Petrescu would accept the new situation." He was reading events with common sense, examining possibilities and choosing the most likely outcome.

By now one could identify key differences between Culianu's writing and the accusations leveled by other opposition writers. He admitted that the Iliescu regime *had* granted fundamental freedoms; he suggested he knew more about events than he was letting on; and he wrote in a no-holds-barred style, unleashing a lifetime of hatred. The anger came with the sharper, deeper thrust of irony. No one else used such a style with such precision; no one else had his international media contacts or his standing in relation to the figure of Eliade.

In Romania Culianu's writings were not well known to the majority of people, but his stories in *Agora* and articles in *Lumea Liberă* did reach a select group of influential readers. *Lumea Liberă* attracted a great deal of interest "for two reasons," said Mircea Raceanu, the Romanian Ministry's former chief of U.S. and Canadian affairs. "First, many prominent people were now writing for it, and secondly, the accusations they leveled were correct." Culianu's most conscientious readers, taking the time to synthesize and analyze the multivalent, bitter attacks from New York, seemed to be the Romanian Information Service itself.

Culianu's last thirteen pieces in *Lumea Liberă* shifted from direct attacks to subtler indirect commentary. He wrote about Elie Wiesel, who came from a town not far from his, discussing whether an exile should "keep silent" or "shout" about injustice. The anger now was more veiled; the threats had frightened him. Still, each article managed to criticize his country's new regime. The Wiesel piece, for instance, called Romania "a prison camp with open gates from which the liberated prisoners will not exit — where the executioners of a little while ago have been consecrated as the legitimate government of their victims."

Ioan traveled to New York to see his elderly mentor Hans Jonas and to meet Cathy O'Leary at the New School for Social Research. When he returned to Chicago, he had lunch with Greg Spinner. They talked about his work, Greg's summer, and other projects. At

. . . . . .

the end Ioan mentioned, "I'm getting into some dangerous territory in my writing." Greg pressed him, but he refused to elaborate.

❋ ❋ ❋

In the fall of 1990 Culianu returned to his high rise on Lake Michigan, teaching a special course in the formation of sects, the History of Heresies in Christianity and Buddhism, and the required survey course, History of Christianity. In his last columns for *Lumea Liberă* Culianu turned to general and scholarly topics like the Inquisition, Claude Lévi-Strauss, the Cajun culture he witnessed in New Orleans, and Umberto Eco. He explored themes such as the confusion of fiction and history and murder for invented motives. At Thanksgiving he headed to New Orleans for the American Academy of Religion conference with Wiesner and Moshe Idel, where they met Andrei Codrescu. Codrescu and Culianu decided to speak in English, finding Romanian to be too filled with sad memories. At a Cajun restaurant they talked late into the night about the kindness of Eliade, who had helped both of them as young men, and about the twisted turn of events in their country.

The city moved him deeply. He called his sister in France several times from New Orleans. "It is our place in the world," he said, admiring and identifying with Cajun society for preserving its culture and language despite persecution. When he came home he wrote his most mysterious columns, "The Most Important Romanian in the World" and "A Unique Chance," detailing his experience of the Iron Guardist attacks in the late 1970s. By then he was receiving telephone threats as well as letters. The telephone threats were "incredibly dirty," he told Tudoran. They were beginning to frighten him.

There was nothing new about such harassment. He was the victim of threats that followed a pattern. In the United States, in thousands of foreign language newspapers unknown to the general public, reporters have produced outstanding investigative pieces that have earned them threats in their communities. Some of the most daring reporters have included Triet Le, writing on the Vietnamese far right for the Virginia-based *Cultural Vanguard*, and Manuel de Dios Unanue, covering drug smuggling for New York's *El Diario/La Prensa*. Le and Unanue were found murdered in 1990 and 1992, respectively, in crimes the police tried to ignore. In all some thirteen writers in ethnic newspapers in America have been killed in recent years. Many of the killings have followed a model similar to Ioan Culianu's murder.*

The sequence of Culianu's harassment also followed a formula described by a former Securitate colonel to journalist Petre Bacanu: letters first, then telephone calls, then a break-in or personal visit. Then, if the writer did not stop, he was killed. Culianu turned to fiction in part to understand the experiences he was having, in a story aptly called "The Secret Sequence." First published in Italy in *Leggere* and later in the United States in the *New York Review of Science Fiction*, the story detailed the career of an obscure heretical prophet, John of Cappadocia, who saw the world as a vast mental process in which all human minds are part of a universal mind, designed to think all thoughts possible. When all permutations had been exhausted, then the universe would cease. As with most of his and Wiesner's fiction, the story ended with the narrator's feeling of danger: "All of a sudden I perceive all the threat of the sonorous night looking at me from across the window and interrupt these lines, superfluous as everything else, yet part of a whole of which nothing, not even the cessation of my existence, could reveal to me the secret sequence."

Late in December he called Tess in Poitiers, where Dan was working on his doctoral thesis on Eliade. "I'm going to give up the articles," he said. He mentioned that other writers were now criticizing the regime, and he was anxious to return full-time to the many book projects he wanted to complete. She welcomed his decision.

* Committee to Protect Journalists, *Silenced by Death: Journalists Killed in the United States* (New York: Committee to Protect Journalists, 1993).

. . . .

A FORKING PATH

On Chicago's North Side, where Foster Avenue meets Ash-
land, outside Carol's Café you can smell *ciorba* — sour cream soup —
and *sarmale* — cabbage stuffed with ground pork, rice, tomato, peppers, and onion. Inside you can read the latest newspapers from Cluj
or Braşov, sitting next to a young woman in a skintight black dress or
men in factory garb or mismatched ties and jackets. The men are
smoking, sharing the day's news, and listening to the panpipe or
violin music of the Carpathian Mountains. Head further south and

you reach the Little Bucharest Restaurant, where every September a two-day Romanian Festival attracts up to thirty thousand visitors who see Chicago's mayor presented with a four-hundred-pound roast pig.

The 1990 census listed 21,275 Romanians in or around Chicago, though the actual figure may be much larger. They arrived in roughly three waves: after the Peasant Revolt of 1907, after the rise of communism in 1945 (when Iron Guardists settled there), and before the revolution of 1989. Most are hardworking; many are prosperous. Many of the newest immigrants came in the 1980s, when deprivation became unbearable at home. One such young man, call him Adrian Szabo, inserted himself in Borgesian fashion into the Culianu story.* Adrian grew up on a farm in Transylvania that his family had owned for five generations. The family prospered until 1956, when much of their land and livestock were taken in the Communist regime's ruthless collectivization. In the mid-1980s Adrian survived twenty-two months of virtual imprisonment as a soldier in a work camp.

In the winter of 1985 he and two friends, on their third try, finally made it across the Yugoslavian border, wrapped in white sheets so they would be concealed against the snow. They traveled by night, sleeping in barns or abandoned cars and stealing their food from peasants' smokehouses. Making it finally to Austria, Adrian survived both Austrian and Italian detainment centers before coming to the United States. Built like a middle linebacker, handsome, sandy-haired, with a small mustache, Adrian worked as a trucker in Chicago, Houston, and Los Angeles, eventually returning to Chicago in the fall of 1989.

Back in 1985 Szabo had met a fellow Romanian who liked to use a mobster-sounding nickname. Call him "Johnny."** Short, with steroid-pumped muscles, a little cross-eyed, Johnny had a crew cut and favored black Italian leather jackets. He looked like a bouncer. Adrian and Johnny would go out, shoot pool, play with model race cars, and hang out at East European nightclubs like Nelly's Saloon on Elston Avenue. Johnny bragged to Adrian and others about

* "Adrian Szabo" is a pseudonym.
** "Johnny" is a pseudonym.

· · · · · ·

his exploits — insurance scams, assaults, burglaries — and something about his straightforward style appealed to Adrian. Sometimes, late at night after many beers, they would idly plot some new scheme to make it big.

In the summer of 1990 Adrian was working for a friend who had his own Illinois-based trucking firm. He had a regular run from O'Hare to New York's John F. Kennedy International Airport. One day he was sitting at a favorite Greek café near O'Hare. A man in his late forties, maybe early fifties, balding, with silver-rimmed eyeglasses, well dressed in a slate-colored shirt, overheard him and his friends. He came over. "You guys speak Romanian?" he asked.

Adrian returned that day to the Air Austria freight dock, where he saw the same man again, with his suit jacket off, sleeves rolled up, reviewing a consignment of boxes. "Adrian!" the man said. He introduced himself as Nicolae Constantin. "I've got an idea for you. Driving deliveries to New York. Just like you do now, except I'll pay you a lot more."

Constantin handed him a business card for a company that specialized in "shipping and forwarding." It had a different address in each corner — Chicago, New York, Paris, and Vienna. In the center it had a logo of a pyramid with an eye at the top, rays shooting out, as in a Masonic symbol appearing on the dollar bill and detailed, ironically, in Giordano Bruno's writing. "Call me," Constantin said. "Let's talk."

●   ●   ●

On a completely different level from the immigrant worlds of Chicago, highly placed Romanian diplomats traveled a great deal during the year after the revolution. In Paris, French intelligence noticed that the embassy was "more active in political and military spying than during the Ceaușescu era," foreign affairs reporter Tad Szulc noted. "French intelligence found this to be incomprehensible." Such activities capitalized on the international connections of the former Securitate. Convinced that surveillance of intelligence service spying on Romanians abroad was continuing, *România Liberă* chief editor Petre Bacanu observed, "I feel more frightened outside of the country than when I'm at home."

Various men came to the United States several times in 1990

with Romanian diplomatic passports or visas granted in some cases through the Romanian national airline, Air Tarom. *Lumea Liberă* received reports that former Securitate agents were involved in trucking and smuggling in the Midwest. One of them, it appeared, was using the alias of Nicolae Constantin.

A poet must lift the censorship of the transcendental.

— Lucian Blaga

* * * * * * * *

MEMORIES OF THE FUTURE

At the close of fall term in 1990, Ioan Culianu confronted a situation he had not faced in fifteen years. He had no new signed book contracts, no new pressing deadlines, no imminent lecture tours. He was assured of tenure at one of the preeminent schools for the study of religions. He had nothing to prove to anyone. Bursting with new theories of religion and history to explore, he faced the future without a firm agenda, seeking a new breakthrough in his career.

He was busy certainly — engaged to be married, writing, teaching, and planning his international conference on after-death journeys to be held the next May on the university campus. He looked forward to speaking at the Chimera II conference on magic, also scheduled for May. He was publishing two issues a year of his journal *Incognita* with the modest goal of radically altering the methodology of humanities studies. He was planning his first trip home in eighteen years, and he talked frequently with his sister in Poitiers, France. Still, as the fall nights chilled and the elm leaves on the quad rolled up into small clenched fists, he confronted an almost unique situation. He was, as he had longed to be, *free.*

He began writing new book proposals rapidly. During the next few months he proposed five major book projects for mainstream trade publishers, including HarperCollins and Macmillan. Four of the five proposals offered a due date of December 31, 1991 — an impossible research agenda. Like his favorite fictional character, Borges's detective Erik Lönnrot in "Death and the Compass," he seemed to have discovered an organizing principle of world events and was pushing hard to pursue it to its ultimate end.* He acted, on the other hand, as if he felt suddenly very pressed for time.

By far his largest book project was a proposed multivolume *Encyclopedia of Magic* for Oxford University Press. Drawing on his experience in helping Eliade assemble his multivolume *Encyclopedia of Religion*, he gathered an international board of experts, including Harvard's Lawrence Sullivan, Hebrew University's Moshe Idel, and Chicago colleague Michael Fishbane, to oversee the project. He proposed a three-year timetable, complete with international conferences, to finish the first major scientific reference on magic in forty years. The creation of a new encyclopedia would be "one of the most challenging tasks that faces both the scholarly world and the world of publishing in the 1990s," he had written in his book proposal.

It was a hugely ambitious undertaking, for which the only model was Lynn Thorndike's eight-volume *History of Magic and Experimental Science*. Published sporadically over the years 1923–58, Thorn-

---

* For more on the comparison to Borges's Lönnrot, see Horia Patapeivici, "Ioan Culianu, Perfection and Death," *Cotidianul* (Bucharest), July 18, 1994, pp. 34–37.

dike's work suffered from a shallow understanding of and "contempt" for magic, Culianu complained. *Magic* was not a sloppy term covering everything from carnival hucksters to aboriginal shamans. Rather, it referred to the world of the imagination "that dominated Western science for thousands of years" when culture was based on faith. Culianu wanted to chronicle worldwide metaphysical arts and practices that sought to reunite the conscious and the unconscious, devoting to the subject the precision and passion a physicist brought to the behavior of subatomic quarks and neutrinos.

The multivolume project would take shape through four phases. Phase One would assess scholars active in the field, leading to the establishment of an international steering committee. As editor of *Incognita*, Culianu wrote, "I started Phase One in 1989, by asking the best scholars in different areas to send papers on magic for the January, 1991 issue. . . . Before the deadline [October 1, 1990], we had received more material than we could possibly handle." This response helped him not only to assess scholars, he claimed, but also to understand that the "situation was absolutely ripe" for a truly scientific encyclopedia of the hidden arts.

In Phase Two the core team would assemble a one-volume guideline or "general history of magic," about 350 pages long with bibliographies, similar to *The Eliade Guide to World Religions*. Phase Three would "physically" bring together about fifteen of the best researchers in each subfield to "a conference where they would present their invited papers." Phase Four would feature an international congress, "entailing the participation of no less than 150 scholars, to be held in April or May 1992, having as a seat either Harvard or the University of Chicago," where teams would be formed and final entries culled. His proposed due date for the encyclopedia and one-volume index was July 1, 1994. In all it "was an unbelievable undertaking with significant implications for the study of religion, myth, history, and even cognitive science," said Moshe Idel. "Nothing like it had ever been tried before."

●　●　●

By December 1990 Culianu was looking forward to spending the Christmas holiday with Hillary Wiesner. He had been seeing less of her than in the previous turbulent year of his life, while she took courses at Harvard and worked on her doctoral thesis. That month Hillary's friend Cathy O'Leary and her lover visited them in Cambridge. They brought glow-in-the-dark wands for a fantasy game called Talisman that Ioan and Hillary loved to play. After a home-cooked dinner, Cathy and Hillary decided they wanted ice cream for dessert. Ioan offered to go out shopping. Half an hour later he returned with two shopping bags stuffed with seven different flavors of Häagen-Dazs and Ben and Jerry's. They got so caught up in their dessert and magic wand fest that they never played their game. "It was typical of him," said O'Leary. "Even a trip to Walgreens was an adventure." His love of shopping extended to almost any item advertised by mail. "He bought into the Columbia record *and* CD clubs," said Wiesner, "and would buy whatever came advertised with his credit card bill." One such item he bought that winter, without her knowledge, was an extra life insurance policy naming her as the beneficiary.

A few days later a visiting journalist for Romania's most prominent democratic weekly, 22, interviewed him in Hyde Park. After the revolution the most popular form of writing became the interview. Writers quite simply rediscovered each other after years of isolation, shedding the layers of irony and ambiguity that had by necessity marked public discourse in the Communist era. The novelist and journalist Gabriela Adameşteanu was on a North American tour compiling a "series of remarkable interviews" with prominent exiles. Named for the date of the revolution and fiercely critical of the government, 22 was the single most influential independent news magazine in the country.

Adameşteanu came to see Culianu on the day a stock market guru had predicted an earthquake in the Midwest. They met at Mircea Eliade's favorite restaurant. Dark and attractive, Adameşteanu drank coffee and smoked as she tape recorded their conversation. She was struck by Culianu's youth. "When I had seen his list of publications, I thought this must be someone very old," she said. She noticed a difference between him and other Romanians in exile: he seemed more American, with his penny loafers, khaki pants, and flannel shirt. "Perhaps because he belonged to the West while at the same time knowing Romania," she said, "he seemed to understand things happening there that I could not see."

The interview ranged over many topics, including American culture, the New Age movement, and the Eliade controversy. They dwelled at length on current politics. Culianu protested that he did not know much about politics, but he took it for granted that the revolution was a sham, blasting Eastern Europe as a "tragic waste of time, human lives, and talent." Adameşteanu asked about a scenario suggested by the newspaper *România Mare*, the rabid far rightist newspaper directed by former Communists. "If there had been a revolution," he replied, "*România Mare* would not exist."

He ripped into Securitate, calling it a force "of epochal stupidity and yet unseen profundity," and emphasized the KGB role in the revolution. While the Russian secret police had been unsuccessful in their homeland, he said, they had been too effective in Romania through their minions, Securitate. She countered by quoting an opposition writer who had said Securitate only controlled a part, not the whole, of society. "He's right," Culianu responded, delineating the connection of far right and far left that he saw as the main cause of the country's murderous stalemate: "Except that Securitate creates diversions, dominates local politics, dominates Vatra Românească, dominates the means of communication. And it has an extraordinary power to influence. It can always say, we did it [the revolution], and so you can't lay any claim to it."

Culianu took even Adameşteanu aback with his vitriol. "I had talked to every other prominent Romanian in exile," she said. "There was a difference with him. First because he emphasized the KGB role, and second because he saw the revolution, not as a stolen revolution, but as simply a method of keeping power through flexibility."

When the interview was finished he noticed her checking her tape recorder. "You recorded?" he asked, his face turning white. He had forgotten she was taping.

That night a snowstorm hit Chicago, delaying her for hours. After he dropped her off at O'Hare airport, he drove home slowly through the windblown snow of the midwestern blizzard. When he got home he telephoned his sister in a panic, telling her what he had said.

"I wouldn't worry," she replied. "It's nothing so bad."

On December 22, 1990, the one-year anniversary of the revolution, Culianu officially stopped writing for *Lumea Liberă* by "mutual agreement," said his editor, Cornel Dumitrescu. He had done "his patriotic duty." The situation in Romania began to appear hopeless, and he wanted to get on with his research. The editors, having received several written complaints about "that philo-Semite, Culianu, who attacked their country's role in the Holocaust," wanted to end "Scoptophilia" at the same time he did.

⁂ ⁂ ⁂

Christmas 1990 at Dorothy and Kurt Hertzfeld's home in Amherst was a far different celebration for Culianu than Christmas 1989. The previous year he had been on the telephone, faxing friends and racing from room to room with his hastily written BBC broadcasts and political broadsheets. This year he played chess against the computer and helped prepare the holiday food. He clowned on a home video, making the V for Victory sign that had become his habit after the revolution, and swinging a pendant to hypnotize Hillary, telling her he was a CIA agent. Opening gifts, he put his arm around Hillary on the couch while nieces and nephews crowded the floor with wrapping paper.

In January 1991 Ioan telephoned his sister to suggest that he and Hillary meet her and Dan in France in the spring, and then invite Grazia Marchianò and Elémire Zolla to drive with them all to spend Easter in Bucharest. Tess suggested an alternative: Ioan could come to Romania for the summer Romanian-American Academy conference, the first to be held in Romania by the major scholarly and civic association. "It was also a critical meeting for the opposition," said Mircea Sabau. Culianu said he would think about it.

⁂ ⁂ ⁂

In the winter term in Chicago he taught Gnosticism and Manichaeanism and The Western Tradition of Magic. Like most of his courses in these years, the latter was meant to lead to a book, in this case *Memories of the Future: The Combinatory Art of Raymundus Lullus and Its Mystical Use.* Culianu described the book in a detailed proposal for HarperCollins. He planned to link Bruno's art of memory with discoveries in artificial intelligence, complexity theory, and psychology in an effort to compare the different ways in which cognition creates the universe. He considered the art of memory the

. . . . . .

most important tradition of mysticism in the West. "It all started in the year 1274, or perhaps much earlier, with the wheel of Sefir Yetsira," Culianu wrote in the book proposal, quoting his short story "The Language of Creation." "Its wheels, arrayed with Hebrew alphabets, would produce the sublime language of Creation, the language behind the world, seen and unseen."

The proposal focused on the Jewish mystical conjectures that the proccesses of the universe can be mimicked in a physical construction of spheres or alphabetical wheels inscribed with the Hebrew alphabet. "Thus, the movement of the wheels was . . . the movement of the celestial bodies, and language was the whole universe," Culianu wrote. He saw in this mystical practice a unifying theme of his life: "Nowhere else in history is the idea expressed more clearly that these two systems — the system of language and that of the world — are not only analogous, but consubstantial; by manipulating language one can, actually and concretely, manipulate the surrounding world."

The mystical art of memory became something about more than memory in 1274, he said, when a forty-year-old Catalan named Raymundus Lullus was struck by a revelation in the wild mountains of Palma de Majorca. Lullus invented a machine made of wheels on which he wrote the Hebrew alphabet. This machine looked physically like the mental system of concentric circles devised later by Bruno (to which Bruno attached astrological symbols). What both men had stumbled on was the essential principle of the computer: logic works by infinitely repeating and varying the same simple digital computations.

If we understood that our mind and the world outside of it both functioned on the same principles as a binary computer, he observed, we could predict events in the world based on the patterns of the past. His proposed deadline for submitting *Memories of the Future* was December 31, 1991.

*   *   *

Culianu wrote up three more book proposals in the winter months of 1990 and 1991. Two were part of the same project—a three-volume *History of Mind* for Macmillan, featuring separate volumes on science, religion, and philosophy. The overall purpose of these volumes was to uncover the logic patterns he had begun to explore in *The Tree of Gnosis*, in the history of the three great cultural creations of mankind. Taken alone, it was a staggering project, but coupled with *The Encyclopedia of Magic*, the scope of his attempt to find a universal "world key" seemed staggering.

All of the themes of his work, and of his life, came together in the final proposal, titled *The Birth of Infinity: The Nominalist Revolution, 1250–1450*. Taking as its subject the late medieval "nominalist" thinkers including William of Occam, Nicholas of Autrecourt, and Nicholas of Cusa, Culianu wanted to show that the scientific revolution could not have happened without first a philosophical revolution that fundamentally altered man's relation to the world. "Modernity and its ideas of the infinity of the universe," he wrote, are the product of theological speculation first, and only later scientific experiment. Nicholas of Cusa had to propose that the earth was only one planet in an infinite universe before Galileo could point his telescope at the moon. One cannot discover something unless one first imagines the possibility of its existence.

He drew on the previous work of scholars such as Allen G. Debus, who said that scientists like William Harvey, who contrived the heart-centered theory of blood circulation in 1628, relied without knowing it on the theories of Renaissance metaphysics. Harvey, Copernicus, and the scientific revolution were the *outcome*, not the cause, of a philosophical revolution in tacitly shared assumptions about the world many centuries earlier. Even today we are unaware that we belong to this nominalist world, Culianu wrote. In this argument he had predecessors like Stephen Toulmin, who suggested that we are not aware of the assumptions behind our methods of understanding the world. What we call the "real" world, therefore, is an artificial construct.

At the end of a visit to Chicago Hillary reminded Ioan again to apply for his green card, and he showed her the affidavit he had signed. She was worried about their summer plans. She wanted Ioan to become an American citizen quickly. "When will the card come through?" she asked.

"Soon. Before we go anywhere."

* * * * * * * *

"DR. FAUST, GREAT SODOMITE
AND NECROMANCER"

By the spring of 1991 the questions raised by many journalists about the Iliescu government's legitimacy had thwarted its drive
to attract foreign investment. The United States, which in the 1980s
singled out Ceauşescu's Romania as the only Eastern Bloc country
to receive Most Favored Nation trading status, singled out the
country as the only post-Communist land *not* granted such status.
The June 1990 miners' riots deeply weakened what respectability
the government gained from its victory in earlier elections. By

January 7, 1991, Paul Hockenos was reporting in the *Nation:* "Behind the scenes in Bucharest, power is wielded and contested by rival military factions and the former security apparatus." Because of these questions, foreign business hesitated to invest in a country where a "minority government holds power mainly through an alliance with extreme rightists," noted Reuters News Service.

Out of the chaos three main currents emerged — the rise of a new far right connected with the old security police, the return of former Communists to public and private positions of power, and the persistence of unanswered questions about the revolution and the alleged missing Ceauşescu fortune. Even President Iliescu acknowledged that a new "mafia," made up in large part of former security police, controlled much of the country's ordinary life.*

The trends were linked. Few believed that the rapid rise of the far right, for instance, occurred entirely on its own. "Nationalism," wrote the Polish essayist and activist Adam Michnik, "is the last refuge of communism." While the revival of Romania's mystical fascism struck a chord among some in a disoriented, frustrated, and politically illiterate populace, it was also manipulated. "Far right ideology mainly covered for a grab of a variety of businesses by former security police and officials," concluded *România Liberă* editor Petre Bacanu. As an example he cited the figure of Iosif Constantin Drăgan, the Milan-based Romanian far rightist who had maintained a close relationship with Ceauşescu. Under the new regime, Drăgan was the first and, for several years, the *only* private individual to win a coveted independent television broadcast license. According to *România Liberă*, Dragan was believed to fund *România Mare* and other far rightist media.

While fascism rose in many East European countries in 1991, in Romania it received official sanction because extremist parties provided the support Iliescu needed to govern. Although the President denounced the extreme right in public, citing "Iron Guard provocations" to justify the first miners' attack in Bucharest, the ruling party continued in a Parliamentary alliance with the most rabid nationalist parties. The resurgence of the old Iron Guard's sentiments in

* William McPherson, "Who Won in Romania?" *Washington Post*, December 16, 1991, p. C1.

the writings of prominent communists in *România Mare* seemed to be promoted by some members of the former Securitate.*

In 1990, in short, terms like right and left gradually lost all meaning, as Culianu had suggested in *Eros and Magic.* "There was no logic to the anti-Semitism," complained the elderly leader of Romania's Jewish population, the late chief rabbi Moses Rosen. "It seemed mainly a strategy of people who want or want to keep power." Rosen kept a record of rightist invective in Securitate-funded newspapers, which formed a grotesque subtext to public discussion — the more so because Romania had such a small Jewish population left (most had emigrated to Israel, under business arrangements in which Ceaușescu charged thousands of dollars for exit visas). Here is a typical quote from Constantine Burlacu, who published paeans to the Iron Guard from his Queens, New York, basement: "Unless Jews give up enslaving, terrifying, and murdering mankind, they will not just be chased from every country, but be wiped off the face of the earth." Such rhetoric was popular in the new rightist press. In the same issue of *România Mare,* for instance, one could read that Jews ran the state television for nefarious purposes, and that Rabbi Rosen was an "artful crook . . . and a whole nation has been wound up at his beck and call." This publication claimed a circulation of half a million.

Such activity had to be funded. By the spring of 1991 it was clear that the rumored special accounts secreted abroad by Ceaușescu would never be recovered. Estimated in the hundreds of millions of dollars, perhaps a billion, the money had been gained largely through the sale of exit visas to Romanian Jews wishing to emigrate to Israel and to ethnic Germans returning to what was then West Germany, the sale of arms to Iraq and elsewhere, and the sale of Soviet military technology to the U.S. government.** In the first days after the revolution people clamored to find Ceaușescu's

* To seek out the old Iron Guard, I visited the national "Legionary Library" in Bucharest. The library was in one room of a small building on a dark back street near the main train station, manned part-time by a young engineer whose father had once served the Legion. He had no national constituency that I could discern.

** William McPherson, "Who 'Won' Romania's Mysterious Revolution?" *Washington Post,* Nov. 17, 1991, C1, C3.

money. The Ministry of Justice retained the Canadian accounting firm of Peat, Marwick, Thorne to audit his Swiss and Austrian bank accounts. The trail led to Ceauşescu's brother Marin, who was found hanged in his sumptuous Vienna apartment, his safe cleaned of all papers. After a year the government report was unissued, the investigators strangely silent. "It's a pain of death issue," explained one investigator to the *Washington Post*. "Knowing too much is dangerous." No money was ever found.

Across Eastern Europe, millions of dollars of secret police and government funds disappeared after the respective revolutions, though none more conspicuously and silently than in Romania. Veteran foreign affairs reporter Tad Szulc noted in *Penthouse* that in Romania and other countries such moneys appeared to fund the career changes of former secret police officers — into international intelligence, technology theft, arms sales, murder-for-hire, and even legitimate businesses.

The revolution was continuing in 1991, it seemed, and in the confusion populist and fascist rhetoric became a kind of currency. Rather than condemning the far rightists, for instance, such "reformers" as Prime Minister Petre Roman, who was Jewish, appointed some of the most rabid fascists to key posts. The main beneficiaries of the chaos were those clinging to power.

＊　＊　＊

As March offered endless days of wind and cold, Ioan Culianu escaped to spend Easter in Amherst with Hillary and the Hertzfelds. He prepared for spring term, when he was scheduled to teach the survey course Fundamentals of Comparative Religion, as well as a course based on his upcoming conference, Otherworldly Journeys and Out-of-Body Experiences. He received an offprint of his new essay on Faust, based on the 1987 lecture in Chicago and published in late 1990 in the *Revue de l'Histoire des Religions*. He called it "Dr. Faust, Great Sodomite and Necromancer." In his humorous style he synthesized his life's research on the Faust myth, pushing on to more significant conclusions than he had reached before. Proud of its insights, he showed the essay to his closer colleagues at the Divinity School.

The essay examined the history of Faust myths from ancient times to the present. Building on the work of French thinker André Dabezies, Culianu showed that in the twentieth century in Germany Faust became a hero of nationalist propaganda and the "incarnation of Western man" to Oswald Spengler. Culianu's friend at Chicago, Anthony Yu, liked the essay's ideas enough to discuss a joint course. "I saw in his interpretation hints of the Icarus myth — of the man brought down for flying too close to god — or the Christian myth of the overreacher and I suggested we should examine variants of the myth from the ancient to the present."

The essay concluded with a discussion of myth's role in modern times, when humanity has lost its primitive sense of connection in the cosmos. Culianu agreed with Eliade that the key to myths was not their content but the *process* of storytelling. Myths resulted from a universal "will to repeat" stories, a process that creates a mystical cosmic peace in the speaker and the audience. The story's content did not matter so much; in fact, usually a myth was like "a bud whose meaning never comes to full blossom." The reason why the history of religions was so important in a secular time of disorientation and new fundamentalism was that "changes in Western ideas are occurring far faster than those occurring in other places." Culianu concluded: "Myth, being a privileged conveyor of social meaning, is also the best tool to decipher the more or less hidden purposes of society. . . . *Myth is precisely based on oblivion.* It is not a remedy to oblivion though, but *a mechanism of make-believe intended to establish some perfectly arbitrary and thus illusory continuity in the otherwise tricky and ever-changing world.*" One could offer no more clearer explanation in 1991 than this for the confusion in Romania. Culianu found in Faust not only a key to the fate of his favorite magician, Giordano Bruno, but also resonance for his personal journey. Like Culianu's fiction, the essay linked the separate and hidden threads of his life — his past, his scholarly research, his current life, and violent world events.

* * *

Tess kept pressuring Ioan to return to Romania, but he kept putting off a decision. He felt increasingly uneasy. One Friday night he called his friend Dorin Tudoran. "What did you think of the article I sent?"

Tudoran paused. Culianu had recently sent him an article examining the psychology of the Iron Guard as a fundamentalist movement akin to the Ku Klux Klan or new militia movements in the United States. It was written in Culianu's usual incendiary political style, beginning with a scholarly analysis of a new book on fundamentalism by Martin Riesebrodt, and it made Tudoran uncomfortable.

"Listen, Nene, I think we should hold off on publishing your Eminescu article. Because of your relation with Eliade, the far rightists thought you were one of them. Seeing you attack them openly and accusing them really upsets them."

"I know."

"Securitate is very good at manipulating them. They'll say, 'Look at what this young son is writing about our beloved country.'"

"I know."

"Next time you are threatened, report it to the police."

* * *

In March, Culianu finished his introduction to his and Wiesner's *Eliade Guide to World Religions*. In its opening pages he laid out more clearly than ever before his idea that religions developed as logical systems. Universal beliefs like Creation, he wrote, did not "'originate' in India and 'cross' Iran; they are present in all human minds that contemplate them." But whereas Eliade speculated about such patterns arising from the unconscious, Culianu sought sophisticated tools to understand their cognitive basis.

It seemed odd that he would put the clearest summation of his most daring and controversial ideas in the introduction to a desk reference under his mentor's name. He offered one reason in his introduction by calling for continued research to uncover the cognitive rules that lay behind the development of religions: "In order to perceive these rules, scholars need more than just information: they need *complex* information." Since religions resembled computer software, Culianu suggested in a more utopian vein, we might reverse humanity's dismal track record by "reprogramming" religions to promote respect for the Other. Finally, he enjoyed putting his most important ideas in unexpected places, designed to rile his readers like a mythical trickster subverting the doctrine of his idol. To Hillary he said, "Mr. Eliade had some pretty daring ideas after he died."

* * *

After months of waiting, he learned in April that he was approved for his alien registration card. Finally he had his official papers in his newly adopted country. Former dean Chris Gamwell held a "Green Party" in his Hyde Park apartment for Culianu, catered by Greg Spinner and Michael Allocca. Culianu lunched with Frances Gamwell on April 2, 1991, in part to discuss the party. He had previously mentioned to her that he had been threatened about his political writing, but on this day he told her: "I'm being followed."

"You mean right now? asked Gamwell, looking around her as they walked out of the restaurant inside his favorite Flamingo-on-the-Lake Apartments.

"Probably," he said.

At the Gamwells' party everyone had to wear green; all the food and drink were colored green. Allocca and Spinner served spinach fettucine, pesto lasagna, guacamole, green beer, pistachio ice cream, and cake with green icing. At the party Ioan discussed his and Hillary's plans for the summer trip to Europe and hinted at a triumphal return to Romania. "We're going to have such a party!" he said, holding Hillary around the neck. "Right, sweetie?"

Hillary smiled uncomfortably. She had no desire to go to Romania and advised him against it. She resented his sister's late-night telephone calls, pressuring him to come, and she wondered why they could not simply meet Tess and Dan in France, along with Ioan's mother. Paris, she thought, would make for a real party.

He showed off the U.S. flag flown over the Capitol that she had give him. Now, he said, America welcomes its biggest patriot. At the party everyone clapped when he made a little speech thanking the Gamwells and all of the guests for celebrating with him.

Afterward, cleaning up, Michael Allocca turned to Greg Spinner. "I'm glad he got his green card. At least now he'll be safe."

At night's end, Ioan would not leave. He kept thanking everyone. He was glowing. He took the Gamwells' vacuum cleaner and ran it up the curtains and the walls. Not until everyone else had finished working did he finally bid them good night, walking home toward the icy black Lake Michigan with Hillary. Among other things, his green card approval was also the final step toward tenure, after which he would begin to play a leading role in the future of the Divinity School. And then, he said, they should schedule their wedding.

❋   ❋   ❋

He received the page proofs from Shambhala Press for *Out of This World: Other-worldly Journeys from Gilgamesh to Albert Einstein*, to be distributed by Random House. He hoped the book would vault him beyond the scholarly world into the mainstream of American letters, preparing for his ultimate goal: writing fantasy fiction.

Out of This World was ambitious, hurried, and distinctly his own. In it he examined "side by side the normally separate genres of fiction and factual science, and disparate figures like Bohr and Borges, Einstein and Gilgamesh," wrote Harvard University's Lawrence Sullivan in the foreword. The book's purpose was to present a cross-cultural historical survey of journeys to other worlds, including "altered states of consciousness, as well as out-of-body experiences and near-death experiences." In his introducton Culianu suggested that "mind space . . . has amazing properties, the most remarkable of which is that it is not limited to three dimensions like the physical universe." This was not merely the realm of the imagination, he said, noting that beliefs in otherworldly journeys were universal in time and space and seemed to predate language itself. Yet he left open the question of exactly *where* the journeys did take place. The proofs included an early reaction Carol Zaleski had written for the book jacket: "An invaluable guidebook to the other world's many mansions, as seen through the gates of dream and myth, mystical and shamanic experience, philosophy and imaginative fiction."

Like the Faust essay, *Out of This World* culminated a long journey of his own life. He had begun the research with the monograph published in 1983 by E. J. Brill in Holland, *Psychanodia*. One year later Payot published Culianu's more refined *Expériences de l'extase*, launching his career in France. In that book's preface Eliade praised Culianu's command of the material, hinting that the author "is familiar, too, with other forms of celestial ascension, attested in various shamanisms, in China, in India, in Australia, etc." The book was translated and published in Greece and Italy, leading to Chicago courses like Religion and Science, and Otherworldly Journeys, and now to his Other Realms conference to be held in a matter of weeks.

The book offered a catalog of various routes to worlds beyond conventional perception, including dreams, shamanistic ritual, fourth-dimension theories, ecstatic trances, and fantasy literature. Culianu wanted to establish the common elements of these other worlds, but the scope of his study left little opportunity to go into depth on material as varied as Jewish messianism and ancient Greek visions of the afterlife. The New Age bent of subjects such as out-of-body and near-death experiences indicated his desire to reach a popular audience, but to do so he sacrificed much of the erudition that would have made the book more useful in his field.

The scholar Andrei Oişteanu analyzed *Out of This World* in his introduction to the Romanian edition he translated for Nemira Editions in 1994. Culianu's most important contribution, he argued, was to focus on shamanism. Using drugs or other sacred rituals, shamans guided a tribe by claiming to journey to other worlds and bringing back their testimony, which provided the fundamental connection between the community and the gods. Prior to Culianu, shamanism was a concept applied mainly to sectarian civilizations, with some influences on the West. Culianu claimed to find shamanic patterns in Greek myth, Western otherworldly journeys, even Dante's *Divine Comedy.* He went even further, attempting to change the traditional understanding of magic and witchcraft by saying that all these practices had their cognitive origin in a shamanistic mentality. The idea of the person who sees things others cannot, and whose role is to communicate these things to the people, had motivated Culianu's thought and action since he was a young man reading and modeling himself on Eliade's fictional heroes.

Hidden in Culianu's English version, Oişteanu suggested, was also a direct attack on Eliade, whose 1951 work *Le chamanisme* theorized that shamanism spread by cultural influences from India and Asia. "Nowhere did he acknowledge Eliade's reference work. It was a glaring omission, and it had to be purposeful, since Culianu *had* acknowledged Eliade's book in his French prototype." Along with his introduction to the *Eliade Guide to World Religions, Out of This World* represented his final break with his mentor. By now, though, the break with Eliade was less important than Culianu's new approach to history based on information theory, which suggested the reason myths around the world are so similar is that human minds follow similar, even universal, mental or binary processes.

* * *

On April 5, 1991, the magazine 22 published its multipage spread of Culianu's interview from December. The editors gave it a high-profile centerfold format and titled it from one of his quotes: "The Eastern European World: A Tragic Waste of Time, Human Lives, and Talent." The first of a two-part series, it highlighted his most vitriolic attacks on the KGB's role in the revolution and the new link of far right and far left. (Later in the United States, columnist Jack Anderson confirmed the CIA conclusion that the former Soviet KGB had exercised a controlling influence over events in the Romanian revolution.)

When his mother saw it in Bucharest, she felt a shadow pass over her. What made her fearful were not the strident words but the overall look and the layout's irrational effect — with a picture of her son, looking not at all like himself, flanked on the page by two weeping women icons and a Christ figure. Trained as a scientist, she felt something at a deeper level when she saw the prominently displayed piece. The University of Maryland political scientist Vladimir Tismaneanu was more specific: "He combined the emotionalism of a poet with the depth of a political scientist. It was the most devastating indictment of the union of far right and far left that had appeared thus far." Culianu's most piercing attacks came in his small throwaway lines, such as his indictment of *România Mare*, which seemed to suggest to many readers that he was saying less than he knew.

Culianu did not have time to dwell on the piece, because in Chicago he was asked to show the Eliade sights around the University of Chicago to the former king of Romania, Michael, who wanted to return to his home country in a leading role similar to that of King Juan Carlos of Spain. Michael had assumed the throne for the second time in 1940 in Romania after his father abdicated. Forced to flee in 1947, he had retained a reputation of independence and authority because he had missed the Communist era. Seen as the most serious threat to the post-Communist regime, he was not allowed back into the country, and he was stopping in Chicago during a fund-raising tour of North America.

Culianu was no supporter of the monarchy, but he agreed to host the king out of curiosity. He met Michael, Queen Anne, and their daughter Princess Margareta in Hyde Park, taking them around the Divinity School to meet the faculty who had known Eliade. They enjoyed each other's company. Margareta, an ebullient and attractive woman, asked Ioan to send them his and Eliade's books. That night he telephoned his sister in France. "Sure he's a king," he said, amused at his own reaction. "But at least he's a real king. Perhaps he's the best hope for us." He agreed to support him.

John Crowley was in Chicago and called his friend up for lunch. Chuckling, Culianu told him of the Romanian monarch's political strategy. "He wants to mount a national campaign with all of ten thousand dollars," he said. But Ioan admitted that he had agreed to assist, and was becoming a supporter.

On Saturday night, April 13, 1991, he attended a fund-raiser for the monarch at Chicago's Drake Hotel. It was a strange event, he told Hillary later, filled with suspicious characters lurking in the corners. The next morning Greg Spinner saw him eating a late breakfast at the Salonica Restaurant near campus. "He looked terrible, as though he was hung over or really scared," Spinner said. "He was wearing dark sunglasses and acted nervous and grumpy. He told me, 'I've lost so much time these last few days.' "

A few days later his close friend Moshe Idel came to lecture in Chicago. They saw the movie *La femme Nikita*, about a young woman manipulated by a government into becoming a paid assassin. After dinner at Trader Vic's, he showed Idel the 22 interview.

They spoke Romanian for the first time since the night they first met. "It's very disturbing," Idel told him about the interview.

"There's more." Culianu mentioned that in the lobby of the Drake Hotel a man had accosted him, pushing him up against the wall. The man's overcoat bulged over what seemed to be a gun in

the breast pocket of his jacket. He wore a tie and a grimy white shirt.
"He told me if I got involved with the king, they'd kill me," he said.
"Listen. You'd better not go back," his friend said.

* * *

In April 1991 Dumitru Mazilu, former high official with the ruling
National Salvation Front, was beaten and slashed in Geneva after
completing his book manuscript on the revolution. The two hooded
men who attacked him with razors spoke Romanian. They left with
Mazilu's manuscript, he claimed. He was due to speak to the United
Nations Commission on Human Rights the next day about conditions in Romania.

On April 27 the former U.S. attorney general Edward Levi hos-
ted a birthday party for Christinel Eliade at his Hyde Park apartment. David Tracy was there, as were some of the Romanian women
who were Christinel's closest friends in Chicago. They included
Maria Economou-Zarifopol, Ioan's aunt by marriage, who was then
living in Bloomington, Indiana. After the party Ioan drove Zarifopol
to the Greyhound bus terminal and helped her with her bags.

"He was so happy and excited to be going back to Romania and
seeing his mother," she recalled.

* * *

From May 3 to May 5 he was the Special Scholar Guest at the
Chimera II conference, The Structure of Magic, held in Schaumburg, Illinois. The featured author, John Crowley, had requested
him to speak. With sessions titled Utopias, Cosmology and Con
Games, and Why Chaos Theory Is So Irritating to Real Scientists,
the conference was a heady experience. Spinner came and met
Culianu after breakfast at the Schaumburg Hilton. People walked
up and asked the author to sign his book *Eros and Magic*.

"We adored him," said co-organizer Jennifer Stevenson. "He
demystified eros, talking about how the church put it in the kitchen
with an apron on." In the conference journal Culianu and Wiesner
published "The Secret Sequence." Culianu dined with Crowley and
hatched an idea to bring the writer to Chicago as a guest lecturer.

That night Culianu read to the group from "The Language of
Creation." The story linked the many threads of his life, beginning

by recounting the past of a strange music box that the narrator buys at a Romanian far rightist auction in Holland. The story drew connections from friendships, readings, chance, history, and whole sections of his book proposal for *Memories of the Future*, ending with the narrator's conscious decision to escape his past.

At Ioan's home the next day, Hillary took pictures of him for the upcoming publication of *The Tree of Gnosis*, scheduled to appear in December. Lit by pink sunlight off the lake, the apartment looked beautiful. Ioan's gold and black Chinese screens, one with lilies, the other with cranes, seemed to glow. Ioan and Hillary lay on the pink and blue bedspread and made their summer plans: They would fly to France to attend an international Academy of Religion conference. They would meet Tess and Dan, rent a car, and drive to Romania. He was excited about the trip.

He kept trying to convince her to stay for his Other Realms conference. He was nervous about last-minute preparations. On May 13 Hillary declined, pleading her own work demands. After she left he talked with her mother, in Amherst, on the telephone.

"Hillary tells me you've decided about your plans this summer," she said.

"It's still not sure. Maybe . . . maybe I will go back to Romania alone at the end of summer to see my mother, but I won't take Hillary. It's just too dangerous."

When she got back to Cambridge, Hillary had her photographs of Ioan processed. There must have been something wrong with the camera. All the shots of him showed a double image.

I sensed that the world was a labyrinth, from which it

was impossible to flee.

— *Jorge Luis Borges, "Death and the Compass"*

* * * * * * * *

ROSES AT THE DOOR

In May 1991, Romanian national elections, long clamored for, were announced for that month. Then they were postponed, again, for the fourth time in a year. Journalists complained the government was simply waiting for the moment it knew it would win.

A week before the Other Realms conference, Dorin Tudoran in Washington spoke to Ioan Culianu for the last time. "I have to tell my mother, but I can't," Culianu said.

"Tell her what?"

"I'm not coming. Can you call and tell Tess and Dan?"

"I would, but it's not right for me to call. What's happening?" Tudoran asked.

"Well, I'm afraid this time I do have reasons to be scared."

"Just forget about it." Tudoran himself had already returned to Romania, had even met President Iliescu. He paused. "Is there something new?"

"It's just a feeling. I don't know if it's different, or if it's more serious, but I have a feeling that this time it's serious."

"Talk to the police, Nene."

"I'll think about it."

"Listen to me, tell the police."

* * *

On Tuesday, May 14, Culianu taught Fundamentals of Comparative Religion from 10:00 to 11:30, inviting students to attend the conference on Thursday instead of having class. He enlisted Spinner and Allocca to help him shepherd conference panelists from O'Hare, putting them up at McGiffert House.

Two mornings later, beneath the carved wooden angels of the Swift Hall Lecture Room, Lawrence Sullivan gave the conference's welcoming address, entitled "New Perspectives in the Study of Death and the Afterlife." As Sullivan spoke, Culianu scanned the room for students and colleagues. The university magazine had promoted both his book and the conference in its last issue, in which he had been careful to note that he himself was "skeptical about the supernatural." The turnout was not as bad as he had feared; the conference had even managed to attract some of the witchcraft and goddess crowd from the further reaches of the campus.

The conference offered four sessions over two days, covering the topics Death and Beyond, Death and Ecstasy, Beyond Otherworldly Journeys, and New Scholarly Perspectives. Scholars like New York University's Elliot Wolfson, the University of North Carolina's David Halperin, and Notre Dame's Adela Yarbro Collins presented their work on visionary journeys in Hindu, Buddhist, Jewish, Christian, Islamic, and Greco-Roman cultures. Overall, the sessions fit more into the staid confines of academia than their provocative titles might suggest. Yet it was an unusual gathering because "there was no competitiveness," observed Carol Zaleski. "You had all these world-class scholars simply sharing their work."

One of the most interesting talks, entitled "Death and Near-Death, Today," came from Zaleski. Reviewing the common features of near-death reports, she interpreted the stories as attempts to construct a "personal identity and continuity in the face of death." She began by reviewing death denial in Western culture, starting with Freud's idea that humanity has forgotten how "the enduring remembrance of the dead becomes the basis for assuming other modes of existence." Zaleski suggested and then questioned the notion that we in the West live in a culture of "prolonged adolescence," first denying death and then becoming obsessed with it. She concluded that the current popular fascination with near-death testimony "speaks to an intense and widespread preoccupation in our society with problems of personal identity."

At the conference's end several speakers came up to congratulate Culianu. It was utterly fascinating, said one. You brought back the tradition of the Divinity School, said another participant. "Indispensable for anyone concerned with mysticism or religious experience," John Collins later wrote of Culianu's book on the topic.

On the last night Culianu took Carol Zaleski, Alan Segal, Greg Spinner, and Nathaniel Deutsch out for dinner. It was foggy, and they lost their way several times on lower Wacker Drive in Culianu's futile effort to show off Chicago's architecture to Zaleski. At dinner, Segal recalled, Culianu spoke of his political writing. "He said he was in danger, that it was spooky business. He said he had created some bad enemies and that some of the so-called freedom fighters were actually working for the KGB." No one at the table paid attention. "First of all," Segal said, "I knew about the Romanian situation. And I thought, who would be interested in what an academic had to say?"

By Friday night Culianu was exhausted. He told Greg Spinner, "We'll get together when all this clears up," and headed home to his apartment, where he planned to review the proofs of *The Tree of Gnosis* over the weekend, to rest, and to play chess against his computer. When Spinner pressed him about his summer plans, he told

• • • • • •

him, "I won't go to Romania now, but in September perhaps." It would mean missing the first Romanian-American Academy conference in Romania, a meeting opposition leaders saw as critical, but he had more or less given up on politics.

He could not tell how serious the threats he was receiving were, but he purchased extra mace packets and a special movement detection alarm that could be placed over his apartment door.

On Saturday morning he telephoned his sister in Poitiers. He told her that he and Hillary would come to France only, and he asked if their mother was well enough to travel to Paris. "But why not come to Romania?" Tess asked. "So many people want to see you. You could do so much good there, and it's a good time for you, a critical time."

"I have been receiving some phone calls, not at all pleasant."

"Oh? From whom?"

He laughed. "Oh, Vaca Românească."

She laughed at his pun. *Vatra* was the word for the rightist cultural movement. *Vaca* meant cow. She thought for a moment. "Everyone is threatened," she said. She felt that it was odd to talk with him without a tape machine whirring on the line. She was used to hearing it click on every time an overseas call came to Romania. "You *have* to come."

"Well, maybe."

"If you come you will be safer than if you don't."

He had never thought of it that way, although he had written in one *Lumea Liberă* article that going home would be allowing himself to be co-opted.

Culianu did not mention to his sister a final telephone message he had received, more cryptic than any of the threats. He was told to telephone a particular number at exactly 1:00 P.M. on May 21, his mother's name day. Whose number was it?

After telling his sister he loved her, he hung up and dialed his friend who had arranged for him to pick up a car in France and drive to Romania. "Hold the rental car," he said. "I just might keep my tickets for the moment."

❋ ❋ ❋

All that day he felt drained, so he rested, read, and wrote letters. He purchased Eliade's books at the Seminary Co-op bookstore and packed them in a box along with his own to send to Princess Margareta in Geneva. He packed another copy of *Out of This World* for Gabriela Adameșteanu, editor of 22, addressing it to Bucharest.

He sat down and wrote his mother a long letter, enclosing it with a name day card. He told her of the events of the last week and sent photographs of his day with the king and queen, as well as Christinel Eliade's birthday. In his years of exile, even at the height of surveillance, his name day letters and cards to his mother always got through quickly.

Pausing at times to work out on his exercise bicycle, he reviewed the page proofs of his book *The Tree of Gnosis.* His most ambitious published scholarly work, it offered a survey of gnosticisms from the Manichaeans to the nihilists, focusing on the dualistic contrasts — between good and evil, spiritual and material — that the varieties of the doctrine had in common. His book's introduction gave a name for his theory of logic systems unfolding over time — "morphodynamics" — drawing from the morphology of ideas proposed by the Scottish zoologist D'Arcy Wentworth Thompson. Following Thompson, he suggested that ideas followed a pattern in time, usually that of a tree branching outward. The pattern may be universal, but each bend or gnarl could be twisted by shifts in power, wars, or the whims of rulers. Invoking his image of a Chicago gangster flipping a coin to decide his next move, Culianu observed of the gnostic heretics that "life is a multiple choice mechanism. Myth too. And in myth as in life, the wrong choice can be deadly. It proved indeed deadly for innumerable Marcionites, Manichaeans, Paulicians, and Cathars, who came to grips with various authorities, were persecuted, hunted down, and exterminated. . . . In a certain way it seems astonishing that so much blood was shed for so little."

Moving beyond religions, Culianu traced interpretations of gnosticism to include Darwinism, Marxism, and even the modern science fiction of Philip K. Dick. In his epilogue, he hinted at his future scholarly direction when he stated, "There is practically no sector of the world and human existence that cannot be defined as a mind game."

His book's final lines took up the political implication of his thought that weighed so heavily on him. Referring to events in Romania and elsewhere and to a lifetime on the run from modern

· · · · · ·

totalitarianism, he noted that such games used for power "may seriously jeopardize two of the noblest conquests of Western mind and society: that freedom of thinking out everything to its ultimate consequences should never be interfered with by any authority, and that the dangers of freedom are not lessened by its suppression."

Yale's Harold Bloom called the book "a profound study of Western religious dualism; an immensely learned chronicle of Gnosis; and most originally, a theory of the cognitive dynamics from which religious formulations ensue." For the jacket, Bloom predicted, "It will endure a long time."

*   *   *

On Tuesday, May 21, Culianu brought his packages to campus to mail after class. From 10:00 to 11:30 he taught the Fundamentals course. The day's subject was gnosticism, and he lectured from the middle chapters of his book proof. After class he handed Gwen Barnes a letter of recommendation to type, then headed down to the annual book sale. It was crowded and festive, with music blasting and many of his students asking him about the after-death conference. He joked with a group who circled around him, and then he spotted Alexander Arguelles heading toward him. Alex looked nervous.

"Here," Alex said, "For you." It was a book called *The Dictionary of Imaginary Places*, by Alberto Manguel and Gianni Guadalupi. Arguelles expressed concern over his upcoming presentation to the faculty that afternoon, a redefinition of Spartan law as a quantum leap in ethics in ancient Greece and the model for Plato's later ideal state. Arguelles's approach was based on Culianu's speculative methodology, even paraphrasing Culianu's oft-repeated idea that the human mind had not changed in many millennia, only its operations. Alex was understandably nervous about how his presentation would be received by the faculty.

"It's just a rite of passage," Ioan told him. He patted him on the back. "It's nothing to fear. You'll do fine. See you in a couple hours."

He stopped off in the Swift Hall canteen, then headed up to Gwen's office to drop off the disk with his student recommendation. He picked up his mail and walked to his office. Shutting the door (something he hated to do because it tended to lock on him, and he was claustrophobic), he lifted the telephone receiver and dialed: 011-57-746-273.

A woman answered. He said he had been told to call this number. "No no," she said, with a Spanish accent. "Who are you? Who?" Trumpets blared in the background. He heard a murmur of conversation.

"Gracias," he said, and hung up. He stood up to head to the men's room.

❋   ❋   ❋

Sitting beside Gwen Barnes a few yards away, Divinity School secretary Judy Lawrence daydreamed about one of the soft ice cream cones sold out behind the bookstore. Lawrence was a diminutive, helpful, competent secretary who shared the office with Gwen and another secretary, Peggy Edwards. At about a quarter to one, Judy decided to take a break.

She went out to the elevator and pressed the button. When the elevator arrived, a man was on it. He was tall, perhaps six feet. He had darkish brown hair, fair skin, and light hazel eyes. For a moment the eyes fixed on her. She started.

His eyes terrified her. She later remembered him so vividly because she had never seen a person look at her like that. "He had a pointed, weak chin," she later told police. He was wearing a short-sleeved, white cotton knit shirt. He had dark brown hair and wore thick eyeglasses. He was carrying a canvas tote bag, light blue or gray with navy blue handles. He was slightly paunchy.

He must have punched the elevator buttons for both the third and the fourth floors. Because she had pressed the down button while waiting and the elevator stopped on the way up, he had to have pressed "3." Yet he must have also punched "4," because she saw that the fourth floor button was lit up when she got on.

The Swift Hall elevator was notoriously sluggish. As the seconds ticked she felt so eerie that, at the very last moment before the doors closed, she jumped out. She had never done that in her life. But there was something so spooky about the way he looked at her that she panicked. "He looked almost like a religious fanatic," she later said.

After taking the stairs down and buying her ice cream, she returned to the third floor. With another start, she noticed the same man in the third floor hallway, staring at a plaque, holding his canvas bag. Another man got off the elevator behind her, she recalled later. She walked to the office at the end of the hall. Gwen Barnes was listening on her headphones, and Peggy Edwards was typing. Judy finished her ice cream cone. It was a couple of minutes after one when they heard the shot.

V

. . . .

GAMES OF THE MIND,

1991–1996

It is generally found possible . . . to make some of the

more intelligent leaders of a rebellion perfectly Regular

and to admit them at once to the privileged classes.

— *Edwin A. Abbott*, Flatland

* * * * * * * *

AFTER-DEATH JOURNEYS

From the beginning the case presented difficulties for veteran Chicago detectives Ellen Weiss and Al McGuire. First, in the hope that Culianu might be resuscitated, paramedics moved the body before the scene could be photographed or diagrammed. By the time McGuire and Weiss made it to Swift Hall's third floor, thirty-five minutes after Gwen Barnes's first telephone call, blood was smeared all over the bathroom floor, people had moved freely in and out, and university representatives had grouped key witnesses together in waiting rooms, losing investigators the opportunity to obtain unrehearsed statements.

The detectives tried to pursue leads before they evaporated, in an attempt to follow a trail before it went cold. Neither Weiss nor McGuire finished the first night's work before 2:00 A.M., and they didn't quit much earlier in the days following. The Wentworth District's murder rate was among the heaviest in the city, but neighborhood crime used much bigger firepower — more likely a Magnum or Uzi submachine gun than a .25. A .25 caliber Beretta was small, like a woman's gun that could be slipped into a purse. The ammunition was expensive, and the gun tended to misfire.

Aside from the investigative problems, detectives had to contend with television crews and radio stations clamoring for news. They had, exactly, nothing to report publicly: no weapon, no motive, no witness, nothing. "In my thirty-four years I had never seen anything like it," said their captain, Fred Miller, who put off his planned vacation to oversee the investigation.

They were not completely in the dark, however. Dusting the scene for fingerprints and checking these against the prints of people who had walked in before they got there, they picked up a few clear sets that belonged to no one they had accounted for. Most of the prints would likely be unimportant. But one set, from the top of a partition, came from a spot where a killer would have steadied himself to shoot.

* * *

Around Swift Hall on Tuesday afternoon groups of students formed, talked in frightened voices, then drifted apart, only to regroup around a faculty member or anyone else who might have news. In the utter absence of information, rumors proliferated. To dispel the rumors, Culianu's student Joel Sweek called the secretaries' office, asking for him. Detective Ellen Weiss took the phone. "Professor Culianu is in a meeting," she said. "Can I take your name and number?" For his effort, Sweek was grilled by McGuire, Weiss, and another detective. "Did he have enemies?" they asked. "Was he happy in the department?"

Among themselves the detectives discussed polygraph exams for faculty and students. They checked telephone records and found the call to Colombia; they consulted Culianu's credit card accounts and travel plans and found that his reservations for the trip to Europe were still intact. Spinner, Allocca, and Gwen Barnes all gave statements specifying Culianu's fears and saying that he had canceled plans to return to Romania.

Culianu was an obsessively methodical man, police learned, going for coffee and using the rest room at nearly the same time each Tuesday and Thursday when he taught. McGuire and Weiss checked his class rosters and found that he was not a hard grader. They interviewed students and colleagues several times. "They asked about secret lovers, feuds with faculty or students," said Spinner, "but never about his threats, expressed fears, and writing." One of the faculty taunted the investigators. "Wendy Doniger kept saying to us, 'You'll never solve this,' " McGuire said. "Every time we went over there, it was like few of the faculty wanted to talk to us."

Over the next months the university refused two network television teams the right to film on campus — one from ABC's *Day One*, the other from NBC's *Unsolved Mysteries*. No reward for information was offered; no pressure was placed on the FBI to solve the case. "The university reaction was resounding silence," complained one student, Elise La Rose. Many others echoed her anger at the university's muted public response.

In the dark hours of Wednesday morning, detectives called Gwen Barnes back again, asking if she had noticed anything unusual with Ioan in the previous weeks. Even though Judy Lawrence reported having seen the strange man in the hall to police, investigators did not immediately act on her information. "She seemed hesitant," observed McGuire, "and sort of mesmerized by all the police." Lawrence claimed that she was in a state of shock the day of the murder, and did not fully connect her experience on the elevator with the crime at first. More than three years passed before investigators sent a squad car to chaperon her to the FBI's Chicago headquarters to make a computer composite image of the man. The delay did not affect Lawrence's memory. She remembered that face as clearly as if she had seen it the day before.

* * *

On May 31 Hillary Wiesner flew to Chicago for the funeral with her mother, her sister, and Kurt Hertzfeld. They boarded the same plane as Culianu's new friend John Crowley and Hillary's old friend Carol Zaleski. Still in shock, Wiesner told Zaleski that a Chicago policeman had called her to ask who might have wanted to kill Ioan. When she told him about Ioan's political articles, he asked, "Romania? Where's that?"

She told Zaleski about Ioan's favorite film, by Werner Fassbinder, based on the novel *Necromancer*. In it a figure from a computer game comes alive and tells the boy playing the game he has found a way to get out of his two-dimensional screen. The figure eventually succeeds in leaping out into three dimensions. After a while with his new friend, he whispers, "I've figured a way to get out of here." To Hillary the film encapsulated the meaning of Ioan's life and death.

At her apartment on Woodlawn Avenue, Christinel Eliade held a traditional Romanian sitting for the dead. A large black-and-white picture of Ioan hung above a multitude of burning candles. In the darkened apartment, cakes and coffee were served while people talked about Ioan and remembered him. "His presence filled the room," said Hillary Wiesner, who met Tess Petrescu for the first time that night. Christinel Eliade shooed the others away, leaving the two women alone together.

❀　❀　❀

The next day John Crowley accompanied Hillary, her sister, Nikki, and their mother when they went to Ioan's apartment. "I had never seen anything like it," Crowley said. "He kept detailed photo albums with snapshots of his personal Tarot card readings, going back for years." Culianu had placed a four-foot-high golden crucifix from Assisi on his wall, and a small emerald art deco goddess figure stood in an alcove. "I thought, my God, I've never seen a person like this before. He really took this stuff seriously."

Crowley described his relation with Ioan Culianu as intensely close and often magical, as did many others. They were almost like blood brothers. But the friendship was brief, with no answers to questions of background that confidants might share. Culianu triggered "a sense of self-discovery, and fantastic wish-fulfillment that was mildly hallucinatory," said Greg Spinner. Yet many people realized afterward they did not really know him.

Hillary and Nikki were driven down to Wentworth District police headquarters for questioning, along with Tess Petrescu. Detectives Weiss and McGuire asked about the telephone call to Colombia, about Culianu's finances and possible enemies. "He knew no one in Colombia," Hillary said. "Maybe he was told to make the call as a ploy to throw the investigation off track." She explained his fears and threats over Romanian politics. They listened patiently. The more she talked, the more the story threatened to dissolve amid the cinder block walls, squawking radios, and slamming lockers of district headquarters. For her part, Tess could not speak English well enough to add to the conversation. "I left thinking, well, they're trying, but nothing's going to come of it," said Nikki.

Ellen Weiss traced the telephone number through the FBI's office in Colombia. Agents there reported that the owner of the number had no connection to Culianu. Records showed the call began at 1:02 P.M. and lasted one minute. Detectives concluded that it was a wrong number, which made sense only if it had been a local call, not a long, complicated international number.

* * *

Detectives returned again and again to the murder site, rereading the report of Cook County's medical examiner, Robert Stein. It offered two pieces of evidence. "Examination of the scalp reveals no evidence of power burns or stippling," Stein noted. "Stippling" would have been expected unless the gun was held at least eighteen inches from the head, Stein reasoned. The murderer had a remarkably steady left hand. The second piece of evidence was the entrance wound, located in the "occipital area of the head, 4-and-a-half inches below the top of the head and one-half inch to the right of the external occipital tubical." The bullet's entrance suggested that Culianu was turned slightly when he was shot. The killing was expert, though not necessarily professional. One shot from a small gun in a public place was not the mark of a hit man. "To kill with one shot from a .25, though," Stein mused, "that's not easy. This looked like a Mob-style assassination."

Why was the killer unafraid of a witness entering the men's room? Perhaps an accomplice watched the entrance. Why not two shots to make sure he was dead? "Because if there had been two shots," Stein suggested, "someone would have come running." The former Securitate intelligence chief Ion Pacepa went further: "It's a typical KGB-style type of execution, one shot to the back of the head."

A murder site is a text, and Culianu's colleague Anthony Yu analyzed the bathroom locale of his close friend's murder. "It was ritually significant. It conveys symbolic and physical humiliation, stain, impurity, a most profane site to end a life." Sitting in his book-lined office, Yu turned away from his window. "In fact, I've often wondered if it was a cult killing."

One thing none of the investigators knew was that the date of Culianu's murder carried a deeply religious significance, a fact which the killer highlighted.

*   *   *

At school Dean of Students Jim Lewis consulted with students, deciding to hold the regular Divinity School lunch on Wednesday rather than canceling it. They expanded the scheduled chapel service that preceded lunch. That day's guest minister telephoned Culianu's friends and asked them to speak. Deutsch, Allocca, scholars Franklin Reynolds and Michael Fishbane, and others agreed. Afterward a university psychiatrist was called in to console students.

Of those closest to Culianu at school, Gwen Barnes suffered most vividly. The night of the crime she dreamed she was in a locked, pitch-black room. Far ahead of her was one tiny sliver of light. She was trying to reach the light, but her body was sluggish, her terror growing, when suddenly she woke up. She would experience the dream for several years, long after she left the school. It wasn't until some days after the crime that she recalled she had written a story a few years earlier. It was a whodunit involving a professor killed at the Divinity School. In her version the motive was professional jealousy.

Outside Culianu's office door students left roses, lilies, and notes every day. Some stopped to pray. Others reported Culianu sightings on campus. After meeting with his distraught students, Gilpin promised Spinner, Allocca, and Arguelles that Culianu's books would be transferred into a special collection in the library and that either a special scholarship or a plaque would be set up honoring his memory. Nothing was ever done.

＊　　＊　　＊

Culianu's killing uncoiled a string of strange events, rumors, and instances of disinformation around the world. In Bucharest Elena Bogdan received her son's letter two days after his murder — much faster than a letter seemingly would have arrived had he actually posted it from Chicago on the day of his death. The envelope looked exactly like the others she had received from him for years: it had the University of Chicago Divinity School address and American stamps. Unlike her dozens of other letters, however, it bore no American postmark, only Romanian. The letter's speedy receipt and lack of American postmark could be a coincidence — or someone took it from Culianu's desk that day, flew to Romania, and mailed it to her there.

The date of the crime was ritually significant: May 21 in the Orthodox church is Saint Helen's and Constantine's Day, Culianu's mother's name day. The name day in Orthodoxy commemorates a person's baptism into the sacred realm. During Ioan's years of exile, his mail was routinely delayed and opened, but for nineteen years the card he had sent his mother on her name day always arrived promptly and unopened.

The king in Geneva received Culianu's gift box of books on May 23, but it arrived opened and empty. Gabriela Adameşteanu received the copy of *Out of This World* at a Bucharest hospital, where she was recovering from a near-fatal traffic accident. It came with a note from Ioan inscribed Tuesday, May 21, 1991.

Though the picture was not complete, one could attempt to construct a profile of the killer by his methods. The discovery of the unmatched fingerprint in the strange position on the stall divider suggested that he had not worn gloves. He also had not used a silencer. Both moves suggested someone who wanted to act quickly without calling attention to himself, while at the same time choosing a very risky site. Lacking a silencer, he seemed certain that he could kill with one shot from a small caliber gun, even from a precarious position. The indifference toward leaving a fingerprint might have suggested that the killer knew he had no print on file in

· · · · · ·

America, according to one FBI source. The date of the annual book sale meant that crowds of strangers would be moving in and out of Swift Hall. The day's religious significance, and the site's symbolic humiliation, hinted at a premeditated, viciously mocking act meant to deliver a message.

❋   ❋   ❋

At Rockefeller Chapel on June 3, 1991, University president Hanna Gray and both Divinity School and university administrators and faculty paid homage to Professor Culianu, with students, friends, and older Romanian women and men who appeared as if by silent summons. During the service Bernard McGinn talked about eros as the binding force of the cosmos, and Gwen Barnes and Greg Spinner read from the Bible. Dean Gilpin quoted Culianu, "There is . . . no other resurrection but the river of ideas," and Wendy Doniger delivered a eulogy. "The time is out of joint," she said, quoting *Hamlet.* "O cursed spite, / That ever I was born to set it right!"

Privately Doniger offered a different opinion. "He played with fire with so many things," she said. "He lacked a basic, self-protective human instinct. Culianu didn't understand how serious it all was."

❋   ❋   ❋

In his writing Culianu stressed the deeper messages given in the small, forgotten details and coincidences of our lives. His killing offered a long sequence of such details. In Washington, for instance, State Department officials prepared "guidance" responses on the crime for an upcoming press conference. "The role of the security service in Romania is a matter of continuing concern," the official commentary read. "We have urged the Romanian government to dismantle secret police organs and bring intelligence activities under democratic controls." The final note, marked "if asked," warned: "Of course, any foreign diplomats assigned to the United States are expected to act in accordance with their diplomatic functions."

On the day of the murder a Los Angeles–based dissident began telephoning exiles, saying that Andrei Codrescu had also tried to kill himself. When the rumor reached Codrescu's wife in New Orleans, she panicked, calling her husband, who was alive and on assignment in Brazil. The dissident later became Romania's ambassador to the United Nations. Shortly thereafter Dumitru Mazilu, the troublesome writer who had been attacked in Geneva, was named ambassador to the Philippines, where he was no longer troublesome.

Andrei Codrescu talked about the rumors in his National Public Radio broadcast on the Culianu killing, noting that the disinformation campaign, which included charges that Culianu was homosexual (as if that, even if true, made a murder motive), was typical of the Ceauşescu era. "Maybe Professor Culianu was not killed for political reasons. Maybe the rumors of my death are greatly exaggerated. Maybe a distressed student killed Ioan. . . . Maybe. That would help save face for Romania. It won't bring back my friend."

❀ ❀ ❀

The disinformation intensified in the following weeks. In a June 7 press conference, President Ion Iliescu commented on the crime, stating that a "high American official" had told him it was not a political murder. A State Department expert on East European affairs, however, disclaimed any knowledge of such a comment by an American official. In the television broadcast of the presidential press conference, the reporter's question and Iliescu's reply were sloppily edited, leaving only a sudden snippet of an angry Iliescu denying any political involvement in the "Culianu case" in the middle of another discussion.

The official newspaper *Libertatea* published what it claimed was a Chicago police report asserting that no foreign intelligence service was involved in the crime. The police issued no such report.

Exactly one month after the murder, Radio Bucharest correspondent Mircea Podina delivered a roundup:

> We have learned recently that in the last period of his life Culianu was interested specifically in some secret organization of the Legionnaires in the United States. Among others, these would include the Sons of Avram Iancu. . . . [Hillary Wiesner] took after the assassination from Mr. Culianu's home three bags of unknown content. At the same time, she is the beneficiary of the life insurance policy of the professor, which is valued at $150,000. She also had a joint account with him worth $90,000. . . .

The main conclusion drawn from this investigation and that

was categorically confirmed by the Chicago police department is that there cannot be any implication of the Romanian secret service in this unhappy case.

Absolving Securitate and placing blame on the "Legionnaires" or on Hillary Wiesner, the broadcast pointed the finger squarely at the security police. In all, the disinformation on television and radio and in selected newspaper articles suggested someone behind the crime had access to Romanian national media.

In September 1991 some ten thousand miners entered Bucharest again, attacking not only the opposition party offices but also the government's reform wing centered on Prime Minister Petre Roman. The miners complained of low wages, terrible conditions, and escalating prices under Roman's rapid transition to a free market. In this most mysterious of the four miners' uprisings over two years, no one appeared to be in control, as some of the former student demonstrators attacked by the miners a year earlier now joined them. Arriving at the front steps of Cotroceni Palace, the mob was placated by the president until rioters cried out for Iliescu's removal as well. In the end, many miners complained they had been duped by those in power: "They took advantage," one said in the journal *Flacara*. "They made the miners believe they had participated in something grandiose . . . and thus we beat up the intellectuals."

Abroad, the remnants of Securitate appeared to be just as active as they had always been. In November an FBI official testified that, while other East European countries had scaled back their intelligence operations in the United States, "we cannot say the same for Romania. . . . We're still very concerned about their intentions."

Death threats intensified for other writers. The far rightist newspaper *România Mare* attacked Culianu's friend and University of Maryland professor Vladimir Tismaneanu: "Watch out rat, the rat patrol is after you." In Washington, Dorin Tudoran began receiving threats naming Culianu. "I got calls that said, 'We'll send you after your friend Culianu.'" In San Diego the FBI eventually caught the Romanians making the calls, a father and son team who would not divulge why or for whom they were acting. In Athens, Greece, Culianu's university friend Victor Ivanovici was threatened twice during the week his article on the murder appeared. Most of these messages borrowed the archaic language of the Iron Guard's mystic nationalism. Victor's letters even featured obsolete accent marks. Knowledgeable observers said that this was an old Securitate tactic. In his book *Red Horizons*, Ion Pacepa detailed international smear campaigns in which the Securitate used nationalist rhetoric to intimidate dissidents, sometimes inventing new far rightist groups.

In January 1992 an article in *România Mare* publicly and gleefully celebrated the killing. "Captivated by eros and magic from the Renaissance and trips 'out of this world,'" the writer Leonard Gavriliu said, Culianu "finally has the possibility to do his investigations." The style encapsulated the vicious far right rhetoric as it reemerged in a new, obscene style of the 1990s.

It is impossible to overlook, if you are a Romanian, the abominable crime done by the pygmy from Chicago . . . AGAINST ROMANIAN CULTURE. . . . The corpse from the water closet demolished everything: our prose, poetry, playwriting, arts, cinematography, philosophy, etc., killing all hope we have for tomorrow, *although, note well,* his article was offered for publication after the irreversible fall of the Communist regime.

The hyperbole, twisted reasoning, and obsessive nationalism all marked the new post-Communist rhetoric. The article went further:

But the most terrifying crime of that refugee in the gangster megalopolis of Chicago is divulged . . . in a nauseous apologia dedicated to that excrement over whom not enough water was flushed in the lethal *toilet* prepared for him as if by destiny. . . . That Chicago stench reproaches us for the fact that Eminescu taught us to love our country as the most precious gift in life. In the seething, fermented vision of Culianu's fecal brain, Eminescu and only Eminescu was guilty of the fact that Romanians suffer from patriotism—which could be a psychic disease. [He is one of the] privileged subordinates of those aiming for Romania to be transformed into a divided colony, easily dominated by the magnate of the "supermetropolis" to whom they are sold.

The newspaper was generally sent to East European institutes all over North America. None of them, however, ordered it. The article sparked renewed FBI interest just as Chicago detectives found what seemed to be their first solid lead.

. . . .

UNDER THE SIGN OF CAPRICORN: SUSPECTS

In Prospect Heights, Illinois, a young couple who knew nothing of Romania or Ioan Culianu began to have a series of strange experiences. Twenty-seven-year-old David Jedlicka owned a recording studio, and his wife, twenty-three-year-old Sandy Jedlicka, worked as an account clerk for a major airline. A tall, affable young manager of a new production company that specialized in commercial jingles, Dave had the same birthday as Ioan Culianu, January 5.

Early in the morning about three days after the crime, Dave Jedlicka shook in his sleep. His body jerked. He murmured something.
"Dave?" Sandy said. "You're talking in your sleep."

He spoke for about twenty minutes. Three days later he spoke
again in his sleep, and then again. He began doing so several times a
month. The experiences occurred early in the morning or late at
night, right after he fell asleep or just before he awoke. He would
shake violently and then start talking about people's lives and little events that happened to them. At first the experiences amused
Sandy, but as they continued she became more concerned. She began writing down his words.

David Jedlicka did not believe in the occult and had no interest in
his wife's questions, although his mother was an amateur "chan-
neler." But as time went on, and the experiences of a voice that
called itself Jessie continued, both he and Sandy started to wonder
what was happening to them.

On the night of his mutual birthday with Ioan Culianu, January
5, 1992, after dinner at a local restaurant, Dave came home with
Sandy and watched television before retiring to the bedroom. About
seven the next morning Dave's body jerked. "Have to find the boy
with same birthday as Dave," said Dave in a high, childlike tone.

"Do you mean . . ." Sandy named a friend.

"No."

"Who?"

He spelled out the name, I-o-a-n C-u-l-i-a-n-u. Sandy Jedlicka
wrote it in her red spiral-bound notebook. To her the letters did not
sound like a real name.

"Died soon before Jessie started to talk. He knew things. Tried to
teach. Was his job. Lived in big learning place. Not far," her husband said.

"What big learning place?"

"His family far place. From bad place. Not OK to go. Not OK to
think. So run away." Sandy scribbled down what her husband was
saying. "Learn what he knew." His voice trailed off and stopped.

From start to finish the experience lasted about a quarter of an
hour, perhaps less. This was the first occasion Dave had ever used a
name that neither he nor Sandy recognized, but they did not take
much notice of it until two nights later, when he spoke again, this
time in an older, more educated voice.

"He was educated in theology. Find out what he wrote . . . It's your job to find his books and learn from them. He came from a Communist country. His girlfriend's name begins with H."

Reasoning that such a foreign-sounding name would most likely be found in Chicago, Sandy Jedlicka opened a city telephone book. She found "Ioan Culianu" living at 1700 East Fifty-sixth Street. Shaking a little, she dialed his number. What would she say to him? she wondered. She heard a message saying the phone was disconnected. Thoroughly intrigued, she decided that the "big learning place," if close to his street address, probably was the University of Chicago. She began calling the divisions of the school to find this person.

❋   ❋   ❋

In the same town where the Jedlickas lived, Adrian Szabo and his friend Johnny were arrested for and charged with a crime of "armed violence, aggravated battery, and residential burglary." Suburban detectives had pulled Johnny's name from the victim, a construction company manager who had employed him for a brief time. Johnny was angry about back pay he claimed was owed to him, and on September 24, 1991, he had enlisted his friend Adrian to "help" collect the money. The two pushed their way into the man's home. In the ensuing scuffle Adrian pulled a .32 caliber pistol, hitting the homeowner several times on the head and then running off.

It took three months, but Prospect Heights detectives finally traced Johnny to Anaheim, California, where local police arrested him on December 21 for extradition to Illinois. Slapped with a six-figure bond and facing the prospect of a stiff prison sentence, Johnny quickly named his partner. Johnny told police that Adrian worked for an East European crime organization involved in drug running and murder-for-hire. Detectives located Adrian, an unemployed truck driver and a young father of two girls, through records of the repossession of his Toyota. Around nine o'clock on a morning in early February 1992, as he was kissing his two girls good-bye, Adrian heard a knock on the door. Two detectives and a patrolman burst in and arrested him.

When they had begun the Culianu investigation, Detectives Weiss and McGuire had sent out a notice to police departments about crimes involving a .25, a relatively unusual gun. Recalling the notice, one of the suburban detectives noticed that Johnny, tattooed, short, and muscular, had a .25 caliber pistol. He notified Wentworth District detectives of the arrest. Al McGuire drove up to question the suspect, who had a long record of burglaries, assaults, and charges of public intoxication and was wanted on a charge of rape in Michigan. At first Johnny talked freely, bragging that Adrian "worked for Securitate." Pressed about the Culianu murder, he stopped talking, invoking his Miranda rights and requesting an attorney. McGuire noticed that he was left-handed.

Hoping for a solid lead, McGuire and Weiss then went to Adrian, who at first would say nothing. Learning that *his* bail had been set in the high six figures, Adrian found a private attorney who had handled other cases for Romanian immigrants. By the spring of 1992, feeling betrayed by Johnny and hoping to use his testimony in exchange for a lighter sentence, Adrian was ready to talk "about the murder of Ioan Culianu."

❋   ❋   ❋

In Romania during the first nine months of 1992, the main story was the surging popularity of the far right. The right provided critical support for the Iliescu government to remain in control of the Chamber of Deputies and the Senate. The main far rightist group was Vatra Românească, which was trying to play a leading role in shaping the national agenda. Its main spokesman was Ion Coja, Culianu's former teacher. Vatra held its annual meeting in 1991 during the week of the professor's death. Its leading figures were closely linked to the old Securitate.

Early in 1992 there appeared a newer, younger rightist party that demonstrated the importance of the Eliade legacy to the nation after the revolution. Its leader was none other than the democratic student hero Marian Munteanu. Calling his new party Miscarea Pentru România (Movement for Romania), Munteanu modeled his efforts on the Iron Guard rhetoric of a "new man for a new age," putting a special emphasis on the works of Mircea Eliade. His followers had to study Eliade's writings before they could join.

❋   ❋   ❋

It took several months in the spring of 1992 for Sandy Jedlicka to reach the Divinity School at the University of Chicago. She hap-

260 GAMES OF THE MIND

. . . . . .

pened to call one day after the crime's one-year anniversary. Only
then did she learn from secretary Judy Lawrence that Ioan Culianu
had been murdered. Sandy's heart leaped. The Jedlickas considered
going to the police and the FBI, but they feared that David might
become a suspect. They had no interest in money or publicity. If
anything, Dave resented the experience.

Sandy questioned her husband further about the murder. When
he next spoke, on May 25, 1992, she asked "Jessie" flat out, "Who
killed Professor Culianu?"

"Four of them carried out the plan. More than four made up the
plan."

"Were they from his old country?"

"No."

"Why did they kill him?"

"Because he talked bad about the old country."

Two nights later "Jessie" spoke again. Sandy asked again about
the crime and the killers. "The four boys didn't know each other,
didn't know why they were to do it."

Three nights later, on Saturday, David Jedlicka awoke suddenly,
more agitated than usual. When he began talking, Sandy pulled out
her notebook. "How old were the boys who killed Ioan Culianu?"
she asked.

"One old. Other three only a little older than you."

"Who were they?" Sandy asked.

"One know."

"What?"

Her husband said nothing.

"Were they from here?"

"Some. One from old country."

* * *

During the spring and summer Adrian met with Detectives Mc-
Guire and Weiss and with a new FBI agent assigned to the case, John
Bertulis, in the raucous confines of Cook County Prison. Adrian
told them about "Nicolae Constantin." In December 1990, Adrian
told investigators, he learned from Johnny that Constantin wanted
to set up a murder. The job involved killing a professor. Adrian
would only have to drive the car. The pay for him, he claimed, was to
be five thousand dollars up front, and five thousand afterward.

By this time Adrian was driving a truck back and forth on a weekly basis from O'Hare to Los Angeles International Airport. He was drinking a lot and was worried, as always, about money. In March or April 1991, he claimed, he agreed, against his better judgment, to meet Johnny. They met at a restaurant on Thornton and York Roads, beside a row of carting companies. It was raining. He claimed Johnny talked for about forty-five minutes about other things. Adrian said his friend took out a yellow envelope, bigger than letter size but not much. Inside, Adrian said, he saw two tall stacks of fifty-dollar bills and a photograph. The black-and-white image showed a pale young man with long sideburns, wearing an ill-fitting Romanian suit, with a fat, seventies-style tie. The photograph had jagged edges, as was common in a Bucharest passport photo shop.

"Mr. Constantin's paying us," Adrian alleged Johnny told him. "You just pick me up."

Adrian told investigators that he ultimately balked at the plan. He claimed he heard nothing more from Johnny until July 1991, when he received a late-night call from his friend, who said he was in Florida. "Is anyone looking for me?" Johnny allegedly asked.

"No, why?"

Adrian said Johnny told him he had committed the crime. "*Un cartus dupa ureche,*" Adrian claimed were his words. "One bullet behind the ear."

The story sounded compelling, but it struck investigators as odd that someone not involved in a murder claimed to know so much about it. Investigators needed something — a bullet, a fingerprint, or someone to whom Johnny had bragged. They learned that a .25 was the gun of choice for the growing Romanian underworld in Chicago. With the assistance of the FBI, the police set to work.

＊　＊　＊

In Romania, in an unexpected move, the king was allowed back home in 1992 for the first time in forty-five years. Huge throngs appeared everywhere he went — from Bucharest to the holy sites of Curtea de Argeş — some numbering in the hundreds of thousands. In Bucharest's University Square, news reports claimed, the crowds lifted his limousine into the air. When his visa expired, Michael was asked to leave. He was never allowed to return. In the world of post-

Communist Romania, those in power learned that they were right to fear the king and anyone associated with him.

Romania in 1992 seemed to be caught in a repetition of the 1920s, observed Hebrew University historian Jean Ancel, who went back to Romania that summer at the request of the Canadian government. In Bucharest he felt an eerie sense of déjà vu. "I saw a fledgling fragile democracy prone to corruption and manipulation, splintering into ineffective parties amid a growing far right. It was a sense of freedom after crisis, in which people felt they could do as they chose without consequences."

Canada had a large concentration of Iron Guardists still living in Toronto, Windsor, and Hamilton. These Iron Guard exiles controlled some immigrant communities and had been blamed for the 1986 murder of a journalist in Toronto. A leading expert on the Romanian holocaust, Ancel was in Romania to investigate allegations of war crimes committed by a number of the exiles in Canada. He felt frustrated in his efforts to gain access to the necessary documents in government archives. "I was telephoned at odd hours. I was watched, I was followed. They wanted to know every move I made."

He noted with dismay the legacy of Mircea Eliade in the 1990s. "Eliade was a young, brilliant intellectual who, at a certain moment, clearly had gone over to the Iron Guard. Many documents place him among the Iron Guard's ideologists," Ancel said. "He was dangerous because he was brilliant in a negative way. He elevated Codreanu and the movement without naming it fascist. He was popular with the youth." In the end, Ancel argued, the rhetoric of communism and postcommunism did not differ much from prewar fascism. "At heart Romanian regimes have legitimated themselves by taking any attack on them as an attack on the nation."

· · ·

In Chicago, Adrian Szabo's trail started off auspiciously. As Adrian had directed them, investigators found bullets from a .25 embedded in the floor of an apartment on the West Side, where Johnny had shot them off one night at a party. (FBI agents had to ask the young Pakistani family living in the apartment if they could tear up and then replace the new carpeting.) Unfortunately the bullets did not match the one that had killed Culianu. They did not even come from the same lot number. McGuire and Bertulis looked for a second .25 that Adrian claimed Johnny had hidden, searching vainly over two frozen days in a railyard behind Adrian's truck repair shop. They then used an electronic testing device to check the walls of a North Side restaurant owned by a Romanian called the Pine Tree Grill, where Adrian alleged that Johnny had purchased his second gun, shooting into the wall to test it. No bullets.

Chicago police sought a connection with the unsolved 1986 killing of a Romanian journalist in Toronto. That crime was similar to the killing of Ioan Culianu: the victim had been threatened beforehand, the gun was small caliber, and the case remained unsolved. The victim's wife heard the murderer speak in Romanian before firing, but the gun he had used was a common .22 caliber pistol. On the other hand, apart from the fact that he was also a writer, the crime victim was quite different from Ioan Culianu. Constantin Dima Drăgan had run a pro-Ceaușescu newspaper called *Tricolorul* (Three Colors, referring to the Romanian flag). He gathered dirt on people and was considered a government operative and a "rat, a weasel," said one source.

The shooting in Toronto appeared to be an act of the Iron Guard because the victim was stabbed after he was shot, allegedly an Iron Guard signature. Toronto detectives also found that the same gun had been used to fire on the Romanian embassy a month earlier, on the anniversary of the Iron Guardist uprising in Bucharest in January 1941.

In Culianu's case, some fellow exiles conjectured, the Iron Guard would have feared Culianu because he had been named executor of Eliade's unpublished scholarly papers. They might have feared he would use his position to undermine his mentor's reputation by publishing the wrong documents. But by 1991 the Eliade papers had long since been dispersed, mostly under the care of Regenstein Library. Eliade's uncompleted volumes had been either edited and published or shelved. There were no secret Iron Guard papers.

Concerning the whispered rumors, Paris dissident Monica Lovinescu put it best: "Whenever they say it's the Iron Guard," she observed, "you can be sure it's Securitate."

※ ※ ※

At a critical point in almost every one of Ioan Culianu's fictional works, the narrator himself is pulled into his story. In May 1992 I received a telephone call from Sandy Jedlicka. The secretary Judy Lawrence had given her my number. Jedlicka and I talked about their experiences. I arranged to visit her and Dave.

We met at Dave's recording studio in St. Charles, Illinois, and drove to a Mexican restaurant for lunch. Born and reared in the small farming town of Chilton, Wisconsin, Sandy had curly reddish hair and a loopy sense of humor. She had come to Chicago to work as a nanny. Dave had grown up in the affluent Chicago suburb of Deerfield. He was tall, awkward, with a light smile. He had attended the Chicago Academy of Music and had met Sandy in a bar where he was playing bass in the band.

Sandy pulled out the red notebook in which she recorded Dave's conversations. When she explained that "Jessie" would not allow her voice to be recorded, I grew more suspicious. I tried not to believe in experiences like that of the Jedlickas, and I suspected many reported incidents to be either hoaxes or the product of our deepest desire to break the bond of ordinary life. We decided that Sandy would call me whenever she heard Jessie speak, and that I would tell the Jedlickas as little as possible about Ioan Culianu's life.

One problem, Sandy said. She had already purchased *Eros and Magic in the Renaissance* and *Out of This World*. Would they suggest too much about the crime?

Culianu's books were hard to find, expensive, and dense even for professional reviewers; I had read them numerous times in order to make sense of them. I reconsidered my suspicions of the Jedlickas, especially after their experiences made them grow increasingly fearful.

❈   ❈   ❈

On Wednesday, June 3, 1992, David Jedlicka was sleeping late after a last-second club date had kept him out the night before with friends. At about ten in the morning he jerked in his sleep. Sandy, who worked from noon to eight and was still home, went to get her notebook. After a few minutes of talking, Sandy asked "Jessie" if she knew the names of the killers of Professor Culianu.

"No."

"Tell me whatever you do know."

"Some live in big city. All of them were boys. In plan, need one boy who can go places and not be strange. One of them knows Ioan. Not the older one. Jessie think was a friend of Ioan's."

"What else?" Sandy asked.

"Was told to be place so can get message. Was dark hair boy. Extra seeing things. Live in big city now."

Through further questioning Sandy Jedlicka determined that the "extra seeing things" were eyeglasses, much like those in the composite image that Judy Lawrence later created. But the last thing her husband said took her aback. "Jessie think boy still at learning place. Think was a friend of Ioan's."

❋ ❋ ❋

In September 1992 Ion Iliescu won a national election in a plebiscite rife with fraud. Even with the fraud Iliescu's party, the Democratic National Salvation Front, polled only 28% of the vote for the Senate and 27% in the Chamber of Deputies. Amnesty International noted that the government was "maintained in power by smaller left wing and right wing, nationalist parties." In its 1993 report "Romania: Continuing Violations of Human Rights" the nonprofit group observed that most of the judges in the country remained in the same posts they held before 1989. Still, the situation in Romania matched closely Ioan Culianu's prediction — that the people themselves would eventually freely elect a government directed by former Communists.

In the weird looking-glass world of post-Communist Romanian politics, the cultural movement Vatra Românească resuscitated Ion Antonescu, the dictator in World War II responsible for the deaths of a quarter of a million or more Jewish and Roma people. Virtually every major publication "competed in turning Antonescu into a national hero," wrote Radio Free Europe's Michael Shafir. A proposed statue to the dictator drew fire from fifteen U.S. senators and representatives, but the main purpose of reviving Antonescu seemed to be to understate and ridicule the role played in the 1940s by King Michael.

In September, in a back street office guarded by an armed policeman, Corneliu Vadim Tudor responded to my questions about the *România Mare* article that extolled Culianu's murder. "I get these documents from young men," Tudor, in his trademark white suit, boomed. "They don't tell me where they come from, and I don't ask." He produced the telephone number of the article's signed author, Leonard Gavriliu. In 1992 my repeated attempts to reach Gavriliu by telephone were unsuccessful. When I finally contacted him after I returned to Romania as a Fulbright Senior Researcher in 1994, Gavriliu denied having written the article.

Confronted with Culianu's assertion he was being threatened by Vatra Românească before he was killed, his former teacher Ion Coja became pensive. "Vatra was infiltrated by SRI," he said. "I even accused [SRI director] Virgil Magureanu of this to his face. He did not disagree."

With all the confusion of its daily politics serving to block rather than to promote reform, Romania lurched into 1993 with many of the same problems as in the past. According to the U.S. State Department's *Country Reports on Human Rights Practices for 1992,* the new constitution allowed the Romanian Information Service "to justify other widely prohibited actions on national security grounds," including illegal entry, search, and mail and wire tapping. Ioan had often mentioned to Hillary his suspicion that his calls home were tapped. Not only could he hear the recorder running, he said, he could hear the monitoring officers playing cards or laughing in the background. Whenever the conversation became sensitive, the line would be cut.* The experience of severed phone lines was shared by other journalists in Romania. The young Associated Press bureau chief in Bucharest, Dan Petreanu, complained that his phone was cut off whenever tried to ask sensitive questions of government officials. "I can practically predict when it will happen," he said.

* Twice my telephone calls to Romania were cut off at critical moments in interviews. The first occasion was in January 1994 as I discussed the murder investigation with Tess Petrescu. The second was on April 5, 1996, when I interviewed Gelu Voican, then Romanian ambassador to Tunisia, about the case. Of the eight pieces of mail Petrescu said she sent to me in the years 1991–94, only one ever reached its destination: a Christmas card.

On December 13, 1994, I lectured on the Culianu case at the American Cultural Center in Bucharest. Three men with two large television cameras interfered with the talk for the first twenty-five minutes, standing in front of me to face the audience, walking up and down the aisles, videotaping most people in the audience and often the notes people were taking. Though the cameras were marked with the logo of Romanian television station, to my knowledge no report has ever aired.

The special dignity of mankind stems not from its

obedience but from its opposition to the world.

— *I. P. Culianu*, Eros and Magic in the Renaissance

. . . .

THE INVESTIGATION

In the 1990s around the world, writing had become a more dangerous act than at any time in the twentieth century. According to the nonprofit Committee to Protect Journalists, in 1992 at least fifty writers were killed around the world; in 1994 the figure jumped to seventy-two. Twenty-seven journalists were killed in the first nine months of 1995 in Algeria alone. These cases were just the documented ones; many more writers had disappeared or been beaten or threatened. The danger was most pronounced for smaller press writers and radio broadcasters, who took bigger chances and had fewer resources when threatened.

In the United States, thirteen writers were killed between 1976 and 1992. The killings occurred mainly in émigré communities, and mostly the murders remain unsolved. In many of the American immigrant cases, the pattern followed that of Culianu's killing — beginning with mailed threats, then telephone and physical threats, private expressed fears never reported to the police, followed by a murder that baffles police so much that they first try to call it a suicide. With conflicting rumors, an absence of witnesses, and other pressing crimes for police to investigate, most of these cases remained open.

Different reasons lie behind the widely noted increase in the attacks on writers in the post-Cold War era, including the *fatwa* on Salman Rushdie or the near-fatal attack on Egyptian Nobel laureate Naguib Mahfouz. The separate causes include power politics, religious fundamentalism, ethnic strife, even occasionally money. But a deeper underlying link is something rarely discussed in news analyses and yet is responsible for much of the danger in the world today: the power of the unconscious. In the collapse of the old world order, some of the most primitive forces of history came bubbling up — hatred of the Other, anti-Semitism, obsessive fantasy. These forces became the weapons of new demagogues and extremists. Writers were often their targets because they work on a psychological frontier where national, tribal, and individual memory intersect. The danger had little to do with "truth" but much to do with the way the mind invents its myths — a process Culianu illuminated in detail.

❋   ❋   ❋

In the middle of June 1992 David Jedlicka started speaking one morning near dawn. Sandy roused herself sleepily, and then snapped awake. She again questioned him about how the crime was committed.

"Every boy had a gun, but they were different shootguns. . . . The boy who shot him is still in big place. Dark hair, important clothes."

"What kind of important clothes?" Sandy Jedlicka asked. "Does Dave have important clothes like this?"

"No. Other boys have same clothes. They don't know why they are told to do it. Boy with extra seeing things tells them what to do." "What kind of important clothes?" she persisted. "Like a uniform?"

"No."

"A priest?"

"No. Short black, leather. Something written on the back." With that he trailed off. She interpreted this to mean that the "boys" wore leather jackets.

* * *

Investigators in four states worked unsuccessfully to corroborate Adrian's story. FBI agents could not find a transport company that matched Szabo's description. Johnny also had an alibi: construction company records showed he had been at work on May 21, 1991. More important, Chicago police could not match his fingerprint to the one found at the murder site. In an FBI-administered polygraph test, his denial of involvement in the crime registered in the range of "truthful."

Now the investigation returned to the man who had first offered the information against Johnny. In the spring of 1993, Adrian Szabo agreed to submit to a polygraph test.

"Were you there at the killing of Professor Culianu?"

"No." His answer registered as "truthful."

"Were you involved?"

"No."

His response on the polygraph registered in the "untruthful" range.

One could not make too much of such a response. It *is* possible, much as Culianu had noted in his stories of forgeries and history, under the stress of prison conditions to tell the truth and register on a polygraph as lying. Adrian told the FBI his "untruthful" results came because "I felt since I knew about it and did not prevent it, I was somehow involved."

* * *

Far more important than the details of a halting investigation was the public record and pattern of events in Romania itself. When the United States considered Romania for Most Favored Nation trade status, for example, opponents like former ambassador David Funderburk argued forcefully that granting MFN status would legitimate an illegitimate regime. Funderburk, who went on to be elected as a Republican congressman from North Carolina, noted the continuing vote fraud and deeper problems of harassment and manipulation of events. In one documented case, a young Romanian diplomat and his family had complained of their votes being altered, and the diplomat had fled with his wife to the United States. Calling home, "he learned that his father had, in January 1993, been interrogated and beaten by the secret police, and had died from his injuries 2 hours after returning home from the interrogation." The perpetrators were never brought to justice.

Summarizing his arguments in a letter to New York senator Daniel Patrick Moynihan, Funderburk recorded the instances of carryover from the Communist era in Romania, emphasizing the maintenance of power by the old Communist nomenklatura, a weak and uneven development toward democratic government, a poor record of encouraging privatization and free enterprise, continued government domination of television, continued operation of the old secret police under another name, and human rights and minority rights violations. Amnesty International recorded the instances of continuing harassment, protesting the lack of resolution of several disappearances during the violent events of 1990 and 1991. Parents of some of the missing students, including Natalia Horia, reported to Amnesty International that they had been threatened by police when they tried to obtain information on the fate of their children. "You give your country a bad name. Perhaps you conspired in your son's disappearance," Horia said she was told.*

In Romania, Funderburk might have added, individuals associated with the first events of the revolution and the trial of the Ceauşescus had been dying or disappearing in mysterious ways. The "suicide" of Ceauşescu's brother in his Vienna apartment was followed by the suicide of Georgică Popa, the Ceauşescu trial judge. Later the pilot of the helicopter in which Ceauşescu had fled, Colonel Vasilei Malutan, died when his helicopter ran into some high-voltage wires. He had just revealed to a parliamentary commission

---

* "Romania," *Amnesty International Report: 1993* (New York: Amnesty International USA, 1993), 245.

that Ceauşescu had been carrying a suitcase with secret documents when he fled. Several other figures died in murky circumstances. One thing was clear: the smaller role-players in the events of the "revolution" perceived themselves to be in danger. The Ceauşescus' prosecutor, Dan Voinea, told reporters he was certain he and the other involuntary trial participants were to be killed once the "trial" organizers had left.

Despite the questions, the United States approved Most Favored Nation trading status with Romania.

❋   ❋   ❋

In February 1994 Tess Petrescu wrote the U.S. ambassador in Bucharest, John Davis, a supporter of the Iliescu regime, to complain of the slow progress in her brother's murder investigation. On February 25 she heard from the State Department's chargé d'affaires, a Chicagoan named Jonathan Rickert: "We regret that United States law enforcement agencies have been unable to solve this crime. Should sufficient evidence emerge, however, to sustain charges in a court of law, no political or other consideration would stand in the way of vigorous prosecution."

The clever mind that staged all these crimes . . . wanted

us to understand its purpose. Consequently, it had to

give us another clue, a clue for the Mars murder. Don't

you see the game is entertaining for our challenger only

to the extent that we can follow it?

    —I. P. Culianu and H. S. Wiesner,

      The Emerald Game

GAMES OF THE MIND

    In the summer of 1994, Culianu's *Eros și magie in Renaştiere* was published in Romania by Nemira Editions, where Dan Petrescu was chief editor. In its first week it sold out its print run of twenty thousand copies. Other Culianu best-sellers followed in Romania, including *Out of this World* and *Mircea Eliade*, the former translated and introduced by Andrei Oişteanu, the latter with an afterword by Sorin Antohi. Just as Culianu had predicted to his sister from Rome in 1972, he had come back "a winner." Translations of his works appeared in Spain, Italy, Japan, France, Germany, Czechoslovakia, Poland, Holland, and elsewhere. Special presentations or whole conferences in his honor were held in Paris and Rome. Several book chapters and entire books on or dedicated to Culianu came out— including John Crowley's *Love and Sleep*; Elémire Zolla's *Ioan Culianu*; the papers from his final conference, *Death, Ecstasy, and Other Worldly Journeys*, edited by John Collins and Michael Fishbane; and, in Romania, Ilieana Mihăilă's *The Magician's Splendors and Sufferings*. His works of fiction attracted a large audience at home.

The political danger for Ioan Culianu began with his fiction, said fellow writers Dorin Tudoran and Andrei Codrescu. Political murder "has always been a way of propping up regimes," said a 1920s Romanian pamphlet on the dangers of artists and intellectuals writing about politics. For Ioan Culianu, telling stories was the best way to understand the forces behind everyday life.

The text of Culianu's story "The Intervention of the Zorabis in Jormania" is striking for its allusiveness and hints at deeper knowledge well before the Romanian "revolution" had even been imagined by most people. In Jormania, Culianu wrote, all the key players' "names end in -an," as did those of many of the key figures in the revolution, such as Petre Roman, Silviu Brucan, and Gelu Voican. Though Culianu was only playing a game in which certain facts corresponded to real events, a close reader might have wondered what else he knew, or what knowledge he frequently hinted in his writing he was hiding. Among his closest readers, Andrei Codrescu surmised in a National Public Radio broadcast, were members of their country's intelligence service.

"Free Jormania," by contrast, was more specific in its description of the intelligence service's behind-the-scenes infighting, the fomented rise of a new far right, and the mysterious disappearances of key figures after the revolution. Each insider is given a name that is a play on words and personalities, such as *Motan* (Tomcat), *Bulan* (Cudgel), *Bostan* (Pumpkin). The story focused on the step-by-step process of a revolution's derailment following a dictator's hasty execution in a faked trial.

If Culianu's fiction brought him attention, his weekly political articles, 22 interview, and pledge of support for the king brought escalating and documented threats. In those articles he purposefully went beyond the edge of danger. With the benefit of hindsight his observations today seem clear and logical, but his bitterly taunting tone against the men he called tools of the KGB was deliberately calculated to enrage his audience at a level deeper than that of conscious thought. A student of magical arts, he could not resist playing with them in his writing. Like Giordano Bruno, Culianu seemed to want to do more than merely write about events, but to use his theories of mass psychology to influence them. As with Bruno, it's astounding that someone would murder him for his writing, but his work and world role in a chaotic time made a sum greater than any one of its parts.

It is hard to separate the degree to which chance, coincidence, or misperception increased the danger in Culianu's last months. In April 1991 he pledged support to the king, saw a five-month-old incendiary interview published in 22, and finalized his long-planned return home. He was slated for an honorary directorship of a new national Oriental Institute, the same post tapped for Mircea Eliade half a century earlier just before he was forced into exile. After months of silence, it might have appeared to those Culianu said were watching him that he was going to become active again. He told Fran Gamwell he was being followed; he told his conference colleagues he was being threatened; he told the poet Dorin Tudoran he was in danger; and he told his sister that he feared to come home. To all of these people he claimed that the perpetrators came from the forces behind the Romanian government.

❋　❋　❋

In October 1995 *Lumea Liberă* and the aggressive Romanian news daily *Ziua* (The Day) published the FBI composite picture of the strange man seen by Judy Lawrence minutes before the Chicago crime. With Dan and Tess Petrescu and others, *Ziua* offered a sixty-million-lei (twenty-thousand-dollar) reward for information leading to the arrest of the murderer. The paper received many obviously spurious tips. *Ziua*'s chief adjunct editor, Gabriel Stănescu, also received a telephone call from Ioan Culianu's former acquaintance Gelu Voican. The former deputy prime minister and intelligence chief criticized the attempt to label Ioan Culianu's murder a political crime, arguing that the government would have no interest in such a counterproductive killing of an American professor at a moment when it sought western acceptance.

Among the tips the *Ziua* offer produced came an anonymous letter with a local postmark and no return address. It alleged this story: Voican directed the assassination of Ioan Culianu, working through three reassigned intelligence officers, one of whom was posted to the Romanian national airline. The letter named the men and claimed the murderer closely resembled the FBI composite of the man.

The receipt of the anonymous letter was confirmed by *Ziua*'s publisher, Sorin Roşca Stănescu, Gabriel Stănescu, and *Ziua*'s crime editor, Sorin Ovidiu Balan. "We are not sure how much to believe it," cautioned Gabriel Stănescu. "It is not supported by material evidence." The detailed letter, listing even the alleged killer's number of children, sounded in some ways as fictional as Ioan Culianu's stories. Informed of the letter Voican, then the Romanian ambassador to Tunisia, called it "a folly, an outrage." He vigorously denied any involvement in the murder of a man he liked and scholar he admired.

Ziua did not publish the letter and there is no evidence to link Gelu Voican to the crime. He left his post in the intelligence service more than a year before Culianu's death. In the end the anonymous letter represents yet another example of disinformation to divert the Culianu investigation. The FBI, however, set to work on the letter's more specific allegations about the name of the killer, learning that a man with the same name, age and family status as the letter reported, *had* worked as a steward on Tarom airlines. As early as 1981 he had applied for a 12-month visa waiver to remain in the United States. Records showed he was approved in 1983 and renewed in 1986. The Chicago bureau of the FBI put out inquiries to every major law enforcement databank for information on any of the four men listed in the anonymous letter. So far it has received no valuable evidence.

No one has been charged to date with the murder of Ioan Culianu. Reviewing the scattered pieces of the Chicago investigation, one law enforcement source felt Adrian Szabo's polygraph result suggested he may have been approached in a first plan that was later abandoned. As for the Jedlickas, nothing they said or did suggested they invented their experience. Friends vouched for their integrity. David Jedlicka expressed the wish that his experience had never happened. He and Sandy had no interest in Romania, or in publicity.*

The critical facts in the story, however, do not come from psychics, informants or highly suspicious anonymous letters. They come from the victim himself, and from his own method of analysis applied to the pattern of events in his death.

* * *

Culianu told many prominent friends of his fears prior to his murder, of threats using far rightist rhetoric, of surveillance, and, finally, personal confrontation. He said his pursuers came from the former intelligence service of his own country. After his murder came more subterfuge: a presidential press conference doctored for broadcast, false radio and newspaper reports, and persistent refusals from top officials to answer questions about the crime. Such disinformation was a "trademark of Securitate," according to Andrei Codrescu. The humiliating manner of the murder, and the choice of a lesser known figure whose disappearance would confuse and demoralize opponents, was another trademark. Culianu's harassment, combined with the disinformation after the crime, at the very least merited a government response.

Over four years I made roughly a dozen interview requests by telephone, fax, letter and in person — to Virgil Magureanu, Ion Iliescu and to the successor of DIE Director Mihai Caraman, Ion Talpes. Magureanu and Talpes did not turn down the requests outright, but each time I telephoned I was told there was no answer yet to my requests. When I did set up an interview with the new SRI spokesman Nicolae Ulieru, he failed to appear. He claimed that he "knew nothing about Culianu."

If the killing's attention to arcane detail and to the political influence of an intellectual abroad fit a pattern of past Securitate killings, it was also effective. In 1990 and early 1991 the Romanian regime still faced domestic unrest and western reluctance to invest in a country it deemed unstable. Prominent émigrés supported a grow-

---

* On the use of psychics in murder cases, see Lois Duncan, *Who Killed My Daughter?* (New York: Delacorte, 1993).

ing domestic opposition. It was a time of confusion even for the former intelligence service itself. "The right hand," concluded FBI agent John Bertulis of the reassignment of past agents, "didn't know what the left was doing."

After the murder, however, the opposition faltered. Andrei Codrescu noted of his fellow émigrés that "people did get scared, and many of them stopped their activities." Only three months after the killing a final riot toppled the government's reform wing. The Iliescu government won in national elections. Today the government no longer courts the far right; the country's press remains free; elections relatively fair; and domestic surveillance or police harassment has slowly diminished but not ended.

A competitive scholar who was adept at making his colleagues think he new more than he did, Culianu appears to have taunted his killers into *perceiving* him as being dangerous in a moment of danger and confusion. He did so with the tone and prescience of his articles, his international prominence as the heir to Eliade, and his relative isolation. Delving into magical arts his entire life, he crossed a line between games and reality. He was playing, but his killers were not. Ioan Culianu's death was the ultimate game of the mind, when even his killers appeared to lose sight of the distinction between truth and fiction.

❋   ❋   ❋

The political interests of those who pulled the strings remains the smallest part of Culianu's story. "I was just thinking," said Anthony Yu when phoned at his home, "what a tragic, inexplicable loss it was." Mac Linscott Ricketts called his death "a catastrophe for scholarship." Culianu was a leading professional in the fields of gnosticism and dualism, hermetic and astral religion, and a growing group of theorists interested in the relation of cognition to history. The questions he left unanswered were raised succinctly by Divinity School Dean Clark Gilpin in his eulogy: "Is there any enduring connection between the human ideas to which universities are accountable," he asked, "and some eternal wisdom present at the primordium?"

From his childhood, Culianu sought a key to the universe. The value was not the answer, he suggested in numerous writings, but the knowledge gained on the way. In his struggle to follow his conscience as he lived an American success, he beguiled many, enraged many, but most of all left a legacy of the dangers of a life of the mind. Culianu kept coming back to the same themes that marked his life from birth, themes that haunted him, fascinated him, and contributed to what killed him. Perception shapes history, he wrote, time reveals hidden truths, and sometimes even forgeries can alter events.

In his last works, book proposals, letters, and stories, he left a puzzling, but coherent attempt at an explanation of the cognitive operations of history. He sought the deepest meanings in the small coincidences of dreams and daily life, and the mystery of human existence in the infinite space of the mind. "If Ioan Culianu had not unexpectedly disappeared," Umberto Eco wrote, "he would have given us more seminal works" revealing the patterns behind the veil of daily life and the relation of chance and fate, truth and fiction, murder and "illusory disappearance." In many ways, Culianu said, these opposites are the same. The deepest tragedy is that, in the only way we understand, they are not.

ENDNOTE

Unlike many other East European countries, Romania has never released its Communist secret police files, never accounted for most of the thousands of Communist Securitate operatives, never returned the family properties seized during the Communist era. At a time when Romania is applying for full membership in NATO and full acceptance in the West, it is especially critical that the assassination of a popular young American professor must be finally resolved.

Those who must speak out are Americans who care about free thought and the rights we take for granted. This crime took place on American soil, in a renowned university, in the middle of a school day. The brutal killing of a talented young scholar cannot be tolerated. As a sign of one American's vulnerability to history, it presents a critical policy issue to those who teach, write, think, or enforce our laws.

WORKS BY IOAN CULIANU

SCHOLARLY BOOKS AND THESES

Mircea Eliade. Orizzonte Filosofico. Assisi: Cittadella Editrice, 1978.

Iter in silvis: Saggi scelti sulla gnosi e altri studi. Vol. 1. Gnosis, no. 2. Messina: EDAS, 1981.

Religione e accrescimento del potere. In *Religione e potere,* by G. Romanato, M. Lombardo, and I. Culianu, pp. 173–252. Turin: Marietti, 1981.

Psychanodia I: A Survey of the Evidence Concerning the Ascension of the Soul and Its Relevance. Etudes Préliminaires aux Religions Orientales dans l'Empire Romain, no. 99. Leiden: Brill, 1983.

Eros et magie à la Renaissance, 1484. Idées et Recherches. Paris: Flammarion, 1984.

Expériences de l'extase: Extase, ascension et récit visionnaire, de l'Hellénisme au Moyen-Age. Paris: Payot, 1984.

Gnosticismo e pensiero moderno: Hans Jonas. Storia delle Religioni, no. 1. Rome: L'Erma di Bretschneider, 1985.

Empeiries tes ekstasis: Extsasi, anabasi kai orase apo ton Hellenismo mechri ton Mesaiona. Metafrasi Lida Palladiou. Athens: Hadjinikoli, 1986.

Espirienze dell'estasi dall'Ellenismo al Medioevo. BCM 926. Translated by Maria Garin. Bari: Laterza, 1986.

Recherches sur les dualismes d'Occident: Analyse de leurs principaux mythes. Doctorat d'Etat, 1986. A.N.R.T., Université de Lille III. Microfiche, Lille-Thèses, ISSN 0294-1767.

Eros and Magic in the Renaissance. Translated by M. Cook. Chicago: University of Chicago Press, 1987.

Eros e magia nel Rinascimento: La congiunzione astrologica del 1484. La Cultura, no. 46. Milan: Il Saggiatore—A. Mondadori, 1987.

I miti dei dualismi occidentali. Milan: Jaca Book, 1989.

Dictionnaire des Religions. Paris: Plon, 1990. With Mircea Eliade and in association with H. S. Wiesner.

Les Gnoses dualistes d'Occident: Histoire et mythes. Paris: Plon, 1990.

Out of This World: Other-worldly Journeys from Gilgamesh to Albert Einstein. Boston: Shambhala, 1990.

The Eliade Guide to World Religions. San Francisco: HarperSanFrancisco, 1991. With M. Eliade and in association with H. S. Wiesner.

I viaggi xell anima. (Translation of *Out of This World.*) Milan: Arnoldo Mondadori Editore, 1991.

The Tree of Gnosis: Gnostic Mythology from Early Christianity to Modern Nihilism. San Francisco: HarperCollins, 1992.

Diccionario de las religiones. Barcelona: Paidos Orientalia, 1993.

282 Works by Ioan Culianu

Dictionarul religiilor. Bucharest: Editura Humanitas, 1993.
Mas alla de este mundo. (Translation of *Out of This World.*) Barcelona: Paidos Orientalia, 1993.
Calatorii in lumea de dincolo. (Translation of *Out of This World.*) Bucharest: Editura Nemira, 1994.
Dictionary of Religions (in Japanese). Tokyo: Shoten House, 1994. (*Dictionary of Religions* has also been published in Dutch, Polish, and Czech translations.)
Eros and Magic in the Renaissance (in Japanese). Tokyo: Shoten House, 1994.
Eros și magie in Renaștiere. Bucharest: Editura Nemira, 1994.
Experiences del extasis. Barcelona: Paidos Orientalia, 1994.
Gnozele dualiste ale Occidentului. (Translation of *Experiences of Ecstasy.*) Bucharest: Editura Nemira, 1995.
Jenseiter dieser Welt. (Translation of *Out of This World.*) Munich: Dideriche Verlag, 1995.
Mircea Eliade. Bucharest: Editura Nemira, 1995.

EDITED VOLUME

Libra: Etudes roumaines offertes à W. Noomen à l'occasion de son soixantième anniversaire. Dordrecht: Presses Universitaires de Groningen, 1983.

FICTION

Il corridore tibetano. *L'Umana Avventura* (Spring 1988): 106–8.
Le coureur tibetain. *L'Aventure Humaine* (Spring–Summer 1988): 106–8.
Tozgrec. *Tempo Presente* 89–90 (1988): 91–101.
La collezione di smeraldi. Romanzo. Milan: Jaca Book, 1989.
The Late Repentance of Horemheb. *Harvard Review* 15–16 (1990): 6–7. With H. S. Wiesner.
La sequenza segreta. *Leggere* (Milan) 18 (1990): 24–29. With H. S. Wiesner.
Hesperus. Romanzo. Milan: Jaca Book, 1991.
The Language of Creation. *Exquisite Corpse* (1991). With H. S. Wiesner.
Hesperus. Bucharest: Editura Univers, 1992.
Pergamentul diafan. Bucharest: Editura Nemira, 1994.
Pergamentul diafan: Ultimele povestiri. Bucharest: Editura Nemira 1996.

ARTICLES

Soarele si luna. *Lucrari stintifice: Cercurile studentseti de folclor* 1 (1971), Baia Mare 1973, 87–97.

Les Xavantes du Mato Grosso. *Revue d'Histoire et de Philosophie Religieuses* 4 (1974): 531-34.

Mit si simbol in proza lui V. Voiculescu. *Ethos* 2 (1975): 258-68.

Nota su "La Vergine delle Rocce" di Leonardo. *Aevum* 49 (1975): 389-93.

La religione come strumento del potere e mezzo di liberazione. *Verifiche* 4 (1975): 236-55.

Il XIII Congresso IAHR. *Aevum* 50 (1976): 169-73. With D. M. Cosi.

La femme céleste et son ombre. *Numen* 23 (1976): 191-209.

Freud-Jung-Wittgenstein. *Ragguaglio Librario* 53 (1976): 126a-130b.

Note sur "opsis" et "theoria" dans la poésie d'Eminescu. *Acta Philologica* 6 (1976): 93-98.

Nota di demonologia bulgakoviana. *Aevum* 51 (1977): 548-51.

La "passione" di Sophia nello Gnosticismo. *Aevum* 51 (1977): 149-62.

L'anthropologie philosophique. *L'Herne 33: Mircea Eliade* (1978): 203-11.

Démonisation du cosmos et dualisme gnostique. *Revue de l'Histoire des Religions* 98 (1979): 3-40.

Erzählung und Mythos im "Lied von der Perle." *Kairos* 21 (1979): 60-71.

Pons subtilis: Storia e significato di un simbolo. *Aevum* 53 (1979): 301-12.

Romantisme acosmique chez M. Eminescu. *Neophilologus* 1 (1979): 74-83.

A Dualistic Myth in Roumanian Folklore. *Dialogue* 4-5 (1980): 45-50.

Les fantasmes du nihilisme chez M. Eminescu. *Romanistische Zeitschrift für Literaturgeschicte* 4 (1980): 422-33.

Iatroi kai manteis: Sulle strutture dell'estatismo grecom. *Studi Storico-Religiosi*, n.s., 4 (1980): 287-303.

Inter lunam terrasque . . . Incubazione, catalessi ed estasi in Plutarco. In *Perennitas: Studi in onore di A. Brelich*, 149-72. Rome: Edizioni dell'Ateneo, 1980.

Some Considerations on the Works of Horia Stamatu. *International Journal of Roumanian Studies* 2 (1980): 123-34.

The Angels of the Nations and the Origins of Gnostic Dualism. In *Studies in Gnosticism and Hellenistic Religions*, edited by R. van den Broek and M. J. Vermaseren, 78-91. Leiden: Brill, 1981.

Les fantasmes de l'eros chez M. Eminescu. *Neophilologus* 1 (1981): 229-38.

History of Religions in Italy. *History of Religions* 20 (1981): 253-62.

Magia spirituale e magia demonica nel Rinascimento. *Rivista di Storia e Letteratura Religiosa* 17 (1981): 360-408.

Ordine e disordine delle sfere. *Aevum* 55 (1981): 96-110.

Le vol magique dans l'Antiquité tardive. *Revue de l'Histoire des Religions* 98 (1981): 57-66.

Les anges des peuples et la question de origines du dualisme gnostique. In *Gnosticism et monde helenistique*, edited by J. Ries, 131-45. Louvain-la-neuve: Peeters, 1982.

Antropologia filosofica a lui M. Eliade. *Ethos* 3 (1982): 243-47.

L' "ascension de l'âme" dans les mystères et hors des mystères. In *La soteriologia dei culti orientali nell'Impero Romano*, edited by U. Bianchi and M. J. Vermaseren, 78–91. Leiden, Brill, 1982.

La grande année et la metempsychose. In *La soteriologia dei culti orientali nell'Impero Romano*, 303–7.

History of Religions in Italy: A Postscript. *History of Religions* 22 (1982): 190–95.

Les fantasmes de la liberté chez M. Eminescu. In *Libra: Etudes roumaines offertes à W. Noomen à l'occasion de son soixantième anniversaire*, edited by I. P. Culianu, 114–46. Dordrecht: Presses Universitaires de Groningen, 1983.

Giordano Bruno tra la Montagna di Circe e il Fiume delle Dame leggiadri. In *Montagna e letteratura*, edited by A. Audisio and R. Rinaldi, 71–75. Turin: Museo Nazionale della Montagna, 1983.

Interferences between Iconography and Folklore in Roumania. *Visible Religion* 2 (1983): 40–57. With C. Culianu.

M. Eliade et la pensée moderne sur l'irrationnel. *Dialogue* 8 (1983): 39–52.

La magie de Giordano Bruno. *Studi e Materiali di Storia delle Religioni* 49 (1983): 279–301.

Le paysage du centre du monde dans le conte "Cezara" de M. Eminescu. *Romanistische Zeitschrift für Literaturgeschichte* 3–4 (1983): 444–58.

The Sun and the Moon. *International Journal of Roumanian Studies* 3 (1981–83): 83–97.

La visione di Isaia e la tematica della Himmelsreise. *Isaia, il Diletto e la Chiesa*, edited by M. Pesce, 95–116. Bologna: Paideia, 1983.

Wer hat Angst vor Hans Peter Duerr? In *Der glaserne Zaun*, edited by R. Gehlen and B. Wolf, 263–64. Frankfurt: Syndikat, 1983.

Eliade et le refus du symbolisme. *3e Millénaire* 13 (1984): 89–93.

Feminine versus Masculine: The Sophia Myth and the Origins of Feminism. In *Struggles of Gods*, edited by H. G. Kippenberg, 65–98. Berlin: Mouton, 1984.

La geomantie dans l'Occident médiéval: Quelques considerations. In *Non nova sed nove: Mélanges de civilisation médiévale*, edited by M. Gosman and J. van Os, 37–46. Groningen: Bouma, 1984.

The Gnostic Revenge: Gnosticism and Romantic Literature. In *Gnosis und Politik*, edited by J. Taubes, 290–306. Paderborn: Schoningh, 1984.

Mircea Eliade et l'idéal de l'homme universel. *Le Club Français de la Médialle, Bulletin* 84 (1984): 48–55.

Mircea Eliade und die blinde Schildkrote. In *Die Mitte der Welt: Aufsatze zu Mircea Eliade*, edited by H. P. Duerr, 216–43. Suhrkamp Taschenbuch 981. Frankfurt: Suhrkamp, 1984.

Un temps à l'endroit, un temps à l'envers. . . . In *Le temps chrétien de la fin de l'Antiquité au Moyen Age IIIe–XIIIe siècles*, 57–61. Colloques Internationaux du CNRS, no. 604. Paris: Editions du CNRS, 1984.

Eros magie et manipulation des masses. *3e Millénaire* 18 (1985): 31–35.

Le mandala dans l'histoire des religions. *Cahiers Internationaux du Symbolisme* 48–49–50 (1984 1985?): 53–62.

M. Eliade at the Crossroads of Anthropology. *Neue Zeitschrift für systematische Theologue und Religionsphilosophie* 27 (1985): 123–31.

Avers si revers in istorie. *Revista de Istorie si Teorie Literatară*, nos. 2–3 (1986): 127–36.

Civilization as a Product of Wilderness: H. P. Duerr and His Theories of Culture. *Nederlands Theologish Tijidschrift* 40 (1986): 305–11.

M. Eliade at the Crossroads of Anthropology. In *On Symbolic Representations of Religion*, edited by H. G. Hubbeling and H. G. Kippenberg, 45–56. Berlin: W. de Gruyter, 1986.

Ascension. In *The Encyclopedia of Religion*, edited by M. Eliade, 1:435a–441a. New York: Macmillan, 1987.

Astrology. In *Encyclopedia of Religion* 1:472a–475b.

Bendis. In *Encyclopedia of Religion* 2:94b–95a. With C. Poghirc.

Dacian Riders. In *Encyclopedia of Religion* 4:195a–196a.

Gnosticism: From the Middle Ages to the Present. In *Encyclopedia of Religion* 5:574b–578a.

Magic in Medieval and Renaissance Europe. In *Encyclopedia of Religion* 9:97b–101b.

Sabazios. In *Encyclopedia of Religion* 12:499b–500b.

Sacrilege. In *Encyclopedia of Religion* 12:557a–563b.

Sexual Rites in Europe. In *Encyclopedia of Religion* 13:186b–189b.

[Sky:] The Heavens as Hierophany. In *Encyclopedia of Religion* 13:343b–345b.

Thracian Religions. In *Encyclopedia of Religion* 14:494a–497b. With C. Poghirc.

Thracian Riders. In *Encyclopedia of Religion* 14:497a–b.

Zalmoxis. In *Encyclopedia of Religion* 15:551b–555b. With C. Poghirc.

M. Eliade et l'idéal de l'homme universel. In *M. Eliade: Dialogues avec le sacre*, 9–16. Paris: Editions NADP, 1987.

"Zapadniki" et "Slavianofily": La portee du conflit. In *Sauf-conduit: La vision russe de l'Occident*, edited by Gérard Conio, 9–14. Paris: L'Age d'Homme, 1987. With C. Culianu.

L' "anéantissement sans nulle compassion" dans la nouvelle "Moara cunoroc" de Ioane Slavici (1881). *Kurier* (Bochum) 13 (1987): 38–49.

Les fantasmes de la peur chez Mihai Eminescu, ou Comment devient-on révolutionnaire de profession. In *Eminescu im europäischen Kontext*, edited by I. Constantinescu, 106–27. Augsburg, 1988.

Urmuz, précurseur de lui-même? In *Vitalité et contradictions de l'avant-garde: Italie-France, 1909–1924*, collected by S. Briosi and H. Hillenaar, 273–78. Paris: Jose Corti, 1988.

Ascension. In *Death, Afterlife, and the Soul*, edited by L. E. Sullivan, 107–17. New York: Macmillan, 1989.

. . . . . .

Astrology. In *Hidden Truths: Magic, Alchemy, and the Occult*, edited by L. E. Sullivan, 151–157. New York: Macmillan, 1989.

Gnosticism from the Middle Ages to the Present. In *Hidden Truths*, 63–68.

Invito alla lettura di Mircea Eliade. *Abstracta* 35 (1989): 38–49.

Magic in Medieval and Renaissance Europe. In *Hidden Truths*, 110–15.

"Dr. Faust: Great Sodomite and Necromancer." *Revue de l'Histoire des Religions* 207, no. 3 (1990): 261–82.

System and History. *Incognita* 1 (1990): 6–17.

"Cultura Romana?" *Agora* 4, no. 3 (July–September 1991): 31–36.

SHORT ARTICLES AND BOOK REVIEWS,
1973 AND AFTERWARD

Dan Laurentiu. *Fiera Letteraria* (Rome) 49 (1973): 15.

Vasile Coiculescu, romancier al iluziei si al sperantei. *Revista Scriitorilor Romani* (Munich) 12 (1973): 164–65.

Mircea Ciobanu si Principele acestei lumi. *Limite* (Paris) 16 (1974): 11.

Review of *Creatie si frumos*, by C. Noica. *Limite* 17 (1974): 10.

Review of *Religions australiennes*, by M. Eliade. *Aevum* 48 (1974): 592–93.

Exil. *Limite* 19 (1975): 13.

Nina Façon (ob. 1974). *Limite* 18 (1975): 20.

Review of *Lo gnosticismo*, by H. Jonas. *Aevum* 49 (1975): 585–87.

Review of *Maya History and Religion*, by J. E. S. Thompson. *Aevum* 49 (1975): 587–90.

Review of *La nostalgia delle origini*, by M. Eliade. *Aevum* 49 (1975): 584–85.

Review of *Pour une science des religions*, by M. Meslin. *Aevum* 49 (1975): 207–8.

Review of *Lo sciamanismo*, by M. Eliade. *Ragguaglio Librario* 51 (1975): 396.

Review of *Le concept de littérarité*, by M. Marghescu. *Limite* 21 (1976): 11.

Doi poeti romani. *Limite* 23 (1977): 15–16.

Review of *L'isola del tonal*, by C. Castaneda. *Aevum* 51 (1977): 583–86.

Review of *Mito e filosofia*, by C. Conio. *Aevum* 51 (1977): 583–86.

Review of *Neuplatonische u. gnostische Weltablehnung*, by C. Elsas. *Aevum* 51 (1977): 187–89.

La XLVI Eranos-Tagung. *Aevum* 52 (1978): 343–46.

Review of *Edipo alla luce del folclore*, by V. I. Ja. Propp. *Aevum* 52 (1978): 383–84.

Review of *Etymologicum magnum romaniae*, by B. P. Hasdeu. *Aevum* 52 (1978): 383–84.

Review of *International Journal of Roumanian Studies* 1. *Aevum* 52 (1978): 637.

Review of *Limbe si gindire in clutura indiana*, by S. Al-George. *Aevum* 52 (1978): 637.

Review of *Mica enciclopedie a povestilor romanesti*, by O. Birlea. *Aevum* 52 (1978): 384.

Review of *La nascita mistica*, by M. Eliade. *Aevum* 52 (1978): 159–60.

Review of *Nederlandse Volksverhalen*, by M. D. Teenstra. *Aevum* 52 (1978): 635.

Review of *Occultism, Witchcraft and Cultural Fashions*, by M. Eliade. *Aevum* 52 (1978): 596–98.

Review of *Production de l'intérêt romanesque*, by Ch. Grivel. *Rapports* (1978): 189–92.

Review of *Vita e pensiero di R. Tagore*, by G. Ottonello. *Aevum* 52 (1978): 637.

Metamorfoza lui M. Eliade. *Limite* 28–29 (1979): 35–36.

Review of *Gesellschaft in mythischen Bahn*, by K. Keller. *Aevum* 53 (1979): 608.

Review of *Histoire des croyances I*, by M. Eliade. *Aevum* 53 (1979): 165–68.

Review of *In Mist Apparelled*, by F. E. Brenk. *Aevum* 53 (1979): 209.

Review of *Letture sulla religione greca*, by P. Scarpi. *Aevum* 53 (1979): 201.

Review of *Macrobe*, by J. Flamant. *Aevum* 53 (1979): 190–93.

Review of *Medieval Heresy*, by M. Lambert. *Aevum* 53 (1979): 427.

Review of *Norms in a Changing World*, by Portman-Rietsema. *Aevum* 53 (1979): 209.

Review of *La paralisi e lo spostamento*, by R. Rinaldi. *Aevum* 53 (1979): 608.

Review of *Philosophie du catharisme*, by R. Nelli. *Aevum* 53 (1979): 428.

Review of *Prometeo Orfeo Adamo*, by U. Bianchi. *Aevum* 53 (1979): 172–76.

Review of *Recherches sur la lune I*, by S. Lunais. *Aevum* 53 (1979): 209.

Review of *Redeunt Saturnia Regna*, by V. Schmidt. *Aevum* 53 (1979): 205–6.

Review of *Symboles et mythes dans la pensée de Plutarque*, by Y. Vernière. *Aevum* 53 (1979): 209.

Review of *Bartholomaeus Anglicus*, by R. J. Long. *Aevum* 54 (1980): 391–92.

Review of *Cahiers Roumains d'Etudes Littéraires 1978*. *Aevum* 54 (1980): 557–58.

Review of *La critique des idées littéraires*, by A. Marino. *Aevum* 54 (1980): 557.

Review of *Cultura cattolica*, by G. Romanato and Molinari. *Problemi di civilita* 6 (1980): 11–12.

Review of *De vita libri III*, by M. Ficino. *Aevum* 54 (1980): 397.

Review of *La guistificazione delle immagini religiose*, by V. Fazzo. *Aevum* 54 (1980): 183–85.

Review of *Hermeneutica lui M. Eliade*, by A. Marino. *Aevum* 54 (1980): 541–43.

Review of *Hommages à M. J. Vermaseren*. *Aevum* 54 (1980): 205–6.

Review of *Magie*, by H. G. Kippenberg and B. Lucchesi. *Aevum* 54 (1980): 206–7.

Review of *Mithriaca IV*, by M. J. Vermaseren. *Aevum* 54 (1980): 206.

Review of *Opere VII*, by M. Eminescu. *Aevum* 54 (1980): 536–37.

Review of *Pour une sociologie du texte*, by P. V. Zima. *Romanistische Zeitschrift für Literaturgeschichte* (1980): 113–14.

Review of *Religion u. Klassenbildung*, by H. G. Kippenberg. *Aevum* 54 (1980): 201.

Review of *Stanze*, by G. Agamben. *Aevum* 54 (1980): 386–87.

Un colloquio sulla nozione cristiana di tempo. *Rivista di Storia e Letteratura Religiosa* 17 (1981): 328–29.

Review of *Apocalypse*, by V. Tanase. *Limite* 32, no. 2 (1981): 28–29.

Review of *Courtly Love*, by R. Boase. *Aevum* 55 (1981): 360–63.

Review of *Cults and Beliefs at Edessa*, by H. J. W. Drijvers. *Aevum* 55 (1981): 172–74.

Review of M. Eliade, etc. *Aevum* 55 (1981): 611.

Review of *Gannat Bussame*, by G. J. Reinink. *Aevum* 55 (1981): 377.

Review of *Luce e Gnosi*, by G. J. Filoramo. *Aevum* 55 (1981): 190–92.

Review of *Mysteria Mithria*, by U. Bianchi. *Aevum* 55 (1981): 169–72.

Review of *Soteriologia di Cibele e Attis*, by G. Sfameni Gasparro. *Aevum* 55 (1981): 168–69.

Review of *Textbuch zur Neutest: Zeitgeschichte*, by H. G. Kippenberg and Wevers. *Aevum* 55 (1981): 190–91.

Wanner begonnen de haksen te vliegen? *Universiteitskrant*, January 21, 1981, p. 5.

Ask yourselves in our own hearts. . . . *History of Religions* 22 (1982): 284–86.

Ecology and Indo-Iranian Reconstruction. *History of Religions* 22 (1982): 196–98.

The Marvelous Ointments of Dr. Duerr. *History of Religions* 22 (1982): 356.

Review of *Adonis*, by S. Ribichini. *Aevum* 56 (1982): 129.

Review of *Iconographie chrétienne*, by A. Grabar. *Aevum* 56 (1982): 356.

Review of *Idee en Verbeelding*, by J. J. A. Mooij. *Aevum* 56 (1982): 590b–591b.

Review of *Purgatoire*, by J. Le Geoff. *Aevum* 56 (1982): 363–64.

Review of *Unde scrute*, by M. Lovinescu. *Ethos* 3 (1982): 296–97.

Review of *Unter dem Pflaster* 8 (1981). *Aevum* 56 (1982): 590a–b.

Colloquio "Gnosi e polotica." *SMSR* 49 (1983): 417–19.

Mircea Eliade et son oeuvre. *Aurores* 38 (1983): 10–12.

Mistica, cultura e societa. *RSLR* 19 (1983): 348.

Review of *Atharvavedaparisista*, edited by L. van den Bosch. *History of Religions* 23 (1983): 194–95.

Review of *CCCA II*, by M. J. Vermaseren. *Aevum* 57 (1983): 165a–b.

Review of *Light and Color*, by M. Barasch. *Aevum* 57 (1983): 573a–574a.

Review of *Mithriaca III*, by M. J. Vermaseren. *Aevum* 57 (1983): 171a–172a.

Review of *Montaillou in Groningen*, edited by D. A. Papousek. *Aevum* 57 (1983): 365a–366b.

Review of *Mythologie du vampire*, by A. Cremene. *Revue de l'Histoire des Religions* 200 (1983): 413–15.

Review of *Scriitori bisericesti*, by I. G. Coman. *Aevum* 57 (1983): 174a–b.

Review of *La soteriologia*, by U. Bianchi and M. J. Vermaseren. *Aevum* 57 (1983): 172a–173a.

Review of *Symboliek van de aarde*, by H. A. Witte. *Aevum* 57 (1983): 582a–583a.

Review of *Symposium Apuleianum Groninganum. Aevum* 57 (1983): 171a.

Review of *Temple et contemplation*, by H. Corbin. *Aevum* 57 (1983): 580b–581b.

Review of *Zoroaster*, by Gh. Gnoli. *Aevum* 57 (1983): 164a–165a.

Review of *L'attesa della fine*, by G. Filoramo. *SMSR* 50 (1984): 373–75.

Review of *Dieu et Dieux*, edited by M. Taille. *History of Religions* 24 (1984): 288.

Review of *The Early Greek Concept of the Soul*, by J. Bremmer. *SMSR* 50 (1984): 371–73.

Review of *Mythologie du vampire*, by A. Cremene. *SMSR* 50 (1984): 195–97.

Review of *Neue Ansatze*, edited by Gladigow and H. G. Kippenberg. *History of Religions* 24 (1984): 185–86.

Review of *Rausch — Extase — Mystik*, edited by H. Cancik. *History of Religions* 24 (1984): 186–87.

Review of *Le Scarabee International. Aevum* 58 (1984): 618.

Review of *Sphinx-Verlag. Aevum* 58 (1984): 617–18.

Review of *Vor Gott sind Alle gleich*, by G. Kehrer. *History of Religions* 24 (1984): 187–88.

Mircea Eliade et le long combat contre racisme. *Nouvelle Acropole* 81 (1985): 3–4.

L'offense raciste. *Nouvelle Acropole* 81 (1985): 7–8.

Religie si istolrie. *Contrapunct* 4 (1985): 4–8.

Review of *3 Graces*, by M. Eliade. *Limite* 44–45 (1985): 29a–30a.

Review of *Isaia*, edited by M. Pesce. *Journal for the Study of Judaism* 116 (1985): 271–72.

Review of *La lettre du prêtre Jean*, by M. Gosman. *SMSR* 51 (1985): 381–83.

Review of *Mystique culture et société*, edited by M. Meslin. *History of Religion* 25 (1985): 288–89.

Review of *Paltinis*, by G. Liiceanu. *Limite* 44–45 (1985): 20b–21b.

Review of *Il picchio e il codice delle api*, by P. Scarpi. *History of Religions* 24 [25?] (1985): 286–87.

Review of *Qui sa vertu anoblist*, by A. J. Vanderjagt. *SMSR* 51 (1985): 383–3.[?]

Review of *Le regioni del silenzio*, edited by M. G. Cicani. *History of Religions* 25 (1985): 287–88.

Review of *Revelation of Elchasai*, by G. P. Luttikhuizen. *SMSR* 51 (1985): 377–80.

Studii recente despre M. Eliade. *Limite* 46–47 (1985): 24a–25a.

Mahaparinirvana. *Limite* 48–49 (1986): 2–3.

Religie si istorie. *Contrapunct* 1 (1986): 10.

Religie si istorie. *Contrapunct* 2 (1986): 10.

Review of *Anthropology and the Study of Religion*, edited by R. L. Moore and F. E. Reynolds. *SMSR* 52 (1986): 336–37.

Review of *Cosmology and Ethical Order*, edited by R. W. Lovin and F. E. Reynolds. *SMSR* 52 (1986): 324–27.

Review of *Dreams, Illusion, and Other Realities*, by W. Doniger O'Flaherty. *SMSR* 52 (1986): 328–30.

Review of *Geographie sacrée*, by F. Schwarz. *Aries* 5 (1986): 87.

Review of *The History of Religions*, edited by J. M. Kitagawa. *SMSR* 52 (1986): 177–79.

Review of *Sophia et l'âme du monde* (Cahiers de l'Hermetisme). *Aries* 5 (1986): 81–83.

Secretul lui M. Eliade. *Contrapunct* 3–4 (1986): 10.

Foreword by the Editor. *ARA Journal* 10 (1987): 4–5.

Mahaparinirvana. *ARA Journal* 10 (1987): 15–21.

Mahaparinirvana. In *M. Eliade: Dialogues avec le sacre*, 44–48. Paris: Editions NADP, 1987.

I mandarini. *Tempo Presente* 73–74 (January–February 1987): 119a–120b.

Mircea Eliade a la lunga lotta contro il razzismo. In *Mircea Eliade e l'Italia*, edited by Mincu and R. Scagno, 89–91. Milan: Jaca Book, 1987.

Mircea Eliade à la recherche du Graal. *CNAC-Magazine*, Centre G. Pompidou, 39 (May–July 1987): 8–9.

"Mircea Eliade on the 80th Anniversary of His Birth." *ARA Journal* 10 (1987): 1072. Edited by I. P. Culianu.

One, Two, Many Gods. *History of Religions* 27 (1987): 97–98.

Pacatul impotriva spiritului. *Agora* 1, no. 1 (1987): 36–38.

Review of *Ayodhya*, by H. Bakker. *History of Religions* 26 (1987): 436–37.

Review of *The Greek Magical Papyri*, edited by H. D. Betz. *Journal for the Study of Judaism* 18 (1987): 81–83.

Review of *Indian Medicine*, edited by G. J. Meulenbeld. *History of Religions* 27 (1987): 107.

Review of *The Name of God*, by J. E. Fossum. *History of Religions* 26 (1987): 435–36.

Review of *Poimandres as Myth*, by R. A. Segal. *Journal of Religion* 68 (1988): 608.

Review of *Rasa mana ke pada*, by A. W. Entwistle. *History of Religions* 27 (1987): 108.

Alter ego. In *Handbuch religionswissenschaftlicher Grundbegriffe*, 437–38. Stuttgart: Kohlhammer, 1988.

Invitation to the Sabbath. *(London) Times Literary Supplement*, December 15, 1989. Liber, 14.

Invito al Sabato. *(London) Times Literary Supplement*, December 15-21, 1989. Liber, 2, 14.

Note, *Religion in Context*, by I. M. Lewis. *Journal of Religion* 68 (1988): 640.

Review of *Gnostic Scriptures*, by B. Layton. *Journal for the Study of Judaism* 20 (1989): 95-96.

Review of *J. Wach*, by J. M. Kitagawa. *Church History* 58 (1989): 419-20.

Review of *Martyrium und Sophiamthos*, by C. Scholten. *Church History* 58 (1989): 370.

Review of *Servants of Satan*, by J. Klaits. *Church History* 58 (1989): 419-20.

Scrisoare deschisă către Ungureanu Fl[orica]. *Lumea Liberă* (New York), December 9, 1989, pp. 8-9.

Dan Petrescu. *L'Umana Avventura* (Spring 1990): 110.

E'morto il re-occhio all'erede. *Panorama*, February 18, 1990, pp. 94-96.

Naked Is Shameful. *History of Religions* 29 (1990): 420-22.

"O lecție de politică." *Lumea Liberă*, June 15, 1990, p. 11.

La realta? Sono due. *Panorama*, June 3, 1990, p. 107.

Review of *Adam, Eve, and the Serpent*, by E. Pagels. *Incognita* 1 (1990): 108-11.

Review of *The Aesthetics of Thomas Aquinas*, by U. Eco. *Journal of Religion* 2 (1990): 283-85.

Review of *The Encyclopedia of Religion*, edited by M. Eliade. *Incognita* 1 (1990): 104-6.

Review of *Gnosis*, by K. Rudolph. *Journal of Religion* 2 (1990): 303-4.

Review of *The History of Religions*, by J. M. Kitagawa. *Church History* 59 (1990): 135-36.

Review of *Other Peoples' Myths*, by W. Doniger O'Flaherty. *Incognita* 1 (1990): 944-45.

Scrisori deschise. *Lumea Liberă*, January 20, 1990, pp. 9-10.

Viitorul României in 11 puncte. *Lumea Liberă*, January 6, 1990, pp. 19, 30-31.

Scoptophilia (column). *Lumea Liberă*, June 23, 1990, p. 9.

Scoptophilia. *Lumea Liberă*, June 30, 1990, p. 9.

Scoptophilia. *Lumea Liberă*, July 7, 1990, p. 9.

Scoptophilia. *Lumea Liberă*, July 14, 1990, p. 9.

Scoptophilia. *Lumea Liberă*, July 21, 1990, p. 9.

Scoptophilia. *Lumea Liberă*, July 28, 1990, p. 9.

Scoptophilia. *Lumea Liberă*, August 4, 1990, p. 9.

Scoptophilia. *Lumea Liberă*, August 11, 1990, p. 9.

Scoptophilia. *Lumea Liberă*, August 18, 1990, p. 9.

Scoptophilia. *Lumea Liberă*, August 25, 1990, p. 9.

Scoptophilia. *Lumea Liberă*, September 1, 1990, p. 9.

Scoptophilia. *Lumea Liberă*, September 8, 1990, p. 9.

Scoptophilia. *Lumea Liberă*, September 15, 1990, p. 9.
Scoptophilia. *Lumea Liberă*, September 22, 1990, p. 9.
Scoptophilia. *Lumea Liberă*, September 29, 1990, p. 9.
Scoptophilia. *Lumea Liberă*, October 6, 1990, p. 9.
Scoptophilia. *Lumea Liberă*, October 13, 1990, p. 9.
Scoptophilia. *Lumea Liberă*, October 20, 1990, p. 9.
Scoptophilia. *Lumea Liberă*, October 27, 1990, p. 9.
Scoptophilia. *Lumea Liberă*, November 3, 1990, p. 9.
Scoptophilia. *Lumea Liberă*, November 10, 1990, p. 9.
Scoptophilia. *Lumea Liberă*, November 17, 1990, p. 9.
Scoptophilia. *Lumea Liberă*, November 24, 1990, p. 9.
Scoptophilia. *Lumea Liberă*, December 1, 1990, p. 9.
Scoptophilia. *Lumea Liberă*, December 8, 1990, p. 9.
Scoptophilia. *Lumea Liberă*, December 15, 1990, p. 9.
Scoptophilia. *Lumea Liberă*, December 22, 1990, p. 9.

INDEX